ALABAMA GOVERNMENT AND POLITICS

JAMES D. THOMAS & WILLIAM H. STEWART

Alabama
Government
& Politics

UNIVERSITY OF NEBRASKA PRESS

LINCOLN & LONDON

The paper in this book meets the minimum require-
ments of American National Standard for
Information Sciences – Permanence of Paper for
Printed Library Materials, ANSI Z39.48-1984.

Library of Congress Cataloging in Publication Data
Thomas, James D.
Alabama government and politics.
(State politics and government)
Bibliography: p.
Includes index.
1. Alabama – Politics and government – 1951-
I. Stewart, William Histaspas, 1939-
II. Title. III. Series.
JK4516.T49   1988   320.9761   87-16242
ISBN 0-8032-4182-8 (alk. paper)
ISBN 0-8032-9181-7 (pbk. : alk. paper)

CONTENTS

DANIEL J. ELAZAR

Series Introduction

Most of the American states are larger and better developed than most of the world's nations. Each has its own story, its own character as a civil society; each is a polity with its own uniqueness. They share a common tradition of governance, but to view them as the same because their institutions resemble one another would be like assuming the nations of continental Europe to be the same because they share a common commitment to parliamentary institutions, or the nations of Africa to be the same because they emphasize presidential rule.

The American states exist because they are civil societies. They were first given political form and then acquired their other characteristics. It is their polities that are crucial to their being. Each of those polities has its own constitution, its own political cultural synthesis, its own relationship to the federal union and to its section. These in turn have given each its own law and history; the longer that history, the more distinctive the state.

It is in and through the states, no less than the nation, that the great themes of American life play themselves out. The advancing frontier and the continuing experience of Americans as a frontier people, the drama of American ethnic blending, the tragedy of slavery and racial discrimination, the political struggle for expanding the right to vote—all found, and find, their expression in the states.

The changing character of government, from an all-embracing concern with every aspect of civil and religious behavior to a limited concern with maintaining law and order to a concern with providing the social benefits of the contemporary welfare state, has been felt in the states even more than in the federal government. Some states began as commonwealths devoted to establishing model societies based on a religiously-informed vision (Massachusetts, Connecticut, Rhode Island). At the other end of the spectrum, Hawaii is a transformed pagan monarchy. At least three were independent for a significant period of time (Hawaii, Texas, and Vermont). Others were created from nothing by hardly more than a stroke of the pen (the Dakotas, Idaho, Nevada). Several are permanently bilingual (California, Louisiana, and New Mexico). Each has its own landscape and geographic configuration which time and history transform into a specific geo-historical location. In short, the diversity of the American people is expressed in no small measure through their states, the government and politics of each of which have their own fascination.

Alabama Government and Politics is the first book in the Center for the Study of Federalism and University of Nebraska Press series State Government and Politics. The aim of the series is to provide books on the government and politics of the individual states of the United States that will appeal to three audiences: political scientists, their students, and the wider public in each state. Each volume in the series examines the specific character of one of the fifty states, looking at the state as a polity—its political culture, traditions and practices, constituencies and interest groups, constitutional and institutional frameworks.

Each book in the series reviews the political development of the state to demonstrate how the state's political institutions and characteristics have evolved from the first settlement to the present, presenting the state in the context of the nation and section of which it is a part, and reviewing the roles and relations of the state vis-à-vis its sister states and the federal government. The state's constitutional history, its traditions of constitution making and constitutional change, are examined and related to the workings of the state's political institutions and processes. State-local relations, local government, and community politics are studied. Finally, each volume reviews the state's policy concerns and their implementation, from the budgetary process to particular substantive policies. Each book concludes by summarizing the principal themes and findings to draw conclusions about the current state of the state, its continuing traditions, and emerging issues. Each volume also contains a bibliographic survey of the existing literature on the state and a guide to the use of that literature and state government documents in learning more about the state and political system.

Although the books in the series are not expected to be uniform, they do focus on the common themes of federalism, constitutionalism, political culture, and the continuing American frontier, to provide a framework within which to consider the institutions, routines, and processes of state government and politics.

Both the greatest conflicts of American history and the day-to-day operations of American government are closely intertwined with American federalism—the form of American government (in the eighteenth-century sense of the term, which includes both structure and process). American federalism has been characterized by several basic tensions. One is between state sovereignty—the view that in a proper federal system, authority and power over most domestic affairs should be in the hands of the states—and national supremacy—the view that the federal government has a significant role to play in domestic matters affecting the national interest. The other tension is between dual federalism—the idea that a federal system functions best when the federal government and the states function as separately as possible, each in its own sphere—and cooperative federalism—the view that federalism works best when the federal government and the states, while preserving their own institutions, cooperate closely on the implementation of joint or shared programs. Alabama has been one of those states that have traditionally held to ideas of state sovereignty and dual federalism, although in practice it has not been averse to cooperating with the federal government when it has suited its purposes to do so.

Alabama's relationship to the federal government has been typical of that of other southern states, aggressively self-assertive in matters relating to slavery and civil rights issues, first to protect the "peculiar institution" and then the "southern way of life," while at the same time actively involved in the search for federal aid in matters of infrastructure and economic development. This uniquely southern pattern of conflict and cooperation has been well documented. Alabama was one of the first states to open an office in Washington during World War I to secure federal military facilities to bolster the state's sagging economy. It was one of the active beneficiaries of the New Deal, not only through the general New Deal programs, but through the Tennessee Valley Authority, which made possible the Huntsville space research facility.

As it continued to pursue federal aid, Alabama was also the scene of some of the most active resistance to the enforcement of the desegregation decisions of the United States Supreme Court and, as this volume describes, has been at the receiving end of some of the most massive federal court interventions in other issues in recent years. At the same time, Alabama has stuck by its section on most matters, being part of the classic "solid South," and changing as that solid southern pattern was modified in the wake of the civil rights revolution.

CONSTITUTIONALISM

Representatives of the Connecticut River valley towns of Hartford, Windsor, and Wethersfield met in January 1639 to draft a constitution. That document, the Fundamental Orders, established a federal union to be known as Connecticut and inaugurated the American practice of constitution making as a popular act and responsibility, ushering in the era of modern constitutionalism. The American constitutional tradition grows out of the Whig understanding that civil societies are founded by political covenant, entered into by the first founders and reaffirmed by subsequent generations, through which the powers of government are delineated and limited and the rights of the constituting members clearly proclaimed in such a way as to provide moral and practical restraints on governmental institutions. That constitutional tradition was modified by the federalists, who accepted its fundamental principals but strengthened the institutional framework designed to provide energy in government while maintaining the checks and balances they saw as needed to preserve liberty and republican government. At the same time, they turned nonbinding declarations of rights into enforceable constitutional articles.

American state constitutions reflect the melding of these two traditions. Under the U.S. Constitution, each state is free to adopt its own constitution, provided that it establishes a republican form of government. Some states have adopted highly succinct constitutions like the Vermont Constitution of 1793 with 6,600 words that is still in effect with only 52 amendments. Others are just the opposite, for example, Georgia's Ninth Constitution, adopted in 1976, which has 583,000 words.

State constitutions are potentially far more comprehensive than the federal constitution, which is one of limited, delegated powers. Because states are plenary governments, they automatically possess all powers not specifically denied them by the U.S. Constitution or their citizens. Consequently, a state constitution must be explicit about limiting and defining the scope of governmental powers, especially on behalf of individual liberty.

Overall, six different state constitutional patterns have developed. One is the commonwealth pattern, developed in New England, which emphasizes Whig ideas of the constitution as a philosophic document designed first and foremost to set a direction for civil society and to express and institutionalize a theory of republican government. A second is the constitutional pattern of the commercial republic. The constitutions fitting this pattern reflect a series of compromises required by the conflict of many strong ethnic groups and commercial interests generated by the flow of heterogeneous streams of migrants into the large industrial states and the early development of large commercial and industrial cities in those states.

The third is that found in the South and which can be described as the southern contractual pattern. Southern state constitutions are used as instruments to set explicit terms governing the relationship between polity and society, such as those which protected slavery or racial segregation, or those which sought to diffuse the formal allocation of authority in order to accommodate the swings between oligarchy and factionalism characteristic of southern state politics. Of all the southern states, only Louisiana stands somewhat outside this pattern, since its legal system was founded on the French civil code. Its constitutions have been codes—long, highly-explicit documents that form a pattern in and of themselves.

A fifth pattern is that found frequently in the less populated states of the Far West, where the state constitution is first and foremost a frame of government explicitly reflecting the republican and democratic principles dominant in the nation in the late nineteenth century, but emphasizing the structure of state government and the distribution of powers within that structure in a direct, businesslike manner. Finally, the two newest states, Alaska and Hawaii, have adopted constitutions following the managerial pattern developed and promoted by twentieth-century constitutional reform movements in the United States. Those constitutions are characterized by conciseness, broad grants of power to the executive branch, and relatively few structural restrictions on the legislature. They emphasize natural-resource conservation and social legislation.

Alabama shares the southern constitutional tradition of many documents, all built around a common core but adapted to exigencies of secession, reconstruction, resegregation, and desegregation. Hence its constitution does not have the classic character of the New England state constitutions or the enduring character of those of Greater New England in the Midwest and West. At the same time, Alabama's constitutions can be profitably examined for the changes in the American constitutional tradition because they have had to make explicit what other states, not touched by the Civil War and its aftermath, have been able to leave implicit in their fundamental laws.

THE CONTINUING AMERICAN FRONTIER

For Americans, the very word *frontier* conjures up the images of the rural-land frontier of yesteryear—of explorers and mountain men, of cowboys and Indians, of brave pioneers pushing their way west in the face of natural obstacles. Later, Americans' picture of the frontier was expanded to include the inventors, the railroad builders, and the captains of industry who created the urban-industrial frontier. Recently television has begun to celebrate the entrepreneurial ventures of the automobile and oil industries, portraying the magnates of those industries and their families in the same larger-than-life frame as once was done for the heroes of that first frontier.

As is so often the case, the media responsible for determining and catering to popular taste tell us a great deal about ourselves. The United States was founded with a rural-land frontier that persisted until World War I, more or less, spreading farms, ranches, mines, and towns across the land. Early in the nineteenth century, the rural-land frontier generated an urban frontier based on industrial development. The creation of new wealth through industrialization transformed cities from mere regional service centers into generators of wealth in their own right. That frontier persisted for more than one hundred years as a major force in American society as a whole and perhaps another sixty years as a major force in various parts of the country. The population movements and attendant growth on the urban-industrial frontier brought about the effective settlement of the United States in freestanding industrial cities from coast to coast.

Between the world wars, the urban-industrial frontier gave birth in turn to a third frontier stage, one based on the new technologies of electronic communication, the internal-combustion engine, the airplane, synthetics, and petro-chemicals. These new technologies transformed every aspect of American life and turned urbanization into metropolitanization. This third frontier stage generated a third settlement of the United States, this time in metropolitan regions from coast to coast, involving a mass migration of tens of millions of Americans in search of opportunity on the suburban frontier.

In the 1970s, the first post–World War II generation came to a close. Many Americans were speaking of the "limits of growth." Yet despite that anti-frontier rhetoric, there was every sign that a fourth frontier stage was beginning in the form of the rurban, or citybelt-cybernetic, frontier generated by the metropolitan-technological frontier just as the latter had been generated by its predecessor.

The rurban-cybernetic frontier first emerged in the Northeast, as did its predecessors, as the Atlantic Coast metropolitan regions merged into one another to form a six-hundred-mile-long megalopolis (the usage is Jean Gottman's)—a matrix of urban and suburban settlements in which the older central cities came to yield importance if not prominence to smaller ones. It was a sign of the times that the computer was conceived at MIT in Cambridge and developed at IBM in White Plains, two medium-sized cities in the megalopolis that have become special centers in their own right. This in itself is a reflection of the two primary characteristics of the new frontier. The new locus of settlement is in medium-sized and small cities and in the rural interstices of the megalopolis.

The spreading use of computer technology is the most direct manifestation of the cybernetic tools that make such citybelts possible. In 1979 the newspapers in the Northeast published frequent reports of the revival of the small cities of the first industrial revolution, particularly in New England, as the new frontier engulfed them. Countrywide, the media focused on the shifting of population growth into rural areas. Both phenomena are as much a product of the communications revolution as they are of the older American longing for small town or country living. Both reflect the urbanization of the American way of life no matter what lifestyle is practiced, or where.

Although the Northeast was first, the new rurban-cybernetic frontier, like its predecessors, is finding its true form in the South and West, where these citybelt matrices are not being built on the collapse of earlier forms, but are developing as an original form. The present sunbelt frontier—strung out along the Gulf Coast, the southwestern desert, and the fringes of the California mountains—is classically megalopolitan in citybelt form and cybernetic with its aerospace-related industries and sunbelt living made possible by air conditioning and the new telecommunications.

The continuing American frontier has all the characteristics of a chain reaction. In a land of great opportunity, each frontier, once opened, has generated its successor and, in turn, has been replaced by it. Each frontier has created a new America with new opportunities, new patterns of settlement, new occupations, new challenges, and new problems. As a result, the central political problem of growth is not simply how to handle the physical changes brought by each frontier, real as they are. It is how to accommodate newness, population turnover, and transience as a way of life. That is the American frontier situation.

Alabama has enjoyed an ambiguous relationship with the continuing American frontier. Even when it was in the path of the original westward movement, from just after the Revolutionary War until the Civil War, its settlement was in most respects a sideshow. It was settled in due course by a southern stream moving westward, and then quickly passed over, even though, as a poor state, what we usually called "frontier conditions" persisted well into the twentieth century.

After the Civil War, there were pockets of industrialization, principally at Birmingham and Bessemer, but they did not so much represent the urban-industrial frontier as the sporadic application of the plantation economy to urban pursuits in the manner described by W. J. Cash in his classic *The Mind of the South.*

Just as Alabama agriculture played out without ever reaching national peaks, so, too, did its urban industrial base play out in the first post–World War II generation. At the same time, Huntsville became a center of the emerging space frontier. Essentially, however, Alabama was passed over by the metropolitan-technological frontier, changing only insofar as the whole country was changed by the impact of that frontier. It may do better in the fourth frontier stage that has opened up in the United States since the mid-1970s. The new rurban-cybernetic frontier may reshape settlement patterns in the state, particularly along Alabama's Gulf Coast, which is part of the sunbelt megalopolis growing along the Gulf Coast from Texas to Florida.

THE PERSISTENCE OF SECTIONALISM

Sectionalism—the expression of social, economic, and especially political differences along geographic lines—is part and parcel of American political life. The more or less permanent political ties that link groups of contiguous states together as sections reflect the ways in which local conditions and differences in political culture modify the impact of the frontier. This overall sectional pattern reflects the interaction of the three basic factors. The original sections were produced by the variations in the impact of the rural-land frontier on different geographic segments of the country. They, in turn, have been modified by the pressures generated by the first and subsequent frontier stages. As a result, sectionalism is not the same as regionalism. The latter is essentially a phenomenon—often transient—that brings adjacent state, substate, or interstate areas together because of immediate and specific common interests. The sections are not homogeneous socioeconomic units sharing a common character across state lines, but complex entities combining highly diverse states and communities with common political interests that generally complement one another socially and economically.

For example, the South is a section bound by the tightest of social, political, and historical ties even though the differences between the states of the lower and upper South are quite noticeable even to the casual observer. The six New England states consciously seek to cooperate with one another in numerous ways. Their cooperative efforts have been sufficiently institutionalized to create a veritable confederation within the larger American Union. It is through such acts of political will that sectionalism best manifests itself.

Intrasectional conflicts often exist but they do not detract from the long-term sectional community of interest. More important for our purposes, certain common sectional bonds give the states of each section a special relationship to national politics. This is particularly true in connection with those specific political issues that are of sectional importance, such as the race issue in the South, the problems of the megalopolis in the Northeast, and the problems of agriculture and agribusiness in the Northwest.

The nation's sectional alignments are rooted in the three great historical, cultural, and economic spheres into which the country is divided: the greater Northeast, the greater South, and the greater West. Following state lines, the greater Northeast includes all those states north of the Ohio and Potomac rivers and east of Lake Michigan. The greater South includes the states below that line but east of the Mississippi plus Missouri, Arkansas, Louisiana, Oklahoma, and Texas. All the rest of the states compose the greater West. Within that framework, there are eight sections: New England, Middle Atlantic, Near West, Upper South, Lower South, Western South, Northwest, and Far West. Alabama is situated in the heart of the Lower South.

From the New Deal years through the 1960s, Americans' understanding of sectionalism was submerged by their concern with urban-oriented socioeconomic categories, such as the struggle between labor and management or between the haves and have-nots in the big cities. Even the racial issue, once the hallmark of the greater South, began to be perceived in nonsectional terms as a result of black migration northward. This is not to say that sectionalism ceased to exist as a vital force, only that it was little noted in those years.

Beginning in the 1970s, however, there was a resurgence of sectional feeling as economic and social cleavages increasingly came to follow sectional lines. The sunbelt-frostbelt confrontation is the prime example of this new sectionalism. "Sunbelt" is the new code word for the Lower South, Western South, and Far West; "frostbelt" is the code word for the New England, Middle Atlantic, and Great Lakes (Near Western) states. Sectionalism is once again a major force in national politics, closely linked to the rurban-cybernetic frontier.

A perennial problem of the states, hardly less important than that of direct federal-state relationships, is how to bend sectional and regional demands to fit their own needs for self-maintenance as political systems. One of the ways in which the states are able to deal with this problem is through the use of their formal political institutions, since no problems can be handled governmentally without making use of those formal institutions.

Some would argue that the use of formal political institutions to deflect sectional patterns on behalf of the states is "artificial" interference with the "natural" flow of the nation's social and economic system. Partisans of the states would respond not only by questioning the naturalness of a socioeconomic system that was created by people who migrated freely across the landscape as individuals in search of opportunity, but by arguing that the history of civilization is the record of human efforts to harness the environment by means of their inventions, all artificial in the literal and real sense of the term. It need not be pointed out that political institutions are among the foremost of those inventions.

As part of the old southwestern region of the Lower South, Alabama's location has meant that the state was settled primarily by white frontiersmen and adventurers and their black slaves. The former remained a population of plain folks to the point that even the rich and powerful were more in the nature of successful conquerors than gentry, while the latter remained an underclass until our own times. This in turn led to a polarized society divided into two homogeneous populations clearly separated with no pretensions of equality. Managing this problem and, in recent decades, trying to overcome it has been at the heart of Alabama's political agenda.

THE VITAL ROLE OF POLITICAL CULTURE

The same locational factors place Alabama at the very heart of the traditionalistic political culture area. The United States as a whole shares a general political culture that is rooted in two contrasting conceptions of the political order that can be traced back to the earliest settlement of the country. In the first, the polity is conceived as a marketplace in which the primary public relationships are products of bargaining among individuals and groups acting out of self-interest. In the second, the political order is conceived to be a commonwealth—a polity in which the whole people have an undivided interest—in which the citizens cooperate in an effort to create and maintain the best government in order to implement certain shared moral principles. These two conceptions have exercised an influence on government and politics throughout American history, sometimes in conflict and sometimes complementing each other.

The national political culture is a synthesis of three major political subcultures. All three are of nationwide proportions, having spread, in the course of time, from coast to coast. At the same time each subculture is strongly tied to specific sections of the country, reflecting the streams and currents of migration that have carried people of different origins and backgrounds across the continent in more or less orderly patterns. Considering their central characteristics, the three may be called *individualistic, moralistic,* and *traditionalistic.* Each of the three reflects its own particular synthesis of the marketplace and the commonwealth.

The *individualistic political culture* emphasizes the democratic order as a marketplace in which government is instituted for strictly utilitarian reasons, to handle those functions demanded by the people it is created to serve. Beyond the commitment to an open market, a government need not have any direct concern with questions of the good society, except insofar as it may be used to advance some common view formulated outside the political arena just as it serves other functions. Since the individualistic political culture emphasizes the centrality of private concerns, it places a premium on limiting community intervention—whether governmental or nongovernmental—into private activities to the minimum necessary to keep the marketplace in proper working order.

The character of political participation in the individualistic political culture reflects this outlook. Politics is just another means through which individuals may improve themselves socially and economically. In this sense politics is a business like any other, competing for talent and offering rewards to those who take it up as a career. Those individuals who choose political careers may rise by providing the governmental services demanded of them and, in return, may expect to be adequately compensated for their efforts. Interpretations of officeholders' obligations under this arrangement vary. Where the norms are high, they are expected to provide high-quality public services in return for appropriate rewards. In other cases, an officeholder's primary responsibility is to serve himself and those who have supported him directly, favoring them even at the expense of the public.

Political life within the individualistic political culture is based on a system of mutual obligations rooted in personal relationships. In the United States, political parties serve as the vehicles for maintaining the obligational network. Party regularity is indispensable in the individualistic political culture because it is the means for coordinating individual enterprise in the political arena and is the one way of preventing individualism in politics from running wild. Such a political culture encourages the maintenance of a party system that is competitive, but not overly so, in the pursuit of office.

Since the individualistic political culture eschews ideological concerns in its businesslike conception of politics, both politicians and citizens look upon political activity as a specialized one, essentially the province of professionals, of minimum and passing concern to the public, and with no place for amateurs to play an active role. Furthermore, there is a strong tendency among the public to believe that politics is a dirty—if necessary— business, better left to those who are willing to soil themselves by engaging in it. In practice, then, where the individualistic political culture is dominant, there is likely to be an easy attitude toward the limits of the professionals' perquisites. Since a fair amount of corruption is expected in the normal course of things, there is relatively little popular excitement when any is found, unless it is of an extraordinary character. It is as if the public is willing to pay a surcharge for services rendered and rebels only when it feels the surcharge has become too heavy. (Of course the judgments as to what is normal and what is extraordinary are themselves subjective and culturally conditioned.)

Public officials, committed to giving the public what it wants, normally will initiate new programs only when they perceive an overwhelming public demand for them to act. The individualistic political culture is ambivalent about the place of bureaucracy in the political order. Bureaucratic methods of operation fly in the face of the favor system, yet organizational efficiency can be used by those seeking to master the market.

To the extent that the marketplace provides the model for public relationships in American civil society, all Americans share some of the attitudes that are of first importance in the individualistic political culture. At the same time, substantial segments of the American people operate politically within the framework of two political cultures.

The *moralistic political culture* emphasizes the commonwealth conception as the basis for democratic government. Politics, in the moralistic
political culture, is considered one of the great activities of humanity in its
search for the good society—a struggle for power, it is true, but also an
effort to exercise power for the betterment of the commonwealth. Consequently, both the general public and the politicians conceive of politics as a
public activity centered on some idea of the public good and properly devoted to the advancement of the public interest.

In the moralistic political culture, there is a general commitment to
utilizing communal—preferably nongovernmental, but governmental if
necessary—power to intervene in the sphere of private activities when it is
considered necessary to do so for the public good. Accordingly, issues have
an important place in the moralistic style of politics, functioning to set the
tone for political concern. Government is considered a positive instrument
with a responsibility to promote the general welfare, though definitions of
what its positive role should be may vary considerably from era to era.

Politics is ideally a matter of concern and duty for every citizen. Government service is public service, placing moral obligations on those who serve
in government more demanding than those of the marketplace. Politics is
not considered a legitimate realm for private economic enrichment. A
politician is not expected to profit from political activity and in fact is held
suspect if he or she does.

The concept of serving the commonwealth is at the core of all political
relationships and politicians are expected to adhere to it even at the expense
of individual loyalties and political friendships. Political parties are considered useful political devices but are not valued for their own sakes. Regular
party ties can be abandoned with relative impunity for third parties, special
local parties, nonpartisan systems, or the opposition party if such changes
are believed helpful in gaining larger political goals.

In practice, where the moralistic political culture is dominant today, there
is considerably more amateur participation in politics. There is also much
less of what Americans consider corruption in government and less toler-
ance of those actions that are considered corrupt, so politics does not have
the taint it so often bears in the individualistic environment.

By virtue of its fundamental outlook, the moralistic political culture
opens greater possibilities for active government intervention in the economic and social life of the community. At the same time, its strong
commitment to communitarianism tends to keep government intervention

local wherever possible. Public officials will themselves initiate new government activities in an effort to come to grips with problems as yet unperceived by a majority of the citizenry.

The moralistic political culture's major difficulty with bureaucracy lies in the potential conflict between communitarian principles and large-scale organization. Otherwise, the notion of a politically neutral administrative system is attractive. Where merit systems are instituted, they tend to be rigidly maintained.

The *traditionalistic political culture* is rooted in an ambivalent attitude toward the marketplace, coupled with a paternalistic and elitist conception of the commonwealth. It reflects an older, precommercial attitude that accepts a substantially hierarchical society as part of the ordered nature of things, authorizing and expecting those at the top of the social structure to take a special and dominant role in government. Like its moralistic counterpart, the traditionalistic political culture accepts government as an actor with a positive role in the community, but it tries to limit that role to securing the continued maintenance of the existing social order. To do so, it functions to confine real political power to a relatively small and self-perpetuating group drawn from an established elite who often inherit their right to govern through family ties or social position. Social and family ties are even more important in a traditionalistic political culture than personal ties in the individualistic, where, after all is said and done, one's first responsibility is to oneself. At the same time, those who do not have a definite role to play in politics are not expected to be even minimally active as citizens. In many cases, they are not even expected to vote. As in the individualistic political culture, those active in politics are expected to benefit personally from their activity although not necessarily by direct pecuniary gain.

Political parties are not important in traditionalistic political cultures because they encourage a degree of openness that goes against the grain of an elitist political order. Political competition is expressed through factions, an extension of the personal politics characteristic of the system. Hence political systems within the culture tend to have loose one-party systems if they have political parties at all. Political leaders play conservative and custodial rather than initiatory roles unless pressed strongly from the outside.

Traditionalistic political cultures tend to be antibureaucratic. Bureaucracy by its very nature interferes with the fine web of social relationships that lies at the root of the political system. Where bureaucracy is introduced, it is generally confined to ministerial functions under the aegis of the establishment powerholders.

Like Georgia, South Carolina, and Mississippi, Alabama is archetypical of the traditionalistic political subculture in the United States. It is likely that only Mississippi has a more homogeneous political culture statewide. This means that large segments of the population do not see it as their place to participate in politics. In Alabama as in the rest of the South, this found expression in the disenfranchisement of the black population, at one time a majority in the state, and, to a lesser extent, through various devices designed to discourage ordinary white people from voting as well. Meanwhile, the political elite is linked together through a matrix of interlocking family connections and political obligations. However, unlike other southern states, Alabama did not have a distinctive "aristocratic" class or even a clearly distinguished gentry. Rather, there were a number of political families not much different from other white Alabamians who came to dominate the state's politics over the years.

Since the civil rights revolution of the 1960s, disenfranchisement of blacks has given way to black participation and with it greater opportunities for white participation as well. Today political participation in Alabama is governed by a more general openness, tempered by the residues of an older political culture. Whether this will lead to fundamental political cultural change is yet to be seen.

Alabama's political culture reflects the state's homogeneity, poverty, and isolation. The predominance of Americans of Scotch-Irish descent in the white population, the fact that Alabama was never rich and was further impoverished as a result of the Civil War, and the state's isolation from the main impetus of southern, not to speak of American society, have all had their influence. It is significant that the two cities in Alabama with more than statewide influence are at either extreme of the state—Mobile, in the south, a port since its founding by the French in 1702, three generations before the arrival of the Americans, and Huntsville, in the north, brought into prominence as America's first center for space research. Neither city has been very influential in state affairs, although both have been extremely important for the state's economy. More typical of the state are Montgomery, the state capital and center of such planter society as existed in antebellum Alabama, and Birmingham, once a modest iron and steel center.

At two historic moments in American history, Alabama has played a major role, in both cases as locus more than as actor. Both were associated with the great American tragedy of Negro slavery and discrimination against blacks, and in both cases Alabama was the site for the inauguration of civil conflict. In 1861, Montgomery became the first capital of the Confederacy, the site of the Confederate constitutional convention and the founding of the Confederate States of America. Nearly one hundred years later in 1956, Montgomery was the locus of the famous bus boycott that launched the civil rights revolution and the public career of its greatest leader, Martin Luther King, Jr. Although Alabama was singularly free of major battles during the Civil War, it was a major battlesite in the civil rights revolution, which not only began in Montgomery, but reached its climax in Selma, where the confrontation between the civil rights movement and the forces of "law and order" was the proximate catalyst for the Voting Rights Act of 1965.

In some respects, the fact that these historic confrontations took place in Alabama was ironic, just as was the location of America's first opening of the space frontier in Huntsville, for Alabama is a modest, rather self-effacing state with a modest, self-effacing population that does not seek national headlines or know what to do with them when they come. About the only two things that are volatile in Alabama are its weather and its politics, which many say resemble each other.

Alabama politics has been dominated by a succession of tempestuous, flashy characters who, while usually drawn from the same network of political families, have tended to be populist in their orientation. If this sounds like a cultural contradiction, so be it. That is one of the unique characteristics of Alabama, whose traditionalistic political culture is modified by a strong populist streak, reflecting the absence of a dominant gentry.

At the very least, these populist figures gave the hardscrabble farmers and factory workers of Alabama a "good show" in the pattern of southern revivalism. Most of the time, like the revivalist preachers, they could do little to enhance their constituents' lives on earth other than by raising their spirits and entertaining them. Only in our own generation has there been a major change in this pattern, with Alabama government finally beginning to offer the underprivileged some of the help expected in modern states.

Not that earlier generations wished for more. By and large, Alabama governments have reflected the will of their citizens, even their disenfranchised ones, in providing a caretaker rather than an activist state. Alabamians have been reluctant to seek more from their governments. Maintenance of law and order and promotion of internal improvements were the two demands made of government in the nineteenth century. Basic schooling and institutional services were added at the turn of the century, and during the New Deal it was expected that public-works programs would supply jobs for those temporarily in need. As Alabama now provides more of the services expected of government in contemporary society, it responds to the political cultures of its neighboring states and the Union. What was a gulf is now a gap that may widen as easily as close. As Professors Thomas and Stewart show in this book, there remains much at stake in the politics and government of Alabama.

Preface

This study of Alabama government and politics is an outgrowth of a little volume that James D. Thomas prepared, a number of years ago now, for the University of Alabama Bureau of Public Administration. That volume was entitled *Government in Alabama.* The Bureau and its publication program were discontinued in a reorganization in the early 1980s. Because the old volume had no chance of being revised and republished, we began to think of using it as the starting point for a more substantial study of Alabama's political system.

As we were working on the manuscript, Daniel J. Elazar, Director of the Center for the Study of Federalism at Temple University, raised with William H. Stewart the possibility of submitting a study of Alabama government and politics for inclusion in the series of state studies sponsored by the center and published by the University of Nebraska Press. We are very grateful to Professor Elazar and the University of Nebraska Press for the opportunity to contribute our study to the series. Because of the passage of time and the nature of this study, there is relatively little of the original material in it. Nevertheless, language used in the earlier work appears in this study, and we also relied on other works we prepared for the Bureau of Public Administration. We are grateful to the individuals at the University of Alabama who permitted us to use material from our previous works, as well as other bureau publications, in the preparation of this study. We owe a debt of gratitude also to Robert L. McCurley, Jr., Director of the Alabama Law Institute, for permission to use material from publications issued by the Law Institute. We thank Malcolm M. MacDonald, Director of the University of Alabama Press, for permission to use material from books published by the

666666666666666666

press. A number of them were quite useful to us. We wish to express our gratitude also to the other individuals and organizations who gave us permission to use material from their publications.

We acknowledge with much appreciation the helpful comments and suggestions made by the University of Nebraska's anonymous reader, who did a thorough job of reviewing the manuscript, and by Professor Elazar, the general editor of the series. We owe a special debt of gratitude to our colleagues at the University of Alabama. They contributed materials for our use as well as valued advice and counsel in our conversations in the offices and corridors of ten Hoor Hall. Our department chair, Harvey Kline, was particularly supportive with aid and encouragement. We very much appreciate the assistance of the knowledgeable individuals, some in the government and some not, who graciously answered our questions and otherwise supplied information about the state's politics and political processes. In general, Professor Stewart prepared the manuscript on his personal word processor, but the secretaries in the Department of Political Science were always ready to help when we needed it.

Several of our graduate students assisted with the preparation of our manuscript, most recently Dan Gressang, John Ellis, and Jack Schutzbach. The Cartographic Lab in the University of Alabama's Department of Geography supplied our maps. Jack Schutzbach, however, completed the maps showing demographic and voting data. The map showing the voting pattern in the 1984 presidential election appeared in one of Professor Stewart's earlier works and is used by permission of Praeger Publishers. Our families gave us the time and support we needed to complete the manuscript. Because their contributions went so far beyond the call of duty, we dedicate our book to our wives, Miriam and Connie. With so many contributions by others, readers may be wondering about our responsibilities. We take responsibility for any mistakes that may remain in the study.

ALABAMA GOVERNMENT & POLITICS

Alabama

CHAPTER ONE

The Character
of
Alabama

This is a book about state and local government in Alabama, a state whose image was shaped for nearly three decades by George C. Wallace. After an initial loss, he won the office of governor in 1962. Elected in the midst of the strife and turmoil of the civil rights movement, Wallace pledged to fight for segregation forever and soon led Alabama into the vanguard of the states opposing the movement. With the publicity he attracted by his stand at the schoolhouse door in 1963, when he tried personally to block the racial integration of the University of Alabama, he came to symbolize southern resistance to federally supported efforts to achieve racial equality.

Later in the 1960s Wallace took his case to the country. He entered presidential primaries in other states and in 1968 ran for the presidency on his own party ticket. The only candidate for the presidency that Alabama has ever produced, his efforts were surprisingly successful. He attracted almost ten million popular votes throughout the country and won the votes of forty-six presidential electors. Wallace entered the presidential race again in 1972. This time, however, his campaign was cut short by an assassination attempt in Maryland that left him paralyzed and confined to a wheelchair.[1] Since then, Wallace has been less visible nationally, but as we write he is completing his fourth (and, he has announced, his last) term as governor of Alabama—a demonstration of voter support without parallel in Alabama history.

To many Americans, Wallace typified Alabama. But Alabama is more than George Wallace. It has had an interesting, even an exciting, history, and it has produced other national figures. William R. King, for example, was elected vice-president of the United States in 1852. Also in the nineteenth century, Alabamians John McKinley and John A. Campbell served as associate justices of the U.S. Supreme Court. Probably no national convention was more dramatic than the Democratic convention of 1924, when its factious delegates took more than a hundred ballots before settling their differences enough to nominate John W. Davis as their presidential candidate. Alabama senator Oscar W. Underwood, who had been mentioned as a possible nominee back in 1912, played a prominent role at the convention. Charles Summersell tells the story this way:

> While America was campaigning for the presidency in 1924, Underwood's name became a household word throughout the nation. This was due to [Governor William W.] Brandon's dramatic support of Senator Underwood for the presidential nomination in the Democratic convention then meeting in New York's Madison Square Garden. Radio coverage carried Brandon's booming voice into millions of homes at the start of each ballot . . . when Brandon shouted, "Alabama casts twenty-four votes for Oscar W. Underwood."[2]

Underwood was succeeded as U.S. senator by Hugo L. Black, who became a staunch supporter of Franklin Delano Roosevelt's New Deal programs and, later, one of the most important justices ever to serve on the U.S. Supreme Court. Also in the FDR era, William B. Bankhead served as Speaker of the U.S. House of Representatives.

In the course of two centuries, Alabama has become the subject of a national debate, a rallying cry, the name of a successful pop music group, and a symbol of football power. But first of all it was a land with borders and resources, potentials and limits defining what the state could be. It would hardly be possible—nor is it really necessary—in the course of these introductory chapters to give a detailed description of the geographical, social, economic, and political foundations of contemporary Alabama government. We may be able, however, to identify some of the main characteristics of the state's physical and historical environment and suggest how they have been significant in the development of Alabama's complex political culture.[3]

GEOGRAPHY

Alabama is over 300 miles long (stretching from the Gulf of Mexico and the Florida Panhandle to Tennessee) and about 150 miles wide at the points of greatest distance. Its total area is 51,609 square miles, which makes it a bit larger than such populous states as New York and Pennsylvania but smaller than its eastern neighbor, Georgia.

The Gulf Coast is represented by a narrow strip of territory extending along the southwestern tip of the state. The indentation into this area made by Mobile Bay furnishes a harbor for seagoing vessels. Mobile, located at the mouth of Mobile River on the northwestern shore of the bay, is an international shipping center. Two of the state's largest rivers, the Tombigbee and the Alabama, eventually merge and flow into Mobile Bay. This links much of the state's inland waterway system to Mobile. Extending this linkage to the Tennessee River was a goal long sought by those involved in Alabama's commercial development.

Geographers have identified four major physiographic regions or provinces in Alabama. These are the Coastal Plain, the Piedmont, the Valley and Ridge region, and the Appalachian Plateau. One of the commonly identified political regions of the state, Sand Mountain, is the popular designation for the Appalachian Plateau, which extends in a southwesterly direction from the northeast corner of the state. The provinces consist of a number of topographic subdivisions. The Coastal Plain, for example, includes eight subdivisions: the Fall Line Hills, Ripley Cuesta, Flatwoods, Red Hills, Buhrstone Cuesta, Jackson Prairie, the Southern Pine Hills, and the Black Belt.

Black Belt is both the scientific and the popular name for a major portion of the Coastal Plain stretching east to west across the south central part of Alabama. The rich, black soils in this geographic subdivision provided the foundation for the early emergence of a vigorous agricultural economy in the state. Because of its historical importance, we will have a good deal more to say about the role of the Black Belt in the political economy of Alabama.

Contrary to what is perhaps the popular impression, much of the northern part of the state is quite hilly and wooded—not plantation country at all. The highest point in Alabama is Mount Cheaha, which rises 2,407 feet. In the Coastal Plain, elevations range from sea level to 200 feet; in the northern plateau, to 800 to 1,000 feet; and to nearly half a mile in the Talladega Mountains (the location of Mount Cheaha). The mean elevation in the highlands is 800 feet. The statewide average is 600 feet.

Although the state has a remarkably extensive set of river systems, no major rivers actually start in Alabama. Yet it is said that about one-twelfth of the water flowing into the seas from the lower forty-eight states flows through Alabama.[4] The state contains three large river systems—the Tennessee, the Tombigbee (including the Black Warrior tributary), and the Alabama (with such tributaries as the Cahaba, the Coosa, and the Tallapoosa). Other rivers include the Mobile, the Chattahoochee (the southern part of the boundary with Georgia), and the Conecuh, also in the south.

With so many rivers, waterway development and use have figured as prominent issues in Alabama politics, both within the state and in the federal arena. The best example of water transportation politics on an intergovernmental plane involves the Tennessee-Tombigbee Waterway, which now connects these rivers and provides the northern part of the state with a slackwater route to and from the Gulf of Mexico. A massive national project, it was supported not only by Alabama but by other southeastern states as well.[5] Within the state, the waterway system contributed to the development of a sectional division found in Alabama politics from territorial days to modern times. In general, the division lay along the lines of a Tennessee Valley–Black Belt, north Alabama–south Alabama rivalry for influence in the state government.[6]

CLIMATE

The Alabama climate is moderate. Scientifically classified as semitropical, the average annual temperature in the northern part of the state is 60°F; and in the south, 67°. Overall, in summer, daytime highs are usually in the nineties, but sometimes higher, while the nighttime low is around 70°. In the winter, 42° is the average January temperature in north Alabama, while the average is 52° in the coastal areas.

At times hot, dry spells in summer and hard freezes in winter cause serious problems, as in the case of central Alabama fruit growers, who experienced both of these calamities in 1985. In 1986 a severe drought in the southeastern United States caused widespread damage to Alabama's farms. Farmers in midwestern states sent hay to Alabama farmers to help them get their cattle through the summer. But mild temperatures generally prevail and, importantly for agricultural productivity, this makes for long growing seasons. In north Alabama the average growing season (the period without frost) is 198 days; in south Alabama there are only a couple of months of winter between the first and last freeze, which leaves an enviable growing season of almost 300 days. Agricultural productivity has also been encouraged by a general abundance of rain. Over the state as a whole the average is fifty-three inches annually. This is a heavier rainfall than in most states, more than in, say, California, New York, or Pennsylvania. Again, however, there are both seasonal and regional variations. For example, more rain falls in the coastal areas, where the average is about sixty-five inches. In central Alabama the average is fifty inches, and in the northeast it is near the state average at fifty-five inches.

EARLY EXPLORATION

Geography and climate have been kind to Alabama; the state is well endowed with natural resources. An Alabama historian once observed that his state had been given "incalculable wealth in climate, soil, minerals, forest, fauna, flora, water power, and transportation facilities." The first inhabitants to benefit from Alabama's natural resources were, of course, the Indians. The leading Native American groups were the Cherokees, Chickasaws, Choctaws, and Creeks. As A. B. Moore, the historian whom we have just quoted, put it, "By treaty and by war [the Indians] parceled among themselves the territory of the present State of Alabama." The Creeks were the largest of the Indian groups, and they held virtually the entire central and eastern part of the state, while the Cherokees were located along the Tennessee River in the north and northeast, the Chickasaws in the northwest, and the Choctaws in the southwest. Although at times Indian tribes in Alabama served as the allies of European powers, as the Creeks did in the War of 1812, American expansion into Alabama resulted in the eventual removal of the Indians and their relocation in the West, but before that happened they played a major role in the state's history. Alabama's Indian heritage is reflected in the fact that Indian names continue to abound in the designations of towns, counties, rivers, and other places. Even the name Alabama is said to be a derivative of the name of a group of Indians who lived in the area centuries ago.

Alabama was first explored by Spain, at the very outset of its contact with the New World. One of the earliest European voyagers to enter the area was Alonso Alvarez de Piñeda, who sailed from the West Indies and briefly explored Alabama's southern coast in 1519. There were other Spanish expeditions, such as that of Narváez and Cabeza de Vaca in 1528, but undoubtedly the most familiar Spanish explorer of Alabama is Hernando de Soto, who traveled through the area in 1540. It was de Soto who first made extensive contact with the Indians. It was also de Soto who fought the first major battle with the Indians, a fierce encounter with the followers of the famous Chief Tuskaloosa.

Despite the Spanish expeditions of the sixteenth century, it was not until the eighteenth century that permanent settlement took place, and this was made not by the Spanish but by the French, who wanted to colonize the area around the Mississippi River. This initial settlement was old Mobile (Fort Louis), founded in 1702 upriver from Mobile Bay on Twenty-seven Mile Bluff. The principal builder of the community was Jean-Baptiste Le Moyne, sieur de Bienville, who, because of his significance in its settlement, is sometimes referred to as the "founder of Alabama." Because the upriver site was less desirable than he had first thought, Bienville abandoned it and constructed a settlement called Mobile in the present location of the city in 1711. For almost ten years it was the seat of government of French Louisiana. French claims in Alabama were transferred to England in 1763, following the British victory in the French and Indian War. After the Revolutionary War, the United States claimed the territory in West Florida down to 31° north latitude. Spain claimed that its lands in Florida extended much farther north, but under a 1795 treaty it accepted the American claim. Alabama thus played a part in one of the new American nation's first serious diplomatic problems, the question of its southern boundary.

The dispute over West Florida also involved Alabama in a dramatic domestic incident that threatened secession and civil war a half century before it actually happened. As friction continued along the borderlands, the settlers in Alabama wanted Spain out of Florida altogether. This made some of them sympathetic to the appeal of Aaron Burr that the Southwest should secede and form an independent nation that would assume control over the disputed territory. The Burr conspiracy was short-lived, however, and through a combination of diplomatic and military efforts, the United States was able to acquire West Florida in 1810. Of the coastal area of modern Alabama, only Mobile remained in Spanish hands, and it was given up to an American military expedition in 1813.

THE CREATION OF ALABAMA

Traders and woodsmen ventured early into Alabama, and they were soon followed by waves of land-hungry settlers. In time, the settlers began to demand the protection of organized government and, eventually, statehood. Congress responded to these demands with a series of steps that ultimately led to the creation of the state of Alabama. The process began in 1798 when

Congress established Mississippi Territory, an area that was, the statute said, "bounded on the west by the Mississippi; on the north by a line to be drawn due east from the mouth of the Yasous to the Chattahoochee river; on the east by the river Chattahoochee; and on the south by the thirty-first degree of north latitude." Essentially, 32°28' formed the territory's northern boundary, so that it included in its eastern part just about the lower third of modern Alabama. In addition to Indian claims, Georgia also claimed title to lands north of this line until it finally ceded them to the federal government in 1802.

In 1804 Congress changed the northern boundary of Mississippi Territory, making it coterminous with the state of Tennessee. Much of the territory still remained under Indian title, however. As white settlers flowed into the area, conflict with the Indians over these lands became ever more intense. Sharp clashes with the Indians, especially during the Creek War of 1813–14, produced such incidents as the Fort Mims Massacre of 1813, which resulted in the death of almost three hundred Alabama settlers. Step by step, though, the Indians were forced to cede their claims to the white settlers. When an army led by General Andrew Jackson defeated the Creek Red Sticks at the Battle of Horseshoe Bend in 1814, resistance to white settlement effectively came to an end. Creek cessions in 1814 were followed by cessions from the Choctaw, Chickasaw, and Cherokee tribes in the years immediately preceding statehood in 1819. In the years 1828 to 1835 the remaining Indians relinquished the last of their claims. Still, a few Indians continued to resist until 1837, when the last significant battle between whites and Indians took place. Hardly any Indians remained in Alabama by the time of the Civil War. Under the national policy of Indian removal— pursued most vigorously during President Jackson's administration—just about all were moved to the West.

Meanwhile, the settlers in the western and eastern portions of Mississippi Territory were assuming separate identities. In 1817 Congress partitioned the territory, admitting the western part to the Union as the state of Mississippi and establishing the eastern part as Alabama Territory. Two years later Congress responded to a petition from the rapidly growing territory's legislature by authorizing the Alabamians to frame and adopt a constitution in anticipation of statehood. The territorial legislature arranged for a convention, which met at Huntsville and drafted the necessary document. Alabama's settlers saw the process of statebuilding finally completed when Congress approved the new constitution and made Alabama a part of the Union on December 14, 1819.[7] Its state capital was located briefly at

Huntsville and then at Cahaba. Later the state assembly selected Tuscaloosa and, ultimately, Montgomery as the capital city.

GROWTH AND DEVELOPMENT

Most of the white inhabitants of the new state of Alabama came from such southern states as Georgia, North and South Carolina, Tennessee, and Virginia. Many of them were seeking new and fertile lands on which to establish the cotton plantations that, with the invention of the cotton gin, had become profitable enterprises. Despite the growth that had contributed to the territory's rapid transformation into a state, only 1.3 percent of the U.S. population was resident in Alabama in 1819. Although the population had increased tremendously, in 1980 still less than 2 percent of the nation's population made their homes in Alabama. The federal census of 1980 listed the state's population as 3,893,888. The fact that such a small portion of the U.S. population lives in Alabama limits the state's general political influence. In presidential elections, for example, its nine electoral votes would not be sought as eagerly as the much larger blocs that can be awarded by such states as California, New York, or Texas.

In the first census after statehood, that of 1820, Alabamians numbered 127, 901, all of them classified as rural. There were 85,451 whites and 42,450 blacks. The blacks were virtually all slaves of the whites. By the middle of the twentieth century there were 979,617 black people in Alabama out of a total population of 3,061,743, or 32 percent of the population. The proportion of blacks in the population had grown fairly steadily until 1900, when the figure stood at 45 percent. Since then it has been on the decline, although it is still substantial. In recent years, most blacks in Alabama have not lived in rural areas (as the stereotypical image of Alabama would have it) but in urban centers. About 70 percent of blacks have been so located, compared to some 55 to 60 percent of whites. As a result, there are thousands of black votes in urban areas, and they can have an important, and sometimes a decisive, influence on the outcome of an election.

As a demonstration of the significance of waterways in Alabama's first years as a state, the small population of 1820 was concentrated in four river districts—the Tennessee Valley, along the Alabama River, the Tombigbee district, and the Mobile district. By 1830 the population of Alabama had climbed to 309,527, a 142 percent increase during the decade, and it was becoming more dispersed. By then, too, slaves comprised 38 percent of the population, compared to about 33 percent in 1820.

In 1880, the first census following Reconstruction, the population of Alabama was 1,262,505, and urban residents amounted to only 15 percent of the total. A century later the urban proportion was placed at 62 percent. Even among rural residents, however, most are not making their living from agriculture. In recent years, only about 4 percent were farmers.

In 1880 the population of Birmingham, today Alabama's largest city, numbered only 3,086. The biggest city then was Mobile, which is now in second place. Jefferson County, in which Birmingham is located, grew from 8,989 in 1850, a figure that put it in the bottom half of the counties, to 88,501 residents in 1890, when it was the most populous county in the state. Ten years later, its population of 140,420 was about twice the size of Montgomery, then the second most populous county. Birmingham's growth reflects the rapid development of the city and its environs at a time when the proximity of coal and iron ore supported a burgeoning industrial economy.

In 1900, 88 percent of the state's population was rural. It was not until 1960 that a majority of Alabamians resided in urban areas. Even in the 1980s probably most of the adult population had been born and raised in a rural environment, and this characteristic has important political implications. It helps explain why Alabama politics has retained its rural flavor for so long. Alabama crossed the rural-urban divide a full generation or more after the United States as a whole.

Traditionally Alabama has been known as the Cotton State. During the nineteenth century, as Summersell put it, Alabama was indeed a "Cotton Kingdom." Cotton was the chief money crop, and as the basis of the Black Belt's plantation economy, it tended to concentrate the black population in that area. By the end of the century, cotton was both the basis of an increasingly important textile industry and the foundation of the sharecropping system of farm tenancy that arose after the Civil War.

In more recent years, cotton has declined sharply in its significance to the Alabama economy. Fields where cotton once grew are now likely to be employed for the production of cattle, soybeans, and peanuts, to be lying dormant, or to be devoted to urban uses. Problems involved in the production and marketing of cotton, federal farm policies dating from the New Deal, the creation of the Tennessee Valley Authority, and the efforts of the agricultural extension service have all contributed to the diversification and improvement of Alabama agriculture. Early twentieth-century growth in manufacturing, mining, and other extractive industries like lumbering further diversified the Alabama economy. Today Alabama has a predominantly industrial economy and, as we have seen, only a small fraction of Alabamians earn their income from agriculture. But despite this development, the

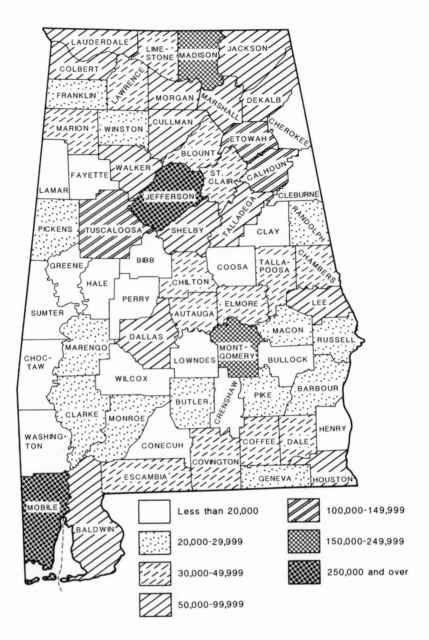

Figure 1. Alabama Population, 1980. (*Source:* Office of State Planning and Federal Programs, Alabama Department of Economic and Community Affairs, *Alabama County Data Book, 1983,* p. 69)

state is not as well off as most of its sister states. In 1981, for example, per capita income was $8,219—only 78 percent of the national average.

In 1880 about half of all Alabamians above the age of ten were illiterate. For blacks as a group, illustrating one of the many negative effects of slavery, about 80 percent were illiterate in 1880. The problem of educating the state's people for life in the twentieth century was thus enormous. Illiteracy has still not been eliminated, but at least it has been sharply reduced, with about 6 percent of the white and 9 percent of the nonwhite school-age population now classified as illiterate.

Alabama's state government was not doing much in 1880 to educate the general population. State contributions to the public school fund amounted to only $130,000. Recognizing the importance of education to the state's social and economic welfare, Alabama's political leaders have made education the state government's primary function. It now spends over a billion dollars a year on education. In 1980, for example, the state contributed $567 million to elementary and secondary education, almost $315 million to higher education, and over $350 million to other educational and cultural programs. In addition, about $215 million in federal funds passed through the state treasury on the way to educational programs administered by local governments. In state support for public education, Alabama now ranks among the most active states in the nation. Yet, combined state and local expenditures are not very impressive, largely because of weak local support.

In 1880 blacks constituted nearly half (45.9 percent) of the state's voting population, but with the rise of Jim Crow legislation around the turn of the century, black participation in Alabama public life was effectively suppressed. Black exclusion from the suffrage was institutionalized in the constitution of 1901, and the names of blacks virtually disappeared from the lists of registered voters. By 1980, for reasons we will examine later, blacks had returned to the polls, representing a full one-fourth of Alabama's registered voters and playing an increasingly important role in Alabama's political life.

POLITICAL ISSUES

Intense political struggles are not a recent phenomenon in Alabama. Throughout the state's history, fiercely contending groups have fought political battles for control of policy-making mechanisms, and from the beginning, political conflict between north Alabama and the Black Belt has

Figure 2. Percentage of Nonwhite Population, Alabama, 1980. (*Source:* Office of State Planning and Federal Programs, Alabama Department of Economic and Community Affairs, *Alabama County Data Book, 1983,* p. 74)

been one of the distinctive characteristics of Alabama politics. In the earliest years of statehood there were controversies over such issues as the location of the capital, the basis of representation in the legislative assembly, and Indian policy. Also, there was a great need to develop Alabama's transportation facilities, particularly its waterways. In addition to its local dimensions, this issue involved the relationship between Alabama and the federal government, which had the means to help develop Alabama's water resources. Alabamians were more likely to cooperate with the federal government in this area than in race relations, where whites generally wanted Washington to maintain, at a minimum, a hands-off policy or, preferably, a vigorous stand against attempts to undermine the institution of slavery.

No issue was more crucial in the state's political development than slavery. From the time the Wilmot Proviso was introduced in Congress in 1846, slavery was the dominant issue in state politics. Groups repeatedly differed over how far the state should go to preserve slavery, but ultimately the state of Alabama did go to war. Obviously the tragedy of the Civil War was the most traumatic event in the history of Alabama and the rest of the South, and it may not yet really be behind us. Affiliation with the Confederacy represented, though, Alabama's last "national" identity (other than American), an identity that had first been Spanish, then French, then English, then American, and finally Confederate. Reestablishment of federal authority after the Civil War had repercussions that affected the state's politics for years.

During Reconstruction, federal policy involved the active encouragement of full black participation in Alabama's political life. Internally, this policy met with varying responses. As a general rule, whites in north Alabama, where there were relatively few blacks, had little sympathy for the efforts of the Black Belt to depoliticize its newly enfranchised blacks. In time, though, southern Alabama whites were able to gain enough support from the northern districts to secure a suffrage article in the constitution of 1901 that virtually halted black voting. Even after the end of meaningful black political participation, however, conservative Black Belt politicians continued to raise the specter of black power against progressive reforms advanced by those who were less race-conscious in their public-policy concerns.

It was because the doctrine of "white supremacy" was generally accepted among whites, including those in north Alabama, that conservative delegates at the constitutional convention of 1901 were able to establish racial segregation and black disfranchisement as official state policies. As a result, for a half-century these policies (and worse practices, including lynching) were hallmarks of race relations in Alabama. But the U.S. Supreme Court's school desegregation decision of 1954 essentially amounted to a declaration that it was time for a change in American race relations. The black civil rights movement was born, and Alabama's political leaders, for the most part, chose to resist it. Beginning in Montgomery with the 1955 bus boycott led by the Reverend Martin Luther King, Jr., civil rights workers brought the state's discriminatory racial policies under increasingly heavy attack. Diehard segregationist opposition to the civil rights movement produced intense racial antagonism that at times erupted into rioting and violence against those who worked for racial integration. Birmingham, with its use of police dogs and fire hoses against black demonstrators, and Selma, where violence broke out against civil rights workers seeking to conduct a protest march to Montgomery, became national (if not international) symbols of racial injustice. By the 1970s, however, national desegregation and voting rights policies had softened these issues, and the civil rights movement in Alabama had turned to new objectives, among them black representation in the councils of government.

Sectional conflicts usually split north Alabama and the Black Belt, with the southeastern Wiregrass counties often supporting the north. Most of the state's wealth and population came to be concentrated in north Alabama, and we would have expected that section to prevail. However, because of their skill at building coalitions with newly rising industrialists—as reflected in the constitutional convention of 1901, in the legislature and in the results of election campaigns—Black Belt conservatives were long able to exercise far greater influence on state policy than the population of the section or its wealth would suggest. It was not until the Second Reconstruction, a century after the first, that the conservatives' hold on the state was effectively broken.

In the late nineteenth and early twentieth centuries, various factions within the Democratic party debated numerous issues in Alabama's political forums. These issues involved such questions as tax policy, the state role in funding public education, methods of nominating candidates for public office, women's suffrage, and the prohibition of alcoholic beverages.[8] Of these, only prohibition seriously rivaled race relations in the attention it received from the people and the politicians.

FACTIONAL POWER STRUGGLES

Group differences based on variations in economic status are of great importance in the political community.[9] In the nineteenth century, the interests of small Alabama farmers frequently were opposed to those of the planters. Geographically, the yeomen were most numerous in north Alabama; the planters, in the Black Belt. The historian A. B. Moore explained how these differing economic interests affected the party alignment of the 1830s and 1840s:

The two parties of the State rested upon social and economic foundations, and, as it happened, became sectional in character. The Whig party was the "broadcloth" party; it drew its strength from the men of slaves and means who lived in the Black Belt and in the western counties of the Tennessee Valley and the business interests affiliated with them. The Democratic party was supported principally by the farmers and the small business classes of the other parts of the State. Generally speaking, the Whig party was a south Alabama party and the Democratic party dominated north Alabama.[10]

In the immediate pre–Civil War years, north Alabama was not anxious to defend what it felt to be primarily a south Alabama interest in the preservation of slavery. At that time factional lines were drawn between Unionists and those who supported secession to varying degrees. Mainly, the Unionists and the less enthusiastic secessionists were north Alabamians. As Moore put it, "mountain whites" in north Alabama "were not pleased with the work of the [secession] convention or with the Southern Confederacy. . . . Secession was distinctly a south Alabama achievement."[11]

During the war years, however, Alabama was generally united in support of the Confederate cause. Even so, the "patriots"—the popular designation for the Confederates—continued to encounter militant opposition from many "mountain whites," also called "tories," who wanted most of all, as Moore said, "that the peace of their hills should be left undisturbed by the war."[12]

In the post–Civil War years the white counties continued to oppose the Black Belt over the role to be played by black Alabamians in state government and politics. North Alabamians, ironically, were at first more likely to oppose black participation, feeling that black votes could be too easily manipulated to serve Black Belt interests. Later, north Alabama tended to oppose Black Belt efforts to curtail black participation, as the sweeping effects of some of the disfranchising techniques adopted in the name of white supremacy also reached potential white voters.

Factional divisions sometimes, though not always, paralleled political party divisions in the state. As strange as it may seem to people familiar with state politics in the twentieth century, Alabama in the nineteenth century was frequently the scene of intense two-party competition, with national issues such as the tariff, federal monetary policy, and internal improvements often dominating the political debate. The earliest interparty conflict was between Democrats and Whigs. With the Whigs' dissolution in the turmoil of the approaching civil war, the planters, particularly those in the Black Belt, began to align themselves with the Democrats. The Democratic party then became the dominant party and, except for a decade during Reconstruction, it has remained so from that day to this.

Following the Civil War and black emancipation, the Republican party undertook the mobilization of Alabama's black voters and assumed control of the state's civil affairs. Because of their Unionist sympathies, many "mountain whites" also joined the Republican ranks, thereby adding another dimension to Alabama politics that has persisted over the years. Supported by the policy of military Reconstruction and led by individuals many Alabamians called "carpetbaggers" (new arrivals from the North) and "scalawags" (native southerners), the party first flexed its muscles in October 1868, when the initial election in which black voters participated took place. Yet, just as earlier the Democratic party had successfully resisted Whig efforts to dominate state politics, after Reconstruction, Democratic power once again established itself.

In 1874 the Republican—or Radical—party was almost totally displaced. Perhaps foreshadowing what was to become the Republicans' seemingly permanent minority role in state politics, the Democratic nominee in the gubernatorial election of 1876 received about twice as many votes as his Republican opponent, and all the counties except Winston, Geneva, and six Black Belt counties supported the Democratic presidential nominee, Samuel Tilden. Later the Populist party, particularly when it was led by Reuben Kolb, became active in the state, and it fought the Democratic party virtually to a standstill in the 1890s. However, this party was also undone to a degree by the racial fears aroused by the Populists' apparent willingness to share political power with blacks. In part because of the specter of revived black power in Alabama, conservative white Democrats were able to defeat the progressive program associated with the Populist movement. Here the real purpose of the suffrage article in the 1901 constitution becomes apparent. The disfranchisement of poor whites along with the blacks would help to preserve Democratic rule by inhibiting the revival of Populism. It would maintain white Democratic rule by preventing any factional appeals to black voters that would give them political power.

But the Democratic party, even though dominant, was hardly a monolithic unit. In the earliest days of statehood, states rights Democrats had

fought the more nationally oriented Jacksonian Democrats. In the immediate pre–Civil War era, a new generation of states rights Democrats struggled
against antisecession Union Democrats. After the permanent failure of the
Populist party in the late 1890s, the popular-versus-elitist battles were
reintensified within the Democratic party, with the factional struggle sometimes characterized as being between the Radicals and the Bourbons. In
more ideological terms, political commentators sometimes spoke of a conflict between the progressive and conservative wings of the Democratic
party. The political scientist V. O. Key, for example, viewed the 1946
gubernatorial primary election between Jim Folsom and Handy Ellis in
these terms and identified the familiar sectional basis of the factional
division:

In the voting, division fell along lines of cleavage that appear in Alabama when
progressive-conservative issues are raised in a compelling manner. Ellis had his
greatest popular strength in the black-belt counties, which are black both in soil and
in a majority of their people, whereas Folsom's strength tended to be higher in the
northern and southern parts of the state where the Negro population is relatively less
numerous. The dominant elements of the black belt bracketed Folsom with the CIO
as a threat to the established order.[13]

This progressive-conservative competition has continued in Alabama,
but recent events have modified the sectional basis of the conflict. Much of
the change can be attributed to George Wallace. As governor in the 1960s he
came down strongly on the segregationist side of the civil rights controversy. Yet the spending programs that he advocated, and the concern he
expressed for the "average citizen," gave him a populist appeal, which
historically has been important in north Alabama. Thus, by combining
segregation with populism, Wallace was able to gain the support of many
segments of the population.[14] Thus the magnitude of the Wallace appeal
upset the traditionally sectional character of Alabama politics. Indeed, a
veteran Montgomery journalist concluded that Wallace "just completely
obliterated it."[15]

Still, other factors besides Wallace's strategy have contributed to the
decline of the old sectionalism. The national Democratic emphasis on civil
rights after World War II led many white Alabama conservatives (after a
brief flirtation in 1948 with the separatist "Dixiecrat" movement) to support
the Republican ticket, especially in presidential elections. This change in
the pattern of party support was at first most striking in the Black Belt.
However, the reenfranchisement of black Alabamians since the mid-1960s

has produced heavy majorities of black Democratic voters in Black Belt counties. Consequently that section is no longer, as Donald Strong put it, "the bulwark of white-supremacist Democracy" that it once was.[16] Finally, some recent elections have witnessed the emergence of a voting pattern that correlates to an appreciable extent with social status. The long-term significance of this alignment is unclear, but what is important here is that it does not follow the geographic alignments of the past.[17]

Recent events thus brought fundamental change to Alabama politics. Black voters became an important component of the Democratic party, and white politicians began openly to seek their support. Urban white conservatives joined the "mountain" Republicans to form a party that could win elections. Political battles involving the issues of progressivism and conservatism were no longer merely "affairs within the Democratic party"; to an appreciable extent they assumed an interparty dimension. Race remained an important feature of the state's political character, but racism was not as palpable as in former years.[18] Conservative whites were likely to identify blacks as being among the "special interests" dominating the Democratic party. These trends were well developed by the time Governor Wallace announced his retirement from Alabama politics in 1986.

The post-Wallace era began in a stormy fashion. Confusion in the Democratic primary of 1986 caused a heated controversy that had a major effect on the state's politics. Because no candidate for the gubernatorial nomination had received the required majority in the first Democratic primary, the state held a second, runoff primary between Lieutenant Governor Bill Baxley and Attorney General Charles Graddick.[19] Graddick received about 9,000 more votes than Baxley (out of almost a million votes cast) and apparently won the nomination. During the campaign Graddick, who was a conservative former Republican himself, called on Republicans to participate in the Democratic primary and vote for him. Some Republican leaders assured their fellow party members that this was perfectly permissible. Prominent Republicans even attributed Graddick's victory to this Republican support.

Considering the nature and extent of the Republican involvement in the Democratic primary, it is perhaps not surprising that some Democratic voters quickly challenged the election. This was a move that Baxley himself soon joined. The contestants based their challenge on the assertion that thousands of "illegal" Republican votes had been cast in the Democratic gubernatorial runoff. Both state law and a Democratic party rule, they argued, forbade those who had voted in the Republican first primary to "cross over" and vote later in the Democratic second primary.

In Alabama, political parties settle contested primary elections. State Democratic chairman John Baker appointed a subcommittee of the state executive committee to deal with the Baxley-Graddick dispute. As the contest moved through its numerous phases, the principals and litigants supporting one or the other of them were also taking the case to the state and federal courts. In one of the more important of these cases, a federal panel agreed that Republican crossover voting was illegal and barred the Democrats from certifying Graddick on the basis of the contested election. The subcommittee had either to declare Baxley the nominee or order a new and untainted runoff. Concluding on the basis of statistical evidence that Baxley had probably received a majority of the legal ballots cast in the election, the subcommittee awarded the nomination to him.

Generally speaking, Graddick's supporters saw him as the candidate best able to break with the "politics of the past" and lead the state into a post-Wallace era more in accord with the views of the modern conservative coalition that had carried Alabama for Ronald Reagan in 1980 and 1984. They tended to identify Baxley as a Wallace protégé and a tool of the "special interests." Naturally they were furious when the Democratic subcommittee "handpicked" Baxley as the party's gubernatorial candidate. They believed that Baxley had stolen the nomination and that, in not calling a new runoff, Democratic bosses had denied the voters the right to elect their governor. Bitterly angry as they were at the Democratic leadership, not many of them could be expected to support the Baxley candidacy in the general election. Meanwhile, Graddick was calling on them to "sharpen their pencils" because he intended to conduct a write-in campaign for governor.

As a result of the dissension in the Democratic party and the support the Republicans received from the national Republican party (including several visits to the state by President Reagan), observers gave Republicans a good chance to win in such key races as those for governor, U.S. senator, and U.S. representative from the Seventh Congressional District. In the general election, however, Representative Richard Shelby, a Democrat, narrowly beat incumbent Republican senator Jeremiah Denton. The Democratic candidate won handily in the Seventh District race to succeed Shelby. Republicans made some gains in county, state legislative, and district elections, but the governorship was the only statewide office that the Democrats lost. Not wanting to split the conservative vote, Graddick dropped his write-in candidacy shortly before the election. As polls had suggested, this virtually assured the election of the Republican candidate, Guy Hunt (a member of the party faithful from north Alabama who was not well known despite his having been the Republican gubernatorial candidate in 1978). The frustrated conservative Democrats had their opportunity to send their message to the party leadership, and they did: "handpicking" the nominee rather than calling a new primary was, to them, a big mistake. The result was that Alabamians elected a Republican governor for the first time in the state's modern history.

How the election would affect the state's political development was not immediately clear, and what lies farther ahead in the post-Wallace era is even less evident. What is obvious is that recent events have produced an Alabama of today that differs markedly from the Alabama of only a few years ago. Race relations have been brought into the twentieth century, and economic development has produced an urban, industrialized society. And by 1986, Alabama, once considered perhaps the most Democratic state in the Union, had witnessed the election of a Republican governor.

CHAPTER TWO

Alabama in the Federal System

In this chapter we examine Alabama from the standpoint of the federal system. The actors and institutions of Alabama state government and politics do not function in a vacuum. Instead, they operate in an environment of many dimensions, one of the most important of which is intergovernmental. Today there are hardly any activities of the state government that do not have some intergovernmental significance.

Seemingly, federalism can be defined with little difficulty. It is a system of government in which powers are divided by a constitution between a central government and state or regional governments. But federalism is a very broad concept that can be interpreted and implemented in a myriad of ways.[1] The most useful models of federalism applicable to the link between Alabama and the federal government in Washington are dual federalism, antagonistic federalism, and cooperative federalism. The concepts of creative federalism and the "new" federalism are subspecies of cooperative federalism, and we will also note these approaches to intergovernmental relations.

Although they overlap conceptually and historically, the models of federalism do clarify Alabama's role in the federal system. While particular forms of federalism have been dominant at various times, national-state relationships during any one of these periods are not all of one kind. In the pre–Civil War period, for example, Alabama supported dual federalism with regard to its state policy on slavery, it was involved in antagonistic federalism when it came to removal of the Indians before Andrew Jackson became president and backed the Alabama position, and it endorsed cooperative federalism on the question of the enforcement of the fugitive slave laws in other states and on internal improvements.

ALABAMA IN A DUAL FEDERAL SYSTEM

The concept of dual federalism stresses the separateness of the national and state governments,[2] and for many years the U.S. Supreme Court frequently based its decisions on this notion of what the federal system should be like. In 1859, in *Abelman* v. *Booth,* the Court asserted that, "The powers of the general [federal] government, and of the states . . . are . . . separate and distinct sovereignties, acting separate and independent of each other, within their respective spheres."[3] Seventeen years later, in the case of *U.S.* v. *Cruikshank,* the Court again observed that the federal government and the state governments were disparate entities: "The powers which one possesses, the other does not. They are established for different purposes, and have separate jurisdictions."[4]

Scholars have for years engaged in a debate over the problem of how appropriate the dual-federalism model is for understanding the relationship of the states to Washington before the New Deal.[5] David B. Walker concludes that nineteenth-century American history "reflected an adherence to dual-federal themes—constitutionally, politically, and operationally."[6] To relate this viewpoint to Alabama, the state's government, its political processes, and its public policies, once established, were to be conducted without federal intrusion. That the assertion of independence from federal intervention has produced conflict between Alabama and the federal government is a well-known fact of American political life.

Even in the territorial period there was conflict between Alabama's interests and the national government over the question of whether the eastern part of the territory should have its own government. Disagreements increased after Alabama entered the Union. In the Jacksonian period, even though the hero of the Creek War was in the White House, there were differences between Alabamians and the federal government over, for example, Indian policy and the tariff. Many Alabamians took strong states' rights positions regarding these questions, especially on the Indian issue, in which they wanted the state policy regarding settlement on Indian lands to prevail. They also opposed the high tariff of 1828, though Alabama's political leadership did not go so far as to endorse South Carolina's nullification position on the tariff act.[7] A century and a quarter later, however, they would resurrect the argument that states could nullify federal actions and attempt to use it against the U.S. Supreme Court's school desegregation decision.

In the immediate pre–Civil War period, most of the important issues in Alabama and other southern states related to slavery. Slaveholders in Alabama and neighboring states insisted, in line with what later came to be called dual-federalist thinking, that slavery was strictly a state policy matter into which the federal government ought not to intrude except to aid in the return of escaped slaves. In the northern states, where abolitionist sentiment was strong, the feeling was that slavery was an evil that the federal government must endeavor to end. When no peaceful solution could be found to the controversy over the constitutional issue of federal versus state power and the human and economic issue of slavery, civil war erupted. The war's outcome made it clear that the federal government was, in fact, supreme and that the states ultimately must yield if their policy objectives differ widely from national norms.

Alabama and the other southern states were the subjects of strongly nationalistic theories of American federalism immediately after the Civil War, during Reconstruction. In this period, which lasted for Alabama until the mid-1870s, the federal government undertook to elevate the political, economic, and social status of blacks through a comprehensive program aimed at conditionally restoring the former Confederate states to their place in the federal system. Because the federal Reconstruction program was not sustained, however, white Alabama elites were soon able to regain political control in the period often referred to as the Redemption, beginning in 1874. Dual federalism then prevailed in that Alabama could set policies pertaining to race relations without paying much regard to national politicians (who may have had considerable sympathy for blacks), national policy-making agencies, or even the Thirteenth, Fourteenth, and Fifteenth amendments, which had been adopted in validation of federal victories on Civil War battlefields. President Theodore Roosevelt, however, was an exception. He signaled his disapproval of Alabama's racial policies by selecting Booker T. Washington as his main contact for advice about Republican party business in Alabama.[8]

Dual federalism meant that the national government would follow a hands-off policy as far as the states' internal affairs were concerned. By 1940, however, the notion that the national government and the states operated in distinct areas had been very largely scrapped as an operational view of the American federal system. "In most of the significant areas of national policy," Reo M. Christenson remarks, "the restraint upon Washington was [now] its sense of self-restraint." Federalism, he argues, when "seen as separate spheres of federal and state power, each protected from encroachment by the other, had suffered such a drastic transformation as to be scarcely recognizable from earlier textbook descriptions."[9]

As we have seen, comprehensive national programs to promote racial equality did not begin in Franklin D. Roosevelt's administration. Nevertheless, starting in the New Deal period the federal government undertook initiatives that would ultimately challenge white rule over blacks in Alabama and other southern states. The social and economic programs of the Roosevelt administration had a great impact on groups on the bottom rungs of the economic ladder, and blacks were more likely to be on this bottom rung than whites. In the post–World War II period there was increasing federal sympathy toward black aspirations for political, economic, and social rights and the realization of constitutional guarantees. White Alabama politicians generally opposed the federal civil rights initiatives, and because they were willing not merely to advocate but actually to carry out a policy of massive resistance to these initiatives, Alabama soon became the epicenter of the civil rights revolution.

ALABAMA IN AN ANTAGONISTIC FEDERAL SYSTEM

In 1954, during the Eisenhower administration, the U.S. Supreme Court decided in *Brown* v. *Board of Education* that state laws requiring racial segregation in public schools violated the Equal Protection Clause of the U.S. Constitution's Fourteenth Amendment. Probably no decision in this century has had more impact on the relationship of Alabama to the federal government than the Brown decision. It stimulated so much additional conflict between Alabama and the federal government as to suggest that the concept of antagonistic federalism best describes the pattern that prevailed in the area of race relations.

The antagonistic theory would have it that the U.S. Supreme Court forced the national government to intervene in state affairs to protect the rights of citizens as the Court defined those rights. To avoid excessive intervention in their internal affairs, then, the states would have to be "constantly on their guard to ward off encroachment and interference from Washington."[10] In this model of intergovernmental relations there is a generalized assumption of hostility between the federal and state governments. When he was inaugurated for his first term in 1963, George Wallace exclaimed: "In the name of the greatest people that have ever trod this earth, I draw the line in the dust and toss the gauntlet before the feet of tyranny and I say . . . segregation now . . . segregation tomorrow . . . segregation forever." In this period, with politicians attempting to "out-seg" one another, antagonistic federalism conditioned the style and substance of Alabama politics for the greater part of two decades.[11]

The federal government also intervened in support of civil rights in areas other than education. As a result of the bus boycott in Montgomery, the U.S. Supreme Court declared that legally required segregation on city buses was unconstitutional.[12] During the administrations of John F. Kennedy and Lyndon B. Johnson, the judicial branch, which had taken the lead in federal intervention efforts, was joined by the federal legislative and executive branches to guarantee full rights to blacks through civil and voting rights laws and executive orders. The specifics of some of the federal policies designed to desegregate various public facilities and to secure for blacks the unhindered right to vote are discussed in later chapters. For now we will simply note that federal initiatives were so extensive that the period of the 1960s and 1970s has been termed the Second Reconstruction.[13]

Simultaneously with federal initiatives to assist blacks came federal intervention into other aspects of state administration. Federal judges, most notably Judge Frank M. Johnson, Jr., who at the time was a federal judge on the District Court for the Middle District of Alabama, ordered improvements in state mental health and retardation facilities and in the prison system. Although they were often attacked by Alabama political leaders, these were measures that the judges saw as necessary to protect the rights of persons confined in public institutions to fair treatment under law. Neal Peirce writes with respect to Alabama that, "there was no state in the country in which the federal courts were intruding themselves so deeply into the basic governmental process, but perhaps none in which their interference was more justified because of the inaction and reaction of state government."[14]

In the late 1960s and early 1970s the state's reputation had sunk so low that it was common in administrative jargon to refer to the "Alabama syndrome." Because federal officials believed that Alabama could not be trusted to carry out federal grant programs properly if allowed to use its own discretion, many conditions and guidelines had to be attached to the programs, even for states that presumably could more safely be trusted. Sharkansky has noted, for example, that in the preparation of the Economic Opportunity Act of 1964 the discretionary role of the states in the administration of the legislation was deliberately kept to a minimum because of doubts about how Alabama would use the freedom that might be delegated to it.[15]

A refinement of this perception of Alabama's position in the federal system during the period of the 1950s to the 1970s was the "Alabama punting syndrome." In Judge Johnson's view the idea of a punting syndrome derived from "the habit that some states have fallen in of ignoring their responsibilities until they are faced with a federal court order."[16] The term describes "the tendency of many state officials to punt their problems with constituencies to the federal courts." As Judge Johnson reviewed federal litigation in Alabama, he found it to be "replete with instances of state officials who could have chosen one of any number of courses to alleviate constitutional conditions of which they were fully aware, and who chose instead to do nothing." In Johnson's opinion the federal courts had "to step into the vacuum left by the state's inaction."[17] His willingness to assume responsibility for necessary policy formation cost him dearly in terms of his social relationships with his fellow Alabamians. Nevertheless, it became common to hear him referred to as "the real governor of Alabama,"[18] and in recent years Judge Johnson has been recognized by many Alabamians for his contributions to improved conditions in the state. The public has also increasingly taken a more benevolent view toward Justice Hugo Black of Alabama, who served on the U.S. Supreme Court during the period of sweeping initiatives in race relations and other policy areas. The state law school observed the centennial of Black's birth with considerable ceremony in 1986.

ALABAMA IN A COOPERATIVE FEDERAL SYSTEM

More recent years have seen a sharp decline in race-oriented antagonism between Alabama and the federal government. In 1976, following George Wallace's unsuccessful presidential campaigns, another southerner, Jimmy Carter, was elected President of the United States. Carter's victory seemed to symbolize, at least in part, a national recognition of the South's growing acceptance of efforts to ensure fair treatment for blacks.

Some of the reduction of tension between Alabama and the federal government may be attributable to a greater symmetry between Alabama and the rest of the states in the Union. That is, Alabama has become more like her sister states, and television has had a great deal to do with this. With this medium of mass communication being projected throughout the country, there has been a resulting tendency toward more uniformity of opinion among similar socioeconomic groups. Also, there has been a considerable migration into Alabama, and this development, too, has had the long-term impact of reducing the amount of difference between Alabama and the other states. The increasingly interdependent national economy has also been, of course, a basic factor linking Alabama more closely to the country as a whole. Recently, for example, Alabama has shared with the nation the problem of high unemployment. Finally, Democratic and Republican activists in Alabama increasingly resemble their partisan counterparts in other regions of the country.

But there is also a continuing asymmetry that sets Alabama apart from some of the other areas in the American federal polity.[19] Alabama has a population that is essentially biracial—about 25 percent black and 75 percent white. Its culture is traditional and remarkably homogeneous. Alabama is mainly Protestant, with the Baptist church as the leading denomination. Non-Protestant denominations are very small in Alabama. Even though the state is mostly urban today, it still has a large rural population, and the flavor of Alabama politics is still more strongly rural than urban. In all of these respects Alabama differs, of course, from the more ethnically and culturally diverse and more heavily industrialized and urbanized sections of the country. Nevertheless, such conflicts as do occur between Alabama and Washington today are more likely than in the old days to resemble those that take place between the other states and the federal government. In the administration of prisons, for example, disputes with the federal courts over the adequacy of state facilities have arisen both in Alabama and elsewhere.

Thus far we have focused primarily on instances of conflict between Alabama and the federal government. Yet, while conflict has attracted more attention, patterns of cooperation probably have been more pervasive. Alabama and the federal government have cooperated in programs of mutual benefit ever since Alabama entered the Union in 1819. According to the idea of cooperative federalism, governments in the United States "do not divide into watertight compartments. . . . [F]ederal, state, and local governments co-operate, their jurisdictions dovetail."[20] Edward S. Corwin defined "the cooperative conception of the federal relationship" as one in which "the states and the National Government are mutually complementary parts of a single governmental mechanism all of whose powers are intended to realize, according to their applicability to the problem in hand, the purposes of good government the world over."[21] With cooperative federalism, according to Dvorin and Misner, "vexatious questions of legal jurisdiction give way to emphasis upon the most effective way of solving urgent social, economic, and political problems."[22]

In the early years there was cooperation between the federal government and Alabama in conducting military campaigns against the Indians, and when national sentiment supported them, there were programs of internal improvements in which the federal government and Alabama cooperated. In

1862, even while the country was torn apart by civil war, Congress passed the Morrill Act, which granted federal lands within the states to assist in establishing institutions of higher learning. After Alabama returned to its former place in the Union, it established (for racial reasons) two of these land-grant institutions, now known as Auburn University (originally for whites only) and Alabama A. & M. University (then for black students). These institutions were initially set up to offer educational programs in the agricultural and mechanical arts and sciences, but today they both function as comprehensive universities.

Later in the nineteenth century, the state—with the aid of federal grants—established agricultural experiment stations to operate in conjunction with the agricultural colleges. Early in the twentieth century the agricultural extension service, another federal-state cooperative activity, was started to educate farmers about improved agricultural practices discovered at the colleges and experiment stations. In 1916 Congress passed the Federal-Aid Road Act to encourage the foundation of a national highway system. This legislation was highly important in the development of Alabama's highway program. Vocational education and maternal and child health programs were also established as federal-state collaborative programs in this era.

With the advent of the Great Depression, the cooperative activities between Alabama and Washington expanded greatly, and one of the most important to affect Alabama directly was the Tennessee Valley Authority, established in 1933 as a multipurpose regional development agency concerned with the economic and social progress of the people living in the valley regions of the seven states served by the authority. In recent years there has been a tendency to regard the TVA as just another power company, and, indeed, the generation and sale of electric power (including nuclear power) are by far the authority's most important activities. The easy availability of electric power through the TVA has been a factor of major importance in Alabama's economic development, especially in north Alabama. Further, one has only to look at the cornerstones of numerous buildings on college campuses and elsewhere to see the impact of other New Deal agencies on Alabama in the 1930s—agencies such as the Public Works Administration, the Works Progress Administration, the Civilian Conservation Corps, and so on.

The adoption of the federal Social Security program meant a greatly expanded role for what was then known as the Alabama Department of Social Welfare. This department administered portions of the Social Security Act making funds available for pensions for needy people not covered by the payroll tax system. Because Alabama was (and is) a relatively poor state, the impact on Alabama of New Deal welfare reforms was probably greater than in more affluent states. Nevertheless, Alabama is a state in which welfare programs have not had a broad base of political support.

In the post–World War II period new programs of cooperative federalism involved Alabama, its local governments, and the federal government in even closer working partnerships. In several instances these new federal-state-local partnerships were devised by entrepreneurial members of the then all-Democratic Alabama congressional delegation, regarded by some as perhaps the most influential and "liberal" in the South. Such postwar programs included, for example, hospital construction (cosponsored by long-time senator Lister Hill of Alabama), public housing (with much of the legislation authored by Senator John Sparkman and Representative Albert Rains), and small-business assistance (advocated by Senator Sparkman, who was Adlai Stevenson's running mate in the 1952 presidential election).

The greatest explosion of federal grant programs occurred in the Great Society era of Lyndon Johnson, particularly in the mid-to-late 1960s. President Johnson called his approach "creative" federalism. Federal grants became increasingly available for such programs as food stamps, Medicaid, job training, and the like, and for activities aimed at reducing problems of recurring poverty.[23] Ironically, during the first Wallace era, at the time of the greatest conflict between Alabama and the federal government over race relations, there was perhaps the greatest dependence on the federal government fiscally and the greatest cooperation administratively between state and local governments in Alabama and agencies in Washington.

Most of the Johnson-era grant programs were narrowly focused project grants that tended to limit the discretion of state and local grant recipients. In 1972, however, during the Nixon administration, the federal government adopted the revenue-sharing program. This program allowed local and state governments a much greater degree of freedom to spend federal funds. In fact, revenue-sharing funds could be spent for any lawful purpose. President Nixon, as President Reagan would after him, identified his approach to intergovernmental relations as the "new" federalism, which encouraged more state and local autonomy. The Nixon and Reagan approaches to federalism signaled a change in the modern relationship between Washington and the states.

In the 1980s federal funds became less abundant. Indeed, program reduction was a major ingredient of Reagan policy. This meant that Alabama and other states would have to assume greater fiscal, technical, and administrative burdens on their own, without as much assistance from Washington.[24] Alabamians would have to dig a bit deeper into their pockets if the assisted programs were to provide the levels of service they had in the past.

FEDERALISM WITHOUT WASHINGTON

In the United States, federalism without Washington refers to "the relationships among the states of the Union either imposed by the Constitution or undertaken voluntarily."[25] The U.S. Constitution obliges the state of Alabama to give "full faith and credit" to the "public acts, records, and judicial proceedings of every other state," to grant the citizens of each state the "privileges and immunities of citizens in the several States" and to return fugitives from justice.[26] Although it is not required to do so, Alabama may enter into interstate compacts (subject to congressional approval), pass standardized laws, and meet regularly in forums of discussion and common action.

The most obvious example of Alabama's joining with other states in concerted action was during the Civil War, when Alabama and ten other southern states associated themselves in a confederation. With the northern victory, and after Reconstruction, the unity of the southern states in support of Democratic presidential candidates and the Democratic party generally was so strong that the concept of the Solid South became one of the most important on the American political scene. When the Democratic hands-off attitude toward race relations changed, however, the raison d'être for southern unity behind the Democratic party ceased. The South has not been solidly behind any Democratic presidential candidate since 1944.

On the other hand, southern unity was demonstrated in the years following the 1954 *Brown* decision, when southern states sometimes worked in harmony in a program of "massive resistance" to school integration. In Congress, southern senators and representatives drafted a "southern manifesto," which declared their opposition to integration and vowed resistance through all legal means.[27] Alabama officials were generally active participants in these efforts to maintain segregation, with the notable exception of Governor James E. Folsom, who was serving his second term in the years 1955 to 1959. He apparently saw nothing out of the ordinary in inviting visiting black congressman Adam Clayton Powell over to the governor's mansion for a drink, and he considered the legislature's interposition resolution (declaring the *Brown* decision null and void) to be nothing but "hogwash."[28]

Alabama has frequently associated with other states in programs of cooperation, including numerous interstate compacts. One of the most notable regional compacts has been the Tennessee-Tombigbee Waterway Development Compact, formed in 1958 to promote federal construction of a waterway to connect the two rivers. Construction of the waterway had received serious consideration since the late nineteenth century as a means of stimulating commercial development in the area, but it was fully realized only in 1985 with the opening of the newly completed canal to barge traffic for the first time. The states of Alabama, Mississippi, Kentucky, Tennessee, and Florida used the compact authority to lobby for continuing and increasing federal appropriations to plan and construct the waterway and to provide assurances to Washington that they would perform needed tasks (such as the relocation of highways and bridges) in the path of the canal.

In the minds of critics, Tenn-Tom was simply a very large pork-barrel project whose benefits would not come anywhere close to covering its costs. The railroads, of course, opposed it as a competing mode of transportation. Some spokespersons for the poor also criticized it as an ineffective use of scarce national monetary resources in the Tenn-Tom Corridor. The money spent on Tenn-Tom, they argued, could be allocated in other ways that would have a much more immediate and positive impact on the lives of the poor. Its supporters, however, saw it as a bonanza well worth fighting for, and they prevailed in Congress.

Alabama officials often meet with comparable officials from other states. Probably the most notable conferences are the Southern Governors' Conference and the National Governors' Association, but officials farther down the line have also been active in associations with their counterparts in other states. Recently, for example, Alabama secretary of state Don Siegelman served as president of the American Association of Secretaries of State and chairman of its national voter-education project.

The most legalistic of Alabama's relations with other states would include the return of fugitives and the provisions of the full faith and credit clause. Generally, Alabama governors honor the requests of governors from other states seeking the return of fugitives from justice who have fled to Alabama, and normally requests of Alabama governors for similar assistance are honored. Occasionally, however, Alabama's requests have been turned down. In 1978 there was an incident in which the governor of

Michigan declined the request to return to Alabama a woman who had been convicted of a serious crime. The reason underlying the decision was that she was now living the life of a model citizen in her adopted state.[29]

Adherence to the full faith and credit clause is generally not controversial. Perhaps the most controversy in this area recently concerned the question of divorce. Before changes in Alabama divorce laws, some communities in Alabama had the reputation of being meccas for those seeking a "quickie" divorce.[30] Dissatisfied husbands or wives would fly in and out of Alabama in a matter of hours with a divorce decree in hand. There were never any serious challenges to the validity of the divorces granted, but there was concern among the parties to the proceedings that they might not be recognized by other states. Changes in the law made Alabama residence more difficult to establish, however, and since their passage this particular field of interstate relationships has been notably quiescent.

In this chapter we have focused our attention on Alabama as a member of the American federal system. We have seen that just as "No man is an Iland intire of itselfe," no state can go it alone, either. To understand fully what Alabama is like, it is necessary, then, to look outside Alabama. This we did, first toward Washington and the kinds of relationships that have prevailed between Alabama and the federal government, and then toward other states and Alabama's relations with them. In the next chapter we turn our thoughts inward again to see how the state constitution shapes the kind of political system Alabama has.

CHAPTER THREE

The Constitution

In 1987 the United States was celebrating the bicentennial of the Constitution. During the long span of two centuries, this one document served as the nation's basic law. In contrast, many states have operated under a succession of constitutions. Alabama has had six.[1]

American state constitutions are written documents traditionally drafted by conventions called to perform that specific task. Alabama's first constitution was written by a convention held at Huntsville before the territory was admitted as a state in 1819. Succeeding constitutions were adopted at other significant points in the state's history. Four were products of the turbulence accompanying and following the Civil War. This accounts for constitutions adopted in 1861, 1865, 1868, and 1875. Later another constitution was adopted in 1901, primarily as a conservative reaction to the Populist challenge of the preceding decade. The first three of Alabama's constitutions were proclaimed effective by the conventions that drafted them; the last three were adopted on what is now the more usual basis of a popular vote.

In large measure Alabama's constitutions of 1875 and 1901 sought to repeal changes imposed on the state during Reconstruction. None of the successive constitutions, however, represented a complete break with the past. Instead there has been much continuity among the state's constitutions, and changes tended to be confined to specific issues. In 1901, for example, the main issue before the constitutional convention was that of "reforming" (read "limiting") the suffrage. Governor Emmet O'Neal made this point in a 1915 address to the legislature when he highlighted the suffrage question as the paramount issue which engaged the attention of our people and hence when the constitutional convention of 1901 assembled, little consideration was given to other matters of reform. This is conclusively shown by the fact that the Constitution of 1875, which had been framed to meet conditions which can never again recur, was practically re-adopted.[2]

A little over a half century later, however, the civil rights movement reversed the bulk of the convention's handiwork.

CIVIL RIGHTS AND LIBERTIES

Alabama still operates under the constitution of 1901. An exceptionally long document, it consisted originally of 287 sections organized into eighteen articles, and it is now supplemented by well over 400 amendments. The Alabama Constitution begins with a declaration of rights. This declaration contains rights of both a substantive and a procedural nature that often parallel those included in the U.S. Bill of Rights. For example, the First Amendment freedoms of religion, speech, press, assembly, and petition are all included in the Alabama Declaration of Rights. Such important procedural rights as those relating to counsel, grand jury indictment, and freedom from self-incrimination are likewise found in the document.

It is important to understand, however, that under the doctrine of national supremacy set out in Article 6 of the U.S. Constitution, individual rights and liberties are protected against state violation not only by the state constitution but also by national constitutional and statutory provisions. Decisions of the U.S. Supreme Court involving interpretations of the Fourteenth Amendment of the U.S. Constitution have spelled out a variety of constitutional rights that must be respected by states in their relations with individuals.[3] The antidiscrimination provisions of such federal legislative enactments as the Civil Rights Act of 1964 and the Voting Rights Act of 1965 have had a similar effect.

THE LEGISLATIVE BRANCH

The description of political institutions in Alabama's constitution begins with the legislative article. The article provides for a bicameral legislature consisting of a Senate and a House of Representatives. It covers the qualifications, elections, and terms of the senators and representatives and contains much language that defines legislative procedures and limits legislative powers.

Early in the state's history, the legislature met annually and enjoyed great freedom in lawmaking. It also had an extensive power of appointment. But, as Professor Malcolm C. McMillan has observed, "a growing distrust of the legislature was one of the most apparent constitutional trends in Alabama in the nineteenth century. After 1819, not a single convention met without placing additional limitations on the legislature."[4]

The terms of the 1901 constitution made these limitations on legislative power both numerous and severe. The convention, for example, wanting to avoid such financial disasters as had occurred with earlier involvement in banking and railroad enterprises, retained the 1875 prohibition that said that the state could not participate in public works projects or lend state money or credit to private businesses involved in such projects. Faced with important technological developments in the automobile industry, Alabama had to amend this provision as early as 1908 to permit the state to participate in such a basic function as the building of roads and bridges.[5] Other limitations dealt at some length with special legislation and sought to reduce the growing volume of this kind of legislation. The depth of the convention's distrust of the legislature is perhaps best illustrated by the provision that set regular legislative sessions for every fourth year, a highly unusual arrangement that was changed first in 1939 to establish biennial sessions and then in 1975, annual sessions.

The convention's arrangements for legislative representation established a legislature of 106 representatives (representing the sixty-seven counties) and thirty-five senators (each representing a single senatorial district composed of from one to several counties). The framers set out an apportionment of the senators and representatives among the counties and districts. Thereafter it was the duty of the legislature, following the federal census taken every ten years, to fix the number of representatives and senators and reapportion them among the counties and senatorial districts on the basis of their total population. Here we see a clear victory in the convention for the rural counties in the Black Belt. Basing representation on white or voting population, as some delegates wanted, would have seriously undermined Black Belt influence in the legislative halls.[6]

Apportionment proved to be such a thorny issue, however, that the legislature failed to carry out the constitutional mandate for periodic reapportionment. With population drifting to the cities, rural overrepresentation became an increasingly serious problem. Rural legislators obviously did not want to eliminate their legislative seats. Also, urban industrialists felt comfortable with a Black Belt–dominated legislature.[7] They were probably apprehensive about the kinds of laws that might be passed by a legislature in which urban working-class residents had greater representation. However, the U.S. Supreme Court decided in the 1962 case of *Baker* v. *Carr* that the federal courts could settle reapportionment suits brought under the Equal Protection Clause of the Fourteenth Amendment of the U.S. Constitution and could thus accomplish a redistribution of state legislative seats so that urban voters would finally get their fair share.[8] Following this decision, urban residents filed apportionment suits in Alabama that culminated in *Reynolds* v. *Sims,* a highly significant case decided by the U.S. Supreme Court in 1964.[9] During this period federal courts made serious modifications in Alabama's constitutional provisions concerning legislative apportionment and in *Reynolds* v. *Sims* established as the national norm the requirement that representation in both houses must be based on population.

THE EXECUTIVE BRANCH

The 1901 constitution provided for an executive branch composed of a governor, lieutenant governor, attorney general, state auditor, secretary of state, state treasurer, superintendent of education, commissioner of agriculture and industries, and a sheriff for each county. Under the original constitutional provisions, these offices were elective, with terms of four years, and incumbents were ineligible to succeed themselves in office. Furthermore, governors could not be elected or appointed to any other state office, or to the U.S. Senate, during the term for which they were elected or within one year after its expiration.[10] These provisions tended to make the governorship a dead-end job. Until George Wallace, only two governors (Bibb Graves and Jim Folsom) had continued in political prominence by being elected to another gubernatorial term following a four-year layoff. The framers obviously did not want the governor to use his position as a stepping-stone to another high political office, and they were quite successful in thwarting possible gubernatorial ambition. Following a bitter fight between Governor Wallace and the state Senate in 1965 over a proposal whose primary objective was to allow Wallace to serve a second consecutive term, a constitutional amendment was ratified in 1968 that removed these restrictions and enabled state executive officers to succeed themselves for one additional term.[11]

To qualify for the office of governor or lieutenant governor, a person must have reached the age of at least thirty when elected and must have been a U.S. citizen for at least ten years and a resident of Alabama for at least seven years prior to being elected. Qualifications for the remaining constitutional executive officers include an age requirement of twenty-five and citizenship and residence requirements of seven years and five years. The state executive officers may be removed from office by impeachment proceedings heard in the Senate on charges brought by the House of Representatives.[12]

In the event of the governor's removal from office, death, or resignation, the lieutenant governor becomes governor. Also, when a governor is impeached (but not yet convicted), is absent from the state for more than twenty days, becomes mentally incompetent (which, under constitutional provisions, is determined by the state Supreme Court), or is otherwise disabled, the powers and duties of the office temporarily devolve upon the lieutenant governor until the problem is resolved.[13]

THE JUDICIAL BRANCH

Alabama's constitution of 1901 originally vested the judicial power of the state in the Senate (sitting as a court of impeachment), a Supreme Court, circuit courts, courts of chancery (equity), courts of probate, justices of the peace, and such other courts as the legislature might establish. The constitution provided for the division of the state into judicial circuits and chancery divisions and for the establishment of separate systems of circuit and chancery courts. A further provision stated that the legislature might merge the jurisdictions of these two sets of courts.

Judges of the Supreme Court and the circuit, chancery, and probate courts were to be selected by popular election. The constitution fixed six-year terms for these judges. The constitution's framers went on to say, however, that the judges of statutory inferior courts might be either elected or appointed as the legislature determined. Justices of the peace were to be elected in precincts for a term set by the legislature. Vacancies in elective judicial offices were to be filled by appointment by the governor.

Constitutional amendments adopted in 1972 and 1973 completely revised Alabama's constitutional provisions concerning the state judiciary.[14] The 1972 amendment abolished the office of justice of the peace. Of much greater significance, however, is the fact that the new judicial article adopted in 1973 established a modern, unified system of courts. The 1973 article provided for a court structure composed of the Supreme Court of Alabama, the Court of Criminal Appeals, the Court of Civil Appeals, the circuit courts, the probate courts, a new set of inferior courts known as district courts, and municipal courts in those municipalities electing to retain their own court rather than having it incorporated into the appropriate district court.

Under the 1973 article, judges continue to be elected, vacancies continue to be filled by executive appointment, and the judicial term of office remains at six years. Now, though, all judges (rather than simply all judges of courts of record) must be attorneys, except for judges of probate—an exception continued from the original provisions of the 1901 constitution. Formerly removable only by impeachment, judges are now subject to discipline, as well as removal, by a court of the judiciary on a complaint filed by a judicial inquiry commission.

OTHER PROVISIONS

The major purpose of the conservative Democrats who dominated the 1901 constitutional convention was "to disfranchise the blacks and although not admitted openly the ex-Populist poor whites who had been disrupting the Democratic Party." Consequently it is not surprising that the framers devoted a large portion of the constitution to voting qualifications and elections. Qualifications for voting included literacy, character, and residence requirements, as well as a cumulative poll tax.[15] As a general rule, these original qualifications are now obsolete. A rising sentiment in favor of eliminating discrimination in voting has been expressed in constitutional amendments (primarily federal, but state amendments also had a liberalizing effect); federal statutes concerning voting rights; and decisions of the federal courts, such as those invalidating the use of poll taxes and durational residence requirements.[16]

Other parts of the constitution deal with such subjects as taxation, corporations, counties and municipalities, banks and banking, and education. With respect to schools, the constitution originally required a system of racially segregated educational facilities. Conservative limits were set on rates of state and local taxes and on the amounts and kinds of permissible indebtedness. Again, many of the original provisions on these and other subjects have been either modified or altogether rescinded by federal actions and by numerous amendments to the Alabama Constitution.

CONSTITUTIONAL CHANGE

Written constitutions may be altered informally by usage and interpretation as well as by formal amendment. Because the U.S. Constitution is written in general rather than specific language, it lends itself to adaptation by interpretation. In fact, only twenty-six amendments have been added to the U.S. Constitution since 1789. Most state constitutions are written with a profusion of specific detail. Largely because of this difference in style, state constitutional change ordinarily takes place by formal amendment. This is not to say that state constitutional change never occurs through interpretation, but the fact remains that in Alabama (as in other states) most constitutional change occurs—and because of the detailed nature of the constitution must necessarily occur—through formal rather than informal amendment.

Alabama's constitution may be formally amended in two ways.[17] First, the legislature may, by a vote of a majority of all the members elected to each house, pass a measure calling a constitutional convention to alter the constitution. The convention cannot be held, however, unless the question has first been submitted to the voters and approved by a majority of those voting in the election.

Conventions are ordinarily held when extensive constitutional revision is under consideration. Further, conventions tend to be opposed by interest groups favored by existing constitutional arrangements, such as provisions that make it difficult to raise property taxes. Thus in Alabama, as in other states, most constitutional change takes place through a second means: narrowly drawn amendments proposed by the legislature and ratified by the voters. The Alabama Constitution makes no provision for the initiative procedure whereby interested citizens may collect signatures on petitions and have amendments voted on without the necessity of legislative action.

In Alabama a legislative measure proposing an amendment to the constitution must receive a vote of at least three-fifths of all the members elected to each house. It is then submitted to the voters, and to become effective, it must receive a majority of the votes cast in the election on the "proposed amendments" (which, by judicial interpretation, means a majority of the votes cast on each particular amendment submitted for voter approval).[18] A curious provision adopted in 1982 (instead of a conventional home-rule amendment) permits the state constitution to be amended by the voters of a single county when a proposed amendment is of only local application. Local amendments, therefore, are now submitted only to the voters of the county concerned.

It is widely held that to be most effective a constitution should concern itself mainly with the fundamentals of government and leave the details for elaboration through more ordinary processes.[19] By concentrating on fundamentals, according to this theory, a society can establish the form of government it wants and protect civil liberties through appropriate constitutional provisions, and at the same time achieve the flexibility necessary for the government to adapt readily to changing conditions. But the quality of fundamentalism is an elusive concept, subject to different interpretations. Thus there developed in American state politics a decided tendency for those having a special interest in public policy to seek special protection for their values by anchoring them firmly in a highly detailed state constitution.[20]

In Alabama, largely as a result of attitudes developed during Reconstruction, the practice of writing details into the state constitution was first undertaken on an extensive scale in 1875.[21] Later the 1901 convention carried the practice to even greater lengths. The delegates' overriding concern with specification eventually produced a constitution consisting of such a great mass of detail, and hence of such rigidity, that formal amendment became increasingly necessary to adapt its provisions to what Alabamians later considered to be their current needs.

The convention's limitations on the state's policy-making authority soon raised these problems of adaptability. The absolute prohibition of state involvement in public works projects was amended as early as 1908 to allow the state government to make appropriations for highway construction. By 1915 Governor Emmet O'Neal had become convinced that the constitution adopted only a few years previously was so unwieldy that nothing short of a constitutional convention could adequately revise the state's basic law. Eight years later Governor Thomas E. Kilby came to a similar conclusion and suggested to the legislature the establishment of a constitutional study commission to facilitate the work of his proposed convention.[22] During the Great Depression, when tax receipts fell sharply, Governor Benjamin M. Miller commissioned the Brookings Institution to make a study of Alabama's state government to see if it could be operated at less cost and with greater efficiency. Constitutional revision was one of the major recommendations made in the Brookings report.[23] The Alabama Policy Commission, a citizens' organization functioning during the 1930s and 1940s, consistently advocated a new constitution for the state. In later years Governor James E. Folsom repeatedly called for a constitutional convention, mainly for the purpose of legislative reapportionment. None of these efforts at constitutional reform achieved the slightest success.

RECENT REVISION EFFORTS

Largely because of federal actions in such areas as voting rights, representation, and race relations, sentiment in favor of a basic revision of the Alabama Constitution had increased substantially by the late 1960s. This concern was heightened by the continuing growth of the constitution through many amendments of only minor importance. At that time, the most serious interest in constitutional revision centered in the legislature, which in 1967 adopted a resolution creating a joint committee to study the problem of constitutional revision. This action was necessary, the resolution's supporters explained, because "the Constitution as a whole is in many respects not well adapted to modern conditions and problems, and urgently needs simplification and restatement."[24]

The low rate of voter participation in constitutional amendment elections contributed to the greater influence of a relatively small number of interest groups in these elections. It was not unusual for 10 percent or less of the state's voters to participate in constitutional referendums, and public interest was not stimulated by the increasing frequency with which the polls were opened for voting on changes in the state's basic law.

Because of stringent constitutional limitations on the power of local governments to tax, to compensate their officials, and to borrow money, most of the constitutional amendments adopted in Alabama do not apply to the whole state but are designed to relax these restrictions in the case of specified cities or counties. People began to perceive the process of submitting matters of a very local nature to a statewide referendum as both illogical and costly, and this caused a demand for home rule to be joined with the general interest in constitutional revision.[25]

Historically, extensive constitutional revision is the function of a convention. However, groups favored by existing constitutional arrangements are apprehensive about conventions because they feel their constitutional advantages may be placed in jeopardy. Consequently, some states have followed the practice of holding a limited constitutional convention, as in the case of Tennessee, and an increasing number of states have turned to the use of relatively small study commissions as the source of proposed revisions.[26]

The joint committee created by the legislature in 1967 suggested the establishment of a commission as an advisory agency to a convention, as had Governor Kilby in 1923. Although revision commissions have been used in connection with conventions, such commissions commonly report their recommendations to the legislature, which must approve the suggested revisions and propose them, if it chooses, as constitutional amendments.[27] By 1969, interest in the Alabama legislature had coalesced in favor of the commission as the most feasible means of accomplishing constitutional revision. Most important, Governor Albert P. Brewer, who had succeeded to the office in 1968 on the death of Governor Lurleen B. Wallace, was an advocate of constitutional reform and gave his support to the movement to create a revision commission.[28]

Governor Brewer proposed the establishment of a commission composed of twenty-one members—seven legislators and fourteen public members. It was to report its recommendations to the legislature in 1971. At the 1969 regular session, the legislature responded to the governor's proposal and created the Alabama Constitutional Commission, broadly empowered to "consider and investigate the necessity for and the extent and nature of desirable amendments to or general revision of the Constitution of 1901 of Alabama."[29] Its membership followed the lines suggested by Governor Brewer.

The members of the commission soon concluded that a thorough revision of the constitution required more time than had originally been scheduled for it. Consequently, the commission made only an interim report in May 1971 and requested that its life be extended for two additional years so it could complete its assigned task. When the legislature responded and did extend the commission's mandate in 1971, its membership was increased to twenty-five to make room for additional legislative representation.[30] The commission selected as its chair Shelby County probate judge Conrad M. Fowler, a highly regarded figure in Alabama government.

In its final report, submitted in May 1973, the commission recommended a complete revision of the constitution and its many amendments.[31] The report was cast in the form of a proposed new constitution for the state of Alabama and included an extensive commentary on the draft constitution. Generally, the changes recommended by the commission were directed toward the reduction of constraints on the legislature, some increase in the governor's authority as chief administrator of the state government (for example, by authorizing executive reorganization of administrative departments, subject to legislative veto), and the eradication of details considered essentially more statutory than constitutional.

Among the more important specific proposals were recommendations that sought to improve legislative–local government relationships through provision for home rule and a limited classification system for the enactment of local legislation on a population basis. A commission on reapportionment was proposed as a method of dealing with this problem. The complicated provisions regarding voting and elections still contained in the constitution (although obsolete in many respects) were to be simplified and updated. The commission also suggested extensive changes in the area of state and local finance—discontinuing the practice of "earmarking" revenues (dedicating tax resources for particular purposes) and modernizing tax and debt limitations, for example.

The commission proposed changes in the governor's veto power (such as the elimination of the pocket veto) and the adoption of annual legislative sessions. At times the legislature has adjourned without passing the appropriation measures necessary to fund the state government. In an effort to encourage timely action on these measures, the commission recommended that whenever the major state appropriation bills had not been passed before the last three days of a regular session, no other legislation could be approved until the money bills had cleared the legislature. If the legislature adjourned without passing these measures, the last appropriation measures enacted would continue in effect until new appropriations had been adopted. As we have seen, the commission's proposed article on the judiciary made substantial changes in the state judicial system.

The legislature had the choice of adopting all or any part of the proposed revisions and submitting those selected to the voters for ratification. It could also, of course, amend or reject any of the proposals. The commission drafted its recommended constitution in such a way that each of its principal articles was complete in itself and could be adopted without affecting other provisions of the existing constitution.[32] Thus constitutional revision could be phased in over a period of time, as particular articles were deemed ripe for consideration, somewhat after the fashion of California in the 1960s and 1970s.[33] This approach could minimize the effect of what has been called "cumulative opposition," or opposition from groups that individually have limited resources yet through their collective opposition have the strength to defeat a proposed new constitution submitted as a single document.[34] When new constitutional articles are submitted separately, it is more difficult for these groups to defeat all of the proposed changes.

When the Constitutional Commission submitted its 1971 interim report to the legislature, it recommended the adoption of ten constitutional amendments. So limited was the interest in the seemingly abstract issue of general constitutional change, however, that only one of the commission's recommendations received the approval of the 1971 legislature. This was a proposal for annual legislative sessions, a recommendation also made by a legislative interim committee that had been established in 1969 to study legislative organization and procedure. By a count of 267,370 to 210,950, the voters, who had been bombarded with negative appeals from tax-conscious interests, defeated the annual-sessions proposal in a referendum held at the same time as the November 1972 general election.[35] Out of a total of 1,052,009 ballots cast in the election, only 478,320 voters expressed themselves on the question of annual legislative sessions. Obviously, much more interest was focused on the elections for president and U.S. senator than on the meetings of the legislature.

When the commission filed its final report with the 1973 legislature, it emphasized the proposed judicial article because it considered this article of the 1901 constitution to be especially in need of revision.[36] The legislature made changes in the article but did pass it, and it was ratified by the voters (73,609 to 44,840) in December 1973.[37] The total vote on the amendment represented only 6.7 percent of the state's registered voters.

Following the adoption of the article on the courts, there was renewed interest among supporters of legislative reform in the possibility of approving yearly sessions of the legislature. Hence the legislature proposed a second annual-sessions amendment in 1975. At a special election held in June 1975, the annual-sessions amendment passed by a vote of 95,330 to 75,966.[38] Typically, only a small percentage of the electorate participated in the referendum.

Interest groups have played a central role in the politics of constitutional revision throughout the history of the 1901 constitution. We have seen, as McMillan put it, that "Black Belt conservatives, big businessmen and industrialists, especially from Birmingham, . . . controlled the convention." These groups were "generally conservative" and had sufficient combined strength "to write their own interests into the Constitution of 1901." We have seen, too, that the coalition identified by McMillan remained dominant politically well after the 1901 convention had dissolved. As he says, its continued operation has been "one of the most constant factors in the state's politics."[39] And over forty years after the constitutional convention was held, the industrial-financial sector of the coalition was still known as the "Big Mules" of Alabama politics.[40]

Political scientists L. Harmon Zeigler and Hendrik van Dalen have noted that the "Big Mules" and the planters were more influential when V. O. Key described their activity in his 1949 classic, *Southern Politics*, than they are today. As these writers observed, there is now a more diverse pattern of group politics in Alabama, which they would attribute mostly to the state's increasing levels of industrialization and urbanization.[41] While the "Big Mules" and agribusiness remain potent forces in Alabama politics, they no longer have the field to themselves. Today they are likely to find themselves opposed in constitutional referendums by such countervailing groups as the teachers' association, labor unions, associations of local officials, and re-form-minded organizations like the League of Women Voters.

Probably the most striking example of interest group activity in the area of recent constitutional change, and one that illustrates the continuing influence of the landowning interests, is the extensive controversy between these interests and education and local government groups over the amendment known as the Lid Bill.[42] This is a lengthy, highly complicated amendment designed to limit property tax increases. Agricultural interests strongly pushed for the cap on property tax hikes, and education and city and county interests opposed it. It was ultimately adopted in 1978 as Alabama, along with many other states, followed the lead of California's Proposition 13 in restricting the growth of property tax revenues.

If Alabama should at some time in the future get a new constitution based on the work of a constitutional commission, the key factor leading to success will probably be executive leadership. Such leadership is critical in rousing public support for the generally uninteresting cause of constitutional reform, diffusing the opposition of interest groups that are generally satisfied with things as they are, and getting the backing of legislators and voters that will be needed if a constitutional draft is to become the basic law of the state. Legislative spokespersons may add considerably to the appeal of broad constitutional change, but unless the governor is actively and consistently involved, it is unlikely that a constitutional reform movement will ever be successful.[43]

When Forrest H. (Fob) James was elected governor in 1978, constitutional revision again became a gubernatorial goal. Soon after the election, the governor appointed a committee to study the subject of constitutional reform and make recommendations for revising the state's basic law. Benefiting from the constitutional commission's efforts, the governor's "working group" recommended the adoption of what amounted to essentially a revised version of the commission's proposed constitution. Among other changes in the commission document, the governor's committee proposed to include in the constitution the initiative, the recall, and the provisions of the Lid Bill.

Governor James's proposed constitution was introduced into the 1979 regular session of the legislature. It passed the Senate and died in the House of Representatives. It experienced opposition in both the preliminary and the legislative stages of its consideration. Some legislators, for example, opposed the recall, arguing that this device for removing elected officials before the expiration of their terms (by petition and election) could be used against courageous officials who took an unpopular stand on a controversial public-policy issue. A provision that would have discontinued the practice of earmarking revenues was opposed by groups interested in maintaining the system of dedicated taxes for the support of such functions as education and highways. Home rule came in for its share of criticism, as did numerous other provisions, either because they had been included or not included in the proposed document.[44] In short, it succumbed to the cumulative opposition that, as we have seen, so often besets a proposed constitution.

In the election of 1982, former state attorney general Bill Baxley raised the issue of constitutional revision in his successful campaign for lieutenant governor. Once in office, he appointed a special committee to undertake the revision effort. Some of the constitutional commission's recommendations had been considered too controversial for successful implementation. Consequently, the 1983 committee concentrated its efforts on a "cleanup" revision that eliminated obsolete material (such as the suffrage article mentioned earlier) and consolidated and condensed other provisions to produce a more streamlined document.[45]

After the failure of constitutional revision in the 1970s there did not appear to be any overriding concern in the state about constitutional change. However, because of the committee's essentially revisionist approach, the 1983 draft constitution did not at first arouse the controversy and opposition associated with the earlier document. Consequently, on its proposal by the legislature, the chance of the state's adopting a new constitution seemed good.[46] The longer the proposed constitution remained before the people, though, the more criticism they raised against it. Some of the strongest criticism was aimed at language regulating the public debt and at the legal uncertainties that the document might produce. Most serious was the charge that the amendment had been improperly passed by the legislature.

Shortly after what would have been Alabama's seventh constitution was proposed, its opponents went to court to challenge the document in an effort to keep it off the ballot. They argued that the legislature did not have the power to propose an entirely new constitution as a single amendment, that a new constitution could only be drafted and submitted for ratification by a constitutional convention. The trial court agreed with this view and, on appeal, so did the state Supreme Court.[47] Consequently, the proposed constitution did not appear on the ballot, and the voters had no opportunity to express their opinions about it. Constitutional revision thus remained an item of unfinished business on Alabama's public agenda.

CHAPTER FOUR

The Legislature

The Alabama legislature is the chief policy-forming unit of the state government. Vested with the state's legislative power, it can pass whatever laws are politically expedient, provided it does not violate the Constitution, laws, and treaties of the United States (the "supreme law of the land") or the state's own constitution. Within this broad area of authority, the legislators establish public programs and agencies and make important decisions about taxing and spending policies and other rules that govern the state of Alabama.[1]

Legislative structure in Alabama follows the bicameral (two-house) model used by every state except Nebraska, where the unicameral (one-house) system is used. Alabama's legislature (which was known as the General Assembly until 1901) has been composed since statehood of a Senate and a House of Representatives. Until 1965 representation in the House was based on the county and in the Senate on districts composed of one county or a group of counties.[2] Where the latter situation prevailed, each county in the district would usually elect the senator in its turn under a rotation system. Since 1965 the legislature's composition has been based on court-ordered district systems of representation designed to implement the "one person, one vote" requirement of federal law.

REAPPORTIONMENT

Federal court decisions during the 1960s brought about a long overdue increase in the urban counties' legislative representation. When the legislators failed to pass an acceptable reapportionment plan after the 1970 census, the federal courts again had to handle the problem. This time, a special three-judge panel issued an order in January 1972 that produced a legislature composed of 105 representatives (instead of 106) and the usual thirty-five senators. In 1966 and 1970, the senators and representatives had been elected on an at-large basis in districts formed of counties. Under the 1972 plan, the legislators were all elected from single-member legislative districts.[3] By basing the apportionment of representation on census tracts, the court was able to arrange the state into 105 relatively small House districts that no longer followed county lines strictly but were remarkably equal in population.[4] The House districts were clustered into sets of three to construct the thirty-five Senate districts.

Although the reapportionment efforts of the 1960s had relieved the legislative imbalance between rural and urban sections, they had failed to affect significantly the racial composition of the legislature. In large measure this was because multimember districts tend to reduce the voting strength of minority groups, especially where voting patterns are polarized. It was this factor that eventually led to the use of single-member districts considered more likely to produce a racially representative legislative assembly.[5]

After the 1980 census, the legislature enacted a reapportionment plan that, in the main, governed legislative elections in 1982. Since the state was subject to the federal Voting Rights Act, the plan had to be submitted to the U.S. Justice Department for approval. It was also challenged in a federal district court as racially discriminatory. The Justice Department raised objections to the plan, finding that it had discriminatory effects, primarily in Jefferson County and the Black Belt. When these adjustments were made, the court finally approved the legislature's efforts. The court ordered a new legislative election to be held in 1983 so that representation in the 1980s would be based on an approved plan.[6] Under this plan of representation, the composition of the legislature remained as it had been established in the 1970s—105 representatives and thirty-five senators, all elected from single-member districts.

LEGISLATIVE ORGANIZATION

Senators must be at least twenty-five years of age and representatives at least twenty-one at the time of their election. The legislators must have been citizens and residents of the state for three years, and residents of their districts for one year, preceding their election.[7]

Over the nation as a whole, senators most frequently serve for four years and representatives for two. In Alabama before 1901, senators and representatives served unequal terms. Under the present constitution, though, both serve four-year terms (a practice that is also followed in Louisiana, Maryland, and Mississippi). Alabamians elect their legislators in the "off-year" election, the general election in which the president is not elected. The legislators' terms begin on the day after their election and end on the day after the election held four years later. During their terms, legislators may be removed only by being expelled (on a two-thirds vote) from the house in which they serve.[8]

The amount legislators are paid is always a controversial subject. As provided in the constitution, members of the legislature receive a salary of ten dollars a day while the legislature is in session and a travel allowance of ten cents a mile for one round trip each session between their residence and the state capital. If these were the only provisions dealing with legislative pay, Alabama would have a very poorly compensated group of senators and representatives. However, in addition to the travel allowance, Alabama legislators receive compensation for expenses other than travel in an amount that the legislature may determine by law. This allows the legislators to compensate themselves more generously than would be permissible under fixed constitutional standards. Today the legislators' compensation for expenses other than travel amounts to $40 a day while the legislature is in session and an additional allowance of $1,900 a month payable throughout the members' term.[9]

Because legislative pay is based largely on the per diem system, the amount of annual compensation is not a firm figure. It varies from year to year (and even among legislators), depending on the length and number of sessions and the amount of interim work for which members receive their legislative pay. Currently the annual compensation is estimated to be a minimum of about $28,000.[10] Extra sessions increase the pay above the minimum. Raising their own compensation, incidentally, is one of the most politically charged issues that the legislators consider. Generally legislators act to hike their pay at the beginning of the term, apparently in the hope that probable voter hostility will subside before members face their constituents at the polls again.

Each new legislature holds an organizational session at which the two houses select their officers, make their committee assignments, and adopt their rules of procedure.[11] The Senate does not have to select a presiding officer, as the lieutenant governor is its presiding officer. However, the

Senate does elect one of its members to the position of president pro tempore (a temporary presiding officer to fill in whenever the lieutenant governor is absent) and the House elects a Speaker from its membership to preside over that body.

In Alabama the presiding officers have an impressive set of powers and duties. They decide the legislators' committee assignments, name the committee chairs, and choose the committees to which bills will be referred for examination. During floor sessions they decide which legislators will be recognized to speak on the bill or issue under consideration, put before the members the issues to be voted on, announce the results of the voting, and settle questions regarding the rules of procedure. Through these and other powers, the lieutenant governor and the Speaker have many opportunities to make their presence felt in the legislative halls. The presiding officers, especially the Speaker of the House, have traditionally served also as channels of gubernatorial influence in the legislature.

Alabama's original constitution provided for annual legislative sessions and placed no limit on the length of these meetings.[12] Later the state waffled on the point, switching to biennial sessions, then to annual sessions, and again to biennial sessions. As noted in chapter 3, confidence in the legislature eroded badly during the nineteenth century. By 1901 (the date of the current constitution) distrust of the legislature had become so intense that the framers of the document included in the basic law an extraordinary provision permitting the legislature to meet in regular session only once every four years, and then for only fifty days.

In practice the fifty-day limit on the length of the session was not as severe a restriction as it seems. It was taken to mean "legislative days," or only those days on which formal legislative meetings took place. A rising sentiment for more frequent sessions became apparent by 1939, however, and the constitution was amended at that time to provide for biennial sessions limited to sixty consecutive calendar days.[13] Between 1939 and 1976 the legislature met in regular session every two years, and every four years in the diminutive (ten-day) organizational sessions held in January following the legislative election. Special sessions could be called at the governor's discretion. By an amendment passed in 1946, both regular and special sessions were limited to thirty-six days, but the legislators were again enabled to use the concept of "legislative" days.[14] The frequency of these meeting (or legislative) days determined the length of the regular and special sessions.

Even though the legislature could (and did, under the theory of the legislative day) prolong its regular and special sessions to a degree, individuals and groups who supported a more expansive role for the state government believed that the session arrangement still did not allow the legislature enough time to give really adequate consideration to the state's legislative needs. Concern about this problem led to a series of recommendations by several study groups that the state change to annual legislative sessions.[15]

Following these recommendations, the legislature enacted a proposed constitutional amendment calling for annual sessions, but the proposal went down to defeat in the election on its ratification. Interest in legislative reform waned for a time but revived with the publication of the Constitutional Commission's final report in 1973. There the commission renewed its recommendation for annual sessions, arguing that "The volume of business with which the legislature is now confronted simply cannot be handled on an intermittent, every-other-year basis."[16]

In March 1975 the legislature acted on the issue and again proposed an annual-sessions amendment to the Alabama Constitution. This amendment was adopted at a special election held in June. The more heavily populated urban counties, particularly Jefferson and Mobile, provided most of the support necessary for its passage.[17] In substance, the amendment formalized the concept of the legislative day (that is, wrote it into the constitution) and allowed the legislature only thirty of these days for its regular sessions each year, within an overall limitation of 105 calendar days. Also, it reduced the permissible number of legislative days in special sessions to twelve and limited them to thirty calendar days.

THE LAWMAKING PROCESS

Although the legislature performs a number of other activities, such as overseeing the implementation of public policy by administrative agencies and confirming administrative appointments (when approval is required of the Senate), its primary function is that of legislation, or passing the laws that establish the state's public policies.[18]

The lawmaking function is closely regulated by both constitutional and statutory provisions as well as by rules of procedure. The process is described in the following pages and is presented in outline form in figure 3.

Alabama's constitution states that no law may be passed except by a bill, which is simply a draft of a suggested law that forms the basis for the legislature's consideration of the proposal. As part-time officials, legislators often lack the time and resources necessary to prepare the legislation in which they are interested. The legislature sought to deal with this problem through the creation in 1945 of the Legislative Reference Service, an agency that serves the legislators as a source of information and assistance in the drafting of legislative documents.[19] Although bills are prepared by a variety of individuals and organizations—such as administrative agencies, the attorney general's office, local officials, interest groups, and individual legislators—probably most of the bills introduced into the Alabama legislature today are prepared by the Legislative Reference Service.

To introduce bills, legislators simply deposit them with the secretary of the Senate or the clerk of the House, depending on the chamber in which the legislator holds membership. As in Congress, revenue bills must originate in the House of Representatives. Otherwise, bills may begin the legislative process in either chamber. Sometimes, in fact, senators and representatives introduce identical bills into both houses at the same time as "companion" measures.[20] In this way, legislators can expedite the passage of their legislation by concentrating on the measure that is moving at the swifter pace.

There is, of course, a great deal of variation in the number of bills introduced into state legislatures. In 1978, for example, 1,967 bills were introduced in Alabama, while in neighboring states the number of bills ranged from 1,136 in Georgia to 3,321 in Florida.[21] As a general rule, many more bills are introduced in the House than in the Senate. At the regular sessions of the Alabama legislature held during the period 1979–1981, for instance, an average of 1,115 bills was introduced in the House (63 percent) and 647 in the Senate (37 percent).

Relatively few of the bills introduced are enacted into law. In the regular sessions from 1978 through 1981 a little less than one-third of the bills introduced were eventually enacted. For reasons that we explain in chapter 10, recently even fewer bills have been passed: in 1982, for example, about 12 percent of the House bills and 22 percent of the Senate bills.[22] Table 1 illustrates the way in which various stages in Alabama's legislative process reduce the volume of legislation that is finally enacted.

There is a constitutional requirement that, to become law, a bill must be read on three different days in each house. In practice, this requirement does not mean that bills must be read in their entirety. When a bill is introduced, it is read only by its title unless (as sometimes happens, especially as a delaying tactic) a reading at length is requested by one of the legislators. The reading of the bill's title at its introduction is considered its first reading. After introduction and first reading, the presiding officer refers the measure to a standing committee.

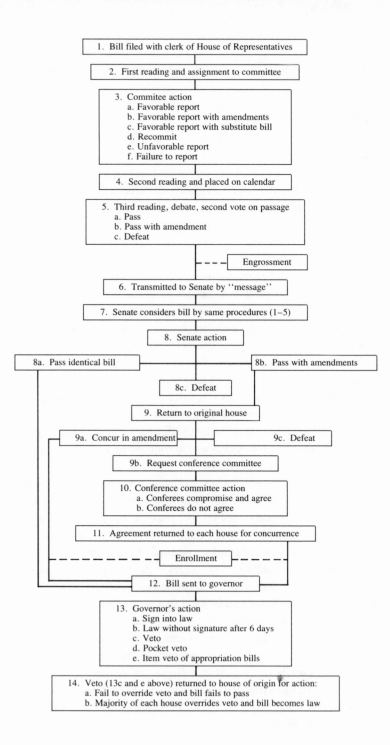

1. Bill filed with clerk of House of Representatives

2. First reading and assignment to committee

3. Commitee action
   a. Favorable report
   b. Favorable report with amendments
   c. Favorable report with substitute bill
   d. Recommit
   e. Unfavorable report
   f. Failure to report

4. Second reading and placed on calendar

5. Third reading, debate, second vote on passage
   a. Pass
   b. Pass with amendment
   c. Defeat

Engrossment

6. Transmitted to Senate by "message"

7. Senate considers bill by same procedures (1–5)

8. Senate action

8a. Pass identical bill   8b. Pass with amendments

8c. Defeat

9. Return to original house

9a. Concur in amendment   9c. Defeat

9b. Request conference committee

10. Conference committee action
    a. Conferees compromise and agree
    b. Conferees do not agree

11. Agreement returned to each house for concurrence

Enrollment

12. Bill sent to governor

13. Governor's action
    a. Sign into law
    b. Law without signature after 6 days
    c. Veto
    d. Pocket veto
    e. Item veto of appropriation bills

14. Veto (13c and e above) returned to house of origin for action:
    a. Fail to override veto and bill fails to pass
    b. Majority of each house overrides veto and bill becomes law

Table 1: Alabama Legislature's Actions on Bills, Regular Session, 1980

Action	House bills		Senate bills	
	Number	Percent	Number	Percent
Introduced	1145	100.0	627	100.0
Reported by committee, house of origin	795	69.4	399	63.6
Amended by committee, house of origin	149	13.0	88	14.0
Amended on floor, house of origin	133	11.6	72	11.5
Passed house of origin	538	47.0	252	40.2
Reported by committee, opposite chamber	484	42.3	215	34.3
Amended by committee, opposite chamber	32	2.8	36	5.7
Amended on floor, opposite chamber	57	5.0	44	7.0
Nonconcurrence	4	.3	2	.3
Veto (pocket)	2	.2	1	.2
Enacted	409	35.7	152	24.2

Source: Computed from final status reports furnished by
Legislative Digest, Montgomery, Alabama.

Following customary practice in American legislatures, standing committees in the Alabama legislature are organized on a policy-field basis (such as public utilities and transportation, agriculture and forestry, finance and taxation, health and welfare, education, and the like), and their main function is to give initial consideration to the bills that lie within their respective jurisdictions. In theory at least, such a division of work "lessens the burden of decisionmaking for legislators" and permits specialization in

Figure 3. Alabama's Legislative Process. (*Source:* Robert L. McCurley, Jr., and James D. Thomas, eds., *The Legislative Process: A Handbook for Alabama Legislators* [University: Alabama Law Institute, 1980], pp. 28–29. Used by permission of the Alabama Law Institute. The chart has been altered slightly.)

considering proposed legislation.[23] As of the organizational session in 1987, there were twenty-five standing committees in the House and seventeen in the Senate.

Committee meetings are not closely regulated, so the committee chairpersons have great influence over committee operations. They call meetings, draw up agendas, and set public hearings largely at their own discretion. Usually they do schedule public hearings on important measures, frequently at the request of committee members.[24] At these hearings, lobbyists and other interested people (including the bill's sponsors) communicate to the committee members their views of the bill's merits.

Bills that the committees report favorably to the whole house receive a second reading (again by title only) and are then listed on the calendar to await the decisive vote on their third reading. Unreported bills simply die in committee. Most bills that are reported are reported favorably. Farmer noted as long ago as 1949 that it had become the tendency in the legislature "to report favorably all bills referred to the committees or not to report them at all."[25]

How effective are the committees as centers of inquiry into the merits of proposed legislation? Our data indicate that in the opinion of most observers of the Alabama legislature the committee system is a weak component of the legislative process. One student of state legislatures, Alan Rosenthal, suggests that committee performance can be evaluated empirically and that committee systems can be generally described as "better-performing," "medium-performing," or "poorer-performing." Alabama is listed in the "poorer-performing" category. These are the state committee systems that, for example, report favorably a large proportion of their assigned bills and either do not function or fail to accomplish much in the way of studying problems and developing legislation in the periods between sessions.[26]

Farmer concluded in her 1949 study that in Alabama most bills failed to receive careful consideration by the committees to which they were referred. She based her conclusion partly on the quantity of bills reported favorably (about 70 percent in 1943) and partly on the relatively small proportion reported with amendments or committee substitutes. Farmer also thought that Alabama's committees had to work under a number of handicaps in considering proposed legislation: their heavy workload, their lack of expertise in the policy areas in which they were expected to legislate, and their lack of staff.[27] The arbitrary referral policies of presiding officers and the number of committees on which legislators served exacerbated the problem.

Twenty years or so after the publication of Farmer's research, the Legislative Reform Study Committee of 1969 observed in its report that "Generally speaking a legislative body is no better than its committee system, and there are many indications that the Alabama committee system is weak."[28] During the 1970s, Harold Stanley dealt at some length with the question of committee effectiveness in a study analyzing voting behavior in the Alabama Senate. In the Senate, Stanley found,

Committees consistently report bills out to the floor as a courtesy to the sponsor without much regard for the bill's merits. The absence of a seniority system makes reappointments to committee coincidental. Most members have had no previous service on the committee. Committees lack sufficient time to make any detailed studies of the bills referred to them. Not having staffs further hinders the ability to carefully consider measures. Referrals of bills to committee follows an inconsistent (but politically purposeful) pattern.[29]

Often, Stanley observed, committee members voted to report a bill to the Senate but with the understanding that they would vote against it on the floor or even fight it. With some exceptions, bills supported by the governor's administration were referred to "rubber stamp" committees (or committees dominated by supporters of the administration) that more or less automatically reported them favorably. For such reasons as these, Stanley concluded, the committees did not, as a general rule, function effectively in screening legislation but left the legislators to face "a calendar thick with bills recommended by one committee or another."[30]

One might imagine that bills would be considered at the third-reading stage (on the floor of the house) in the order in which they appear on the calendar. As a matter of fact, bills that the house leaders deem important are considered out of regular calendar order either by suspension of the rules or by special order of the Rules Committee. In each house of the Alabama legislature, responsibility for screening and prioritizing legislation rests mainly with the Rules Committee.[31] This committee is thus a vital part of the leadership structure. The hundreds of bills not given favorable consideration by the Rules Committee usually "die on the calendar" with the expiration of the legislative session.

Assuming that a bill does reach the floor for action by the house membership, it may then be read at length and is subject to debate and possible amendment on motions made by individual legislators. However, debate is not unlimited in either house, and procedures exist (under the rules of both the House and the Senate) by which the leadership may curtail extensive debate, or filibustering against a bill, and bring about a vote on the pending question. Ultimately a vote is taken on the passage of the bill—assuming, again, that it gets that far. In order to pass the house, the bill must ordinarily receive a simple majority vote. However, some measures (proposed constitutional amendments, for example) require a larger majority. Voting is done by machine in the House of Representatives and by voice vote in the Senate.

Having passed the house of origin, a bill must then run the gauntlet in the second house and pass there exactly as it was framed by the first house. If it does not, the house that originated the bill may request that a committee of members from both houses—a conference committee—be formed to work out the differences in the versions of the bill as passed by the House and the Senate. If the conference committee is able to come up with a compromise bill and both houses adopt it in the form recommended by that committee, then the bill also passes. But if agreement on the exact form of the bill is never reached by both houses, the bill fails to pass the legislature. Bills that do pass the legislature are then presented to the governor for executive consideration.

THE LEGISLATORS

A member of the Alabama legislature is ordinarily a white male of a Protestant religious faith (usually Baptist or Methodist), and is most likely a native Alabamian. He was educated in the public schools of the state and probably at a state college or university. There is also a good chance that he is a lawyer. Generally, the legislator is on the young side of middle age and may have had little if any previous legislative experience, although senators frequently have had experience in the House.[32]

In recent years a number of significant changes have occurred in the composition of the legislature. Substantial increases in the number of business people and teachers, the appearance of black legislators in significant numbers (twenty-four after the 1983 election), a sharp decrease in farmer membership, a small decline in lawyer membership, and a decrease in previous nonlegislative governmental experience (but an increase in legislative experience) are among the most striking developments.[33] Women continue to be badly underrepresented. Their representation at the end of 1983 (nine) amounted to only 6.4 percent of the legislative membership. Nationally, in a recent year, approximately 12 percent of the state legislators were women.[34]

LEGISLATIVE DEVELOPMENT

In the early 1970s a study by the Citizens Conference on State Legislatures (later Legis 50) evaluated all the state legislatures in terms of such measures of effectiveness as independence, functionality, accountability, representativeness, and informational support. Appraised on the basis of these standards, which related essentially to such technical matters as procedures and facilities, not to how well legislative business was actually conducted, the Alabama legislature ranked low. Indeed, the report ranked it last among the fifty state legislatures. (California's was ranked first.)

An interim committee of the Alabama Legislature that had been created in 1969 to study Alabama's legislative system also concluded that legislative improvement was necessary and made dozens of recommendations to deal with specific problems of organization and procedure.[35] A lot of the interim committee's recommendations have been put into practice. As we have seen, the state adopted a constitutional amendment providing for annual sessions in 1975.[36] Orientation meetings of the legislature were held in November and December of 1970, as the committee suggested, and have been continued. Other steps have been taken to regulate the introduction and passage of legislative measures in an effort to facilitate the handling of noncontroversial business and to place the consideration of legislative proposals on a more informed basis. Also, legislation and rules have been passed to regulate the conduct of lobbyists and the practice of lobbying.

Senators accomplished a degree of committee reform by reducing the number of Senate committees to twelve, although this number has now been increased, and (in an effort to regulate bill referrals) by defining committee jurisdictions in the Senate rules. Prefiling of bills between sessions has been permitted, but this has not been coupled with year-round standing committee operations as the study group suggested. Nor has additional time been provided during sessions for committee meetings.

The study committee pointed out that legislators who have little or no staff of their own are dependent on lobbyists and administrative agencies as sources of information. As a means of enhancing legislative independence, it recommended an increase in the legislature's professional staff. Alabama's legislators have responded to the proposals by making some additions to the legislative staff, most notably by the creation in 1975 of the Legislative Fiscal Office. Now the legislators have a legislative agency to estimate the financial effects of proposed legislation, review the executive budgets, and otherwise provide legislators with information about the state's financial operations. Improvements in facilities have also been made. The legislature now has a computer-based bill history and status system, for example, to provide information about legislative action on the bills introduced.[37] And across the street from the capitol the old Highway Building has been converted into a new "Statehouse" with ample facilities for legislators, including private offices.

Members of the interim committee expected that adoption of their recommendations would "restore the people's faith and confidence in the Alabama Legislature."[38] Although many of the recommendations have been adopted, this has failed to happen. A recent survey found "generally strong agreement between the public and the legislature over many issues concerning the state. Differences do exist, and they exist on important matters, but there is more agreement than disagreement."[39] Despite the improvements that have been made and the general congruence between legislative and citizen attitudes, the reputation of the legislature remains poor. There is still criticism that the legislature is irresponsible, that it falls down on the job. In a statewide survey conducted during the spring of 1983, only a little more than a third of the respondents (35 percent) rated the Alabama Legislature as doing a good or excellent job.[40] Obviously the public does not seem to have detected much improvement in the legislature's performance. The actions cited above, however, indicate that the process of legislative modernization in Alabama has advanced to some degree.

CHAPTER FIVE

The Governor

The governor of Alabama, in common with governors in other states, is popularly elected, serves a four-year term, is eligible for reelection (though consecutively for only two terms), and is the state's chief executive officer, taking precedence over all other executive officials. Alabama's constitution sets up an executive branch composed of numerous elective state offices. It goes on to declare, however, that the "supreme" executive power rests with the governor, and it requires the governor to see to it that the laws are faithfully executed.[1]

The constitutional language projects an image of the governor as something of a grand overseer of the state's administrative operations, making certain that the many administrative agencies dutifully carry out the programs and policies enacted by the legislature. Managing state government operations is indeed one of the governor's major functions, given a political environment that favors tax limitation and fiscal accountability.[2] Even so, the governor has many more powers and duties than those related to executive management.

THE ROLES OF ALABAMA'S GOVERNOR

Coleman B. Ransone, Jr., suggests that the American governor's major responsibilities include public relations and policy formation as well as management.[3] As we see it, an Alabama governor's responsibilities involve specific roles associated with the office. Consequently, our discussion of the governor's powers and functions stresses several gubernatorial roles. These roles may be identified as chief of state, chief executive, chief legislator, and chief politician. The next chapter concerns policy and administration and includes a detailed account of the governor's role as chief executive, so this chapter concentrates on the other three.

Chief of State

Students of state government frequently compare the position of governor to that of president of the United States. The analogy is useful and accurate to a certain extent, but there are obvious points of differentiation between the two positions. Differences of scale come immediately to mind, as does the absence in the office of governor of the authority to deal with foreign affairs. In this latter connection, though, we should point out that economic problems have thrust forward international trade as a subject of major interest to recent Alabama governors. In the 1980s, for example, both Governor James and Governor Wallace made trips abroad in the interest of economic development.

Like the president, the governor as the formal or symbolic head of state acts for it on ceremonial occasions and in its formal relationships with other governments. The governor's ceremonial duties include such functions as dedicating public facilities, being present at major events (for example, an Alabama or Auburn homecoming football game), and greeting important visitors to the state. When a disaster such as a drought or a severe storm occurs, the governor may visit the site to symbolize the state's concern for the people involved. If the magnitude of the damage is great enough, the governor may request the president to designate the affected areas officially as disaster areas, thereby qualifying residents for federal emergency assistance and low-interest loans for repairing the damage.

Although the governor's powers that directly concern law enforcement and the administration of justice may not seem large, they are enough to give the governor ample opportunity to exercise influence in these policy areas. The governor is the key figure in rendition proceedings, under which fugitives from justice may be returned to Alabama or from Alabama to another state. Governors in Alabama fill vacancies in judgeships and in prosecutors' and sheriffs' positions, and they may use such appointive opportunities to further their own approach to crime and punishment, as well as to help themselves politically. In 1985, for example, when the sheriff's office in Chilton County became vacant, Governor Wallace appointed to the position a man who had served for some fifteen years as his campaign coordinator in the county.[4] The governor appoints the head of the

Department of Public Safety, the chief state agency concerned with law enforcement. In cases involving particularly serious crimes, the governor offers rewards for information leading to the arrest and conviction of the criminals. Historically prominent among the governor's powers is the clemency power, the granting of reprieves (delays) and commutations (less drastic punishment) to prisoners under sentence of death. Another of these traditional powers—the pardoning power—is not vested in the governor but in a separate board.

The governor is the commander-in-chief of the state's military force— the National Guard—unless, of course, the Guard has been placed under the command of the president. Typically the governor uses the National Guard during periods of natural disaster to maintain law and order and to protect the lives and property of distressed citizens. One of the best-known incidents involving the Guard occurred, though, during the confrontation between federal and state authorities at the University of Alabama in June 1963. Following Governor Wallace's "stand in the schoolhouse door," President John F. Kennedy took control of the Guard away from the governor—what is referred to as the process of "federalization"—to permit integration of the university.

Citizens expect the governor, as the head of the state government, to maintain a peaceful society, and the governor may use the National Guard to do so. The governor would probably respond to a severe breakdown of law and order with a declaration of martial law in the affected area. Then military authorities would temporarily displace the regular local officials until the situation is corrected. Such an incident occurred in 1954. At that time Governor Gordon Persons put military officers in charge in Phenix City and Russell County following the assassination of state attorney general nominee Albert L. Patterson. Persons considered it necessary to strip the local officials of their authority because some of them were suspected of involvement in the murder as well as in other criminal activity in the city that caused it to be referred to sometimes as "Sin City, U.S.A." Military rule continued until order was restored in the community a few months later.

The Chief Executive

Alabama's constitution imposes on the governor the general duty of seeing to it that the laws are faithfully executed. It is under this mandate that the governor is concerned with the way in which the agencies comprising the executive branch (the bureaucracy) administer the state's everyday business. The heads of many executive agencies are either elected by the voters or appointed by boards or commissions, and for this reason they operate somewhat independently of the governor. In Alabama the governor is, however, a stronger executive than the fragmented administrative structure would suggest, because of the governor's informal sources of influence and broad powers of financial management. The Alabama governor controls a finance department with responsibility for such important functions as budgeting, purchasing, central accounting, and releasing funds from the state treasury. Ever since the creation of this agency in 1939, it has been a major factor in strengthening the position of the governor relative to the state bureaucracy.

In some observers' estimation, much of the governor's administrative influence is due to a traditionally strong position of leadership over the legislature. To indicate the nature of the executive-legislative relationship in Alabama, we turn now to the governor's role as chief legislator.

The Chief Legislator

In her book *The Legislative Process in Alabama,* the late Hallie Farmer showed clearly that in Alabama it is the governor who has traditionally served as the "chief legislator."[5] This expression means that, although there are 140 elected legislators in Alabama—and the governor is not one of them—nonetheless the governor has more legislative influence than any member of the House or the Senate. The role is pervasive, evidencing itself at many junctures of the legislative process. As a matter of practice, the function of organizing the legislature (and thus being able to influence its behavior) has been the prerogative of the governor. The House and the Senate have usually elected the governor's designees as Speaker and president pro tempore. According to the rules, the presiding officers make committee assignments and appoint the committee chairs. But these rules have the impact of considerably strengthening the governor's hand in dealing with the legislature, since in practice (especially in the House) committee appointments have been made in cooperation with the governor. The general tendency in matters of state policy has been to defer to executive leadership.

The governor's traditional influence on legislative organization is well illustrated by remarks drawn from Farmer's 1949 legislative study. She observed that after 1915, when authority to make committee assignments was finally vested in the hands of the lieutenant governor, as presiding officer of the Senate,

Only once, so far as the records show, has the Lieutenant-Governor attempted to assert his independence [with regard to committee appointments]. In 1939 that officer announced that the responsibility for the appointment of Senate standing committees rested with him and that he proposed to appoint them without conferring with the Governor. The gossip is that there was much discussion among Senate leaders as to whether they should support this effort to assert the independence of the legislative branch. It was decided not to do so. By unanimous vote the Senate rejected the list of committees submitted by the Lieutenant-Governor and accepted a list submitted by the Governor's floor leader.[6]

Another episode illustrating the governor's influence on legislative organization involved Governor James E. Folsom, who in 1947 was able to secure his choice for Speaker despite "determined and nearly-successful" opposition in the House. It should be added that Folsom was not as fortunate in the Senate, where antiadministration legislators (members of the "Economy Bloc") were selected for such important leadership positions as president pro tempore and chairman of the Rules Committee. During Governor Folsom's second term (1955–59), however, the legislature was not as unfriendly—not in the beginning, at any rate.[7]

What have been the causes of the control that the governor has traditionally exercised over the legislature in Alabama? That is a difficult question. We may note, however, that over the years the rate of turnover in the legislature has been high. Farmer reports, for example, that of the 1,550 legislators who served during the period 1903–1943, 61.5 percent did so with no previous legislative experience.[8] In 1978 the membership turnover rate was reported to be as high as 74 percent in the Senate and 54 percent in the House.[9] New legislators frequently receive favorable committee assignments, including service as chairs of important committees. But with so many new members, the legislature was "inexperienced and uncertain"; the governor may have had "more legislative experience than many members of the Legislature." Many legislators, moreover, were mainly oriented toward their local constituencies and were primarily interested in local measures. With respect to questions of state policy, there was a leadership vacuum that was filled by the Speaker and the floor leaders, and these officers represented the administration.

Although governors in competitive party states may gain influence over their legislatures through the party connection, the one-party status of Alabama probably contributed to legislative weakness. Historically, struggles for political office have been conducted on a personal basis, and candidates for the governor's office have adopted individual platforms regarding proposed state policies.[10] Such personal policy statements tend to be viewed subjectively, by the administration and legislators alike, as commitments to the voters concerning at least the broad outlines of the legislative product.[11]

Important changes in the traditional relationship between governor and legislature became apparent, though, in the 1970s, the middle decade of the George Wallace era in Alabama politics. In a study of the 1971 Senate, which organized as Wallace was inaugurated for his second term, Harold Stanley writes that, "Contrary to custom, the governor did not designate floor leaders in any formal way." Nor, apparently, did Wallace make an overt attempt to influence the selection of the Speaker in 1975. Moreover, he did not seem to influence Lieutenant Governor Jere Beasley's committee assignments in the Senate. In 1979 Wallace's successor, Governor Fob James, followed a policy of nonintervention toward the entire question of legislative organization. James's press secretary was quoted as saying on one occasion that it had been the governor's policy "since election day not to get involved in legislative politics."[12]

At the same time that gubernatorial interest in legislative organization seems to have declined, a growing sense of institutional independence was developing in the legislature. This development was linked in large measure to the publication in the early 1970s of study reports highly critical of the Alabama legislature. As Stanley observes, as early as 1971 the movement "for legislative independence from the executive had gained increasing support. . . . Senators were encouraged by the press, constituents, and other senators to be independent and not just a 'rubber stamp' for the governor." While probably not an outgrowth of the independence movement itself, an ad hoc group in the 1971 Senate formed an antiadministration (i.e., anti-Wallace) faction and challenged executive leadership on a broad front. "The emergence of this group," Stanley continues, "signalled a departure from traditional control of the legislature by the governor."[13] The movement toward legislative independence took root in the 1970s, and by 1980 it was not unusual to see favored executive proposals receive scant consideration in the Alabama legislature.

By 1982 the memory of the governor's traditional role in organizing the legislature had not completely faded. After the election of 1982 it had seemed for a time that an open competition among several contenders might develop for the position of Speaker of the House.[14] But when Governor-elect Wallace, having been reelected to a fourth term, indicated a preference for Speaker, the speculation about the outcome of the House election for the office was laid to rest. Soon, news stories were reporting that the Speaker-designate was organizing the House and consulting with the governor-elect on committee assignments—just as in the old days. Nothing so dramatic happened in the Senate. There the lieutenant governor's nominee was elected as president pro tempore with only limited opposition.

In discussing the governor's legislative influence, we should point out that executive-legislative relationships are shaped by a number of factors that can work to the advantage of the governor. For example, the proceeds of highway bond issues have traditionally been used to generate legislative support for administration programs.[15] Funds that can be spent at the governor's discretion, public works projects (including programs for improved highways), the appointive power, and other forms of patronage may also be used for this purpose. In addition, the governor's greater opportunity for publicity, the incumbent's role as the representative of a statewide constituency, and the governor's popularity with the voters can tip the balance between the two branches toward the executive. As Stanley said, "Despite the dubious validity of a mandate, a governor can normally point to his election as proof that he represents the people of the state and that the state deserves the enactment of his programs."[16] It will be recalled, too, that the constitution gives the governor a number of formal powers by which to influence the legislature—message and veto powers and the power to call special sessions. If the option of succession heightens a governor's influence, as it is widely thought to do, this will also play a role, as the Alabama governor now also has that right.

Some governors, of course, are more politically skillful than others, so success with the legislature varies from administration to administration. At times, confrontations between the governor and the legislature have approached the spectacular—as during the Folsom years and during the period of "antisuccession" opposition to Governor Wallace in the mid-1960s and the activities of the "ad hoc" group in the 1971 Senate. (In Alabama's Democratic legislature, the "ad hoc" legislators were simply those members who, without benefit of any formal organization, were united by their opposition to Governor Wallace.) Nevertheless, the influence that the Governor's Office can bring to bear on legislators is very powerful. It is significant that in neither case was the opposition to Governor Wallace successful in the long run. A politically skillful Alabama governor usually has the resources to cope with hostile legislators and to secure the passage of enough of the administration program to give at least the appearance of leading the legislature.

The governor's legislative influence is perhaps at its greatest in the case of special sessions, which are called at the governor's discretion and which meet at the time spelled out in the governor's proclamation calling the session. Also stated in the proclamation are the subjects on which the governor wants the legislature to take action. The framers of the constitution sought to control the legislature, once it was in session, by inserting a provision to the effect that no legislation may be enacted in a special session on subjects other than those mentioned in the governor's proclamation except by a two-thirds vote in each house.

Although a reduction in the number of special sessions was advanced as an argument for annual legislative sessions, the number of special sessions has continued unabated. Probably a major reason for their persistence was the subject of one of a legislative study committee's objections to the system of biennial and special sessions then in effect. With respect to special sessions, the committee observed that "the Governor sets the agenda." Thus a governor could hope for an increased measure of success in the legislature by focusing attention on the relatively few proposals in the administration program.[17] George Wallace was frequently successful in his use of special legislative sessions. At his call the legislature met three times in special session in 1985. Each time the assembly passed the main agenda items stated in the call for the extra session.

When bills have passed the legislature they must normally be sent to the governor. In Alabama all bills and resolutions passed by both houses have to be presented to the governor except those proposing a constitutional amendment or a constitutional convention. If the governor approves a measure, the executive signature on it enables it to become law. Under certain circumstances a bill may become law after six days without the governor's signature if the legislature remains in session.

When an Alabama governor has objections to a bill, he or she may veto it (which is true in all states except North Carolina), suggest amendments that would remove the objections, or, in the case of appropriations measures, veto only the objectionable items. At one time the governor's power to suggest amendments to bills, sometimes called the amendatory veto, was a practice found in only a few other states, but now more than a dozen have adopted it.[18] When the governor suggests amendments to a bill, the legislature may agree to the executive amendments and resubmit the proposal to the governor as though it had been passed originally in that form. On the other hand, the legislators, by a majority vote of the members elected in both houses, may pass a measure (or an item of an appropriation bill) regardless of the governor's amendments or veto. In practice, however, few bills are vetoed and few vetoes are overridden.

To become law, bills passed during the closing days of a legislative session must be approved by the governor within ten days after the session adjourns. If the governor does not act favorably on these measures, they die, felled by what is usually termed the pocket veto. Although bills are sometimes pocket vetoed, Farmer thought that the amendatory veto had been more significant as a legislative influence.[19] Historically, she pointed out, the most important use of the amendatory veto has been to correct mistakes in bills that the legislature has passed, but at times executive amendments have affected the substance of proposed legislation. In 1983, for example, Governor Wallace used the device to bring about a reduction in a proposed pay increase for legislators.

The Chief Politician

To be elected governor of Alabama, a candidate usually must survive two elections in the party primary and then the general election against the candidate of the opposition party. The two primary elections result from Alabama's majority-vote requirement for nomination. A runoff is required if no candidate receives a majority of the votes cast for the office in the first election.

Viewed broadly, the Democratic nomination has been tantamount to election since the end of Reconstruction in the 1870s. Until Guy Hunt's election in 1986 (which involved a highly unusual set of circumstances), no Republican had come close to ending the Democratic domination of the statehouse. For this reason, the primary is usually much more demanding and expensive than the general election. Coleman Ransone reports, for example, that in 1970 George Wallace's primary campaign cost $930,000, while the general election expenditures amounted to only $96,000. Eight years later, Fob James's primary campaigns had a $3.5 million budget. His general election budget was much smaller.[20]

Campaign costs in gubernatorial elections have increased sharply in recent years, due largely to the use of such modern techniques as employing campaign consultants, conducting polls and direct mailings, and especially buying television time, in addition to such standard methods as buying radio, newspaper, and billboard advertisements, stumping the state, and holding rallies in rented halls.[21] Ransone illustrates the current importance of the broadcast media as a form of political communication in Alabama with an account of the way the James campaign used these media to overcome a severe problem of name recognition. As he concludes, "At least a part of James's success must be attributed to his short but numerous radio and television spots, which had catchy, tuneful 'jingles' as a major ingredient."[22] Add to the media consultants' work a vision of airplanes flitting about the state carrying candidates hither and yon for speeches and news conferences and you will have a pretty good idea of a modern Alabama campaign. (The use of all this modern technology prompted one of our colleagues to remark that sooner or later a candidate would come up with a "new-style" campaign featuring motorcades and a string band and win going away.)

The successful candidate emerges from the campaign as the leader of a large coalition of voters. Almost certainly, more voters have cast their ballots for governor than for any other state officer. A narrow electoral victory damages the winner's image as the state's political leader. But if the margin of the electoral victory is large, that evidence of popularity with the voters adds prestige to the office and lends credence to the governor's claim of having a mandate from the people to carry out policies advocated in the campaign.[23]

On assuming office the governor finds that it, too, is a "bully pulpit." The news media devote a great deal of attention to what the governor says and does, so personal appearances at various events, speeches on ceremonial occasions, messages to the legislature, and news conferences can serve as publicity devices in an effort to drum up support for gubernatorial policies.

One reason why we labeled this role chief politician rather than party chief is that the governor's position as a party leader in Alabama is not as important as it would be in a strong two-party system.[24] The Alabama governor, therefore, is not considered the state party leader in the same way that the president is considered the titular head of the national party. Contrary to the national practice, for example, it has not been regarded as the governor's prerogative to name the chair of the State Democratic Executive Committee. When former state senator John Baker was elected state chair in 1985, for example, there was no discernible Wallace involvement.

There has been factional conflict for control of the state Democratic committee, which actually elects the party chair, and at times governors have been involved in it. Recent governors, though, seem to have taken a hands-off attitude toward matters of internal party organization. In large part this stems from their inability to maintain a continuing influence over party structure and operations. Also, the energy required to exert a sustained influence probably was not worth the effort in terms of political payoff. Alabama's Democratic governor is, however, an ex officio member of the state party committee, and in recent years the committee has appointed the governor to a seat on Alabama's delegation to the Democratic National Convention. Before his election Guy Hunt was quite active in the Republican party, but what his relationship to the party would be as governor remained to be seen.

In the Alabama political setting the governor is a factional leader—the leader of the political coalition, constructed on a framework of personal support, that was responsible for the victory won at the polls. Consequently, the role or function of political leader in this state, which is still basically a one-party state as far as state politics is concerned, involves responsibility for leadership not so much in a political party as in a public policy process that operates largely free of partisan considerations.

CHARACTERISTICS OF ALABAMA'S GOVERNORS

The contemporary period of Alabama political development begins in 1946 with the election of James E. Folsom to his first term. (He took office in January 1947.) Between then and the election of 1986, which marked the end of the Wallace era, seven people (six men and one woman) served as governor.[25]

George Wallace served for sixteen of these years. The average age of the governors who took office during this period was forty-three. (Table 2 notes a number of facts about Alabama's governors at various points in the state's history and provides data for comparisons on some of the points made in the following paragraphs.) The governors were all virtually lifelong residents of Alabama. All of the governors except one were born in Alabama. Albert Brewer (1968–71) was born in Tennessee but moved to the state with his parents at an early age.

There has been a wide geographical dispersion of the homes of successful gubernatorial candidates. Only rural Barbour County supplied more than one governor during the period that began in 1946. After their marriage, George and Lurleen Wallace were both residents of this southeast Alabama county, although Lurleen Wallace was a native of Tuscaloosa County. No governor came from populous Jefferson County (which includes Birmingham) in these four decades, reflecting the continuation of the predominantly rural character of Alabama politics. All but two of the successful candidates were college graduates. Table 2 shows that this was a considerably higher percentage than in any previous period. All of the winning candidates were married.

In terms of occupational background, the governors were split between business (three) and law (three). All but two of the governors had some previous full-time governmental experience. Tables 3 and 4 point out the kinds of prior public background Alabama governors have had over the years. The tables show that governors are more likely to have had previous state experience than national or local experience. They also demonstrate the greater probability of prior legislative service than experience in other public positions. In the period 1947–1985 there was no heavy concentration of experience in a position that would serve as a stepping-stone to the governorship. The Alabama House of Representatives was the only source of previous experience in the backgrounds of two successful candidates. All previous governmental experience was in a state position, with one exception. James E. Folsom was an administrator with a New Deal relief agency during the Depression. There were no successful candidates with local legislative or executive experience in their background. It is also noteworthy that only one person (Brewer) moved from lieutenant governor to governor, and this was due to the death of the incumbent (Lurleen Wallace). Taking Guy Hunt's election into consideration would change the description in several respects. For example, he had prior local government experience in Cullman County.

Postgubernatorial career patterns are portrayed in Table 5. During the earliest period the governorship in Alabama was less likely to be the culmination of a political career than it was subsequently.[26] All the governors in the period 1819–1849 (except for William Bibb, who died in office) occupied other offices following their state executive service. Table 5 shows a pronounced tendency in the earliest period for governors to serve in Congress on completion of their terms. In each period following, however, more governors than not filled no other office after leaving this post. Apparently the governorship came to be looked on as the culmination of a political career.

Table 2: Facts about Alabama Governors

	1819–1849	1849–1874	1874–1907	1907–1947	1947–1985
Average age	42	47	53	56	43
% Born in Alabama	0	20	55	78	86
% College Graduates	38	20	44	55	71
% Married	92	90	100	89	100
% Lawyers	53	72	53	54	42
% with State House Service	25	39	26	21	22
N	7	9	10	10	13

Sources: The statistics presented in this table and the three that follow were derived from several sources, including John C. Stewart, *The Governors of Alabama* (Gretna, La.: Pelican Publishing Co., 1975), Robert Sobel and John Raimo, eds., *Biographical Directory of the Governors of the United States* (Westport, Conn.: Greenwood Press, 1978), Willis Brewer, *Alabama: Her History, Resources, War Record, and Public Men* (Spartanburg, S.C.: Reprint Co., 1975), and Thomas M. Owen, *History of Alabama and Dictionary of Alabama Biography* (Spartanburg, S.C.: Reprint Co., 1978). The subdivisions in the table are those of the authors and, although arbitrary, may make it easier for the reader to interpret the data presented. The first subdivision represents the years from statehood to the immediate pre–Civil War period; the second, the prewar, war, and Reconstruction years; the third, the Redemption through the adoption of the current Alabama Constitution; the fourth, the period down to the beginning of what is identified in the text as the "modern" political era in Alabama politics; and the fifth, the Folsom years through the Wallace years.

PROBLEMS OF THE GOVERNORSHIP

There have been problems related to gubernatorial disability and succession in Alabama, but these have been relatively few in number and rather straightforward in character.[27] Most governors have served throughout their terms without serious illness. Only three have died in office. There has never been an attempt on the life of a governor in Alabama. The assassination attempt against George Wallace occurred while he was campaigning in Maryland in 1972 as a presidential aspirant. After Wallace was shot, Lt. Gov. Jere Beasley served as acting governor when Wallace's hospitalization necessitated his absence from the state beyond the twenty-day limit set by the state constitution.

In its history as a state, Alabama has never had a governor removed from

Table 3: Arenas of Prior Government Experience of Alabama Governors

National	15
State	71
Local	11

Sources: See note for Table 2.
Note: Figures represent numbers of governors having the arena of prior governmental experience in their background. Some governors are counted more than once in the table.

Table 4: Types of Prior Governmental Experience of Alabama Governors

General Administrative	11
Law Enforcement	10
Legislative	58
Judicial	14
Local Government	4

Sources: See note for Table 2.
Note: Figures represent numbers of governors having the type of prior full-time governmental experience indicated. Some governors are counted more than once.

Table 5: Subsequent Governmental Positions of Alabama's Governors

	1819– 1849	1849– 1874	1874– 1907	1907– 1947	1947– 1985
Subsequent gubernatorial term	0	0	0	1	2
State or local judge	0	0	1	1	1
State legislator	5	1	0	0	0
Federal judge	1	0	1	0	0
Member of Congress	7	2*	2	1	0
Miscellaneous federal posts	1	1	0	1	0

Sources: See note for Table 2.
Note: Some governors have occupied more than one office following the expiration of their terms.
*Two former governors in the post–Civil War era were elected to the U.S. Senate but were not permitted to serve.

office. The constitution does, of course, provide for the impeachment of the governor and other state officials, but these provisions have never been applied.

The provisions relating to succession to the governorship have been, as we have seen, only infrequently used. And there apparently has been no controversy about when a lieutenant governor becomes the acting governor. As mentioned above, the constitution of 1901 states that the lieutenant governor assumes this title when the governor has been out of the state for twenty days. However, as a matter of practical politics, the lieutenant governor must walk a fine line in these rare situations. It must not appear that the authority of the "real" governor is being usurped. Serious political damage would probably be done if it seemed that the lieutenant governor was too overtly using the time as acting governor as a launching pad for a future gubernatorial campaign. Some believed this happened when Jere Beasley served as acting governor.

TRENDS IN THE GOVERNORSHIP

It is possible to discern both long- and short-term trends in the development of the governorship in Alabama. Generally the office has developed along lines evident throughout the nation. The national evolution in the office of governor is apparent in the titles of such widely read books on the governorship as Larry Sabato's *Goodbye to Good-Time Charlie* or, earlier, Leslie Lipson's *The American Governor: From Figurehead to Leader.*[28]

Most studies of the American governorship point out that around the time of the Declaration of Independence those who wrote the new state constitutions made the governor a much weaker figure than the colonial governor had been. In general, the earliest state constitutions established the legislature as the most powerful organ in state government—being given, for example, much of the appointive power formerly vested in the governor. Later on, during a state constitutional revision movement during the mid-to-late nineteenth century, legislative abuses of power received the most attention, and a movement arose to place increasingly restrictive limitations on state legislatures. To some extent those changes (such as the executive veto) strengthened the governor's hand as against the legislature. In the next period of comprehensive revision, from about 1890 to the beginning of World War I, there was a further strengthening of gubernatorial power, primarily through a rationalization of administrative structures. Since World

War I, the governor has become an even more important state official, due largely to efforts to make administrative management more effective.

Alabama's original 1819 constitution provided for several other executive officials in addition to the governor (the secretary of state, the attorney general, the state treasurer, and the comptroller of public accounts), but only the governor was popularly elected. Possibly reflecting the influence of the first state constitutions, the other executive officials were selected by the General Assembly. In other states, when constitutions were being revised a few years later, one effect of the Jacksonian movement was to transfer the right to select state officials from the legislature to the people. In Alabama, however, it was not until 1868 that the constitution provided for a decentralized system of electing the principal officers in the executive branch of the state government. Since then the most fundamental change in the governor's position occurred in 1939. At that time a reorganization of the state bureaucracy, discussed in the next chapter, resulted in a major increase in the governor's executive powers.

THE JOB OF GOVERNOR

To this point we have treated the governor's powers in terms of clusters, with each cluster representing a set of functions performed in a particular gubernatorial role. In practice, however, the governor's powers and functions are not this compartmentalized. Instead, the governor's roles blend into and supplement one another to produce a highly complicated mix of political and ministerial powers and duties.[29] The amalgam of these duties and powers amounts to what writers call the "job" of the governor. Charles Press and Kenneth VerBurg aptly summarized the nature of the governor's job when they wrote that "The job of governor . . . is little else if not the responsibility to lead a state and give a sense of direction in attacking its problems."[30]

Policy development in response to definite problems is the governor's main responsibility in the state government. This responsibility is more involved than simply making policy pronouncements. It entails the continuing exercise of primarily political skills in an effort to persuade others— legislators, administrators, and the public—that gubernatorially preferred ways of dealing with problems and concerns should become the public policies of the state.[31]

Obviously some governors have been more successful than others in leading the state and giving it "a sense of direction in attacking its problems." Thomas E. Kilby's administration (1919–23) brought a wide range of social and governmental reforms. Governors Benjamin M. Miller (1931–35) and Bibb Graves (1927–31, 1935–39) provided effective leadership in dealing with the state's economic problems during the Great Depression, as did Frank M. Dixon (1939–43) in reorganizing the state government and promoting civil service reform. Perhaps no Alabama governor was a more outstanding policy leader, however, than Braxton B. Comer (1907–11). According to Moore, he "not only brought the corporations to book and sponsored sound social legislation, but he conspicuously promoted education." Later governors such as James E. Folsom—with his emphasis on paving farm-to-market roads, reapportionment, pensions for the needy aged, and education—and Lurleen Wallace—with her concern for conditions in the state's mental institutions—also made contributions by focusing attention on serious state problems. Not all of the state's governors became such important figures in Alabama history as Governor Comer but, as Press and VerBurg point out, whoever serves as governor of the state "does make a difference."[32]

To help perform the many duties assigned to the office, the governor has a staff composed of a number of attorneys, secretaries (including executive, appointments, and press secretaries), legislative assistants, and other support personnel. In addition, two state agencies that have major responsibilities in the areas of planning, economic development, and grants administration—the Alabama Development Office and the Department of Economic and Community Affairs—provide staff support to the governor and (as a way of emphasizing their role) are attached to the Governor's Office. The Department of Finance is the governor's most important staff agency. We referred to its functions earlier in this chapter, and we do so again in the next chapter.

It should be obvious from the many references to him in this chapter and elsewhere in the book that the qualities of the contemporary Alabama governorship are most attributable to one individual, George C. Wallace, who completed his fourth and final term as governor in January 1987. No other person so dominated this office; he served fully twice as long as any of his predecessors. However, considering his immense popularity and his political acumen, Wallace has not left as much of an imprint on the governorship as might have been expected. In the minds of many, Wallace much preferred running to governing. Consequently, the state's political development has had a static quality about it, a quality that Bass and DeVries describe as the Wallace "freeze."[33]

Wallace eventually recanted his segregationist views, and his policies in recent years stressed reconciliation, economic development, and the continued promotion of education. He sought to be the governor of "all the people," and blacks came to be among his strongest supporters. He especially expressed compassion for the poor and the infirm. Historians in later years will undoubtedly assign George Wallace an impressive place in Alabama history. He made a lot of it.

CHAPTER SIX

Policy and Administration

The executive (or administrative) branch of Alabama's state government is composed of over 250 separate departments, boards, commissions, institutions, and other agencies. The traditional function of these administrative organizations is to implement policy, that is, to provide the services, undertake the regulatory activities, and otherwise administer the programs and policies enacted by the legislature. Everywhere in the United States, however, administrative agencies have increasingly become important policymakers themselves. This has come about through the exercise of the discretion they have available in interpreting the laws they enforce and through the issuance of a wide variety of rules and regulations.[1]

THE GOVERNOR AS CHIEF EXECUTIVE

In constitutional theory the governor functions as head of the administration. In fact, the governor's directing power is considerably diluted. The executive heads of seven administrative units are popularly elected, for example, and many others do not owe their positions to the governor. Instead they hold their positions because of some other office they occupy (ex officio is the legal term) or because they were designated by a board or commission, perhaps at the behest of a special-interest group.[2] Officials selected independently may enjoy a considerable degree of immunity from the chief executive's direct powers of supervision. But the governor of Alabama is not a mere titular chief executive.

Some of the most important agencies are headed by individuals who were appointed by the governor and who serve at the governor's pleasure. In the mid-1970s, 40 of 201 governing authorities were appointed by and at the sole discretion of the governor.[3] Eleven were appointed by the governor with senatorial approval. These included many of the critically important agencies of state government—for example, the Department of Finance, the Department of Revenue, the State Highway Department, and the Department of Public Safety. Even when the governor is not formally vested with the power to select an agency head, such selection may occur informally. Normally a board empowered to choose an agency director will show great deference to the governor's wishes, particularly if some of the board members owe their own appointments to the governor or if the governor is also a member of the board. This is true in the case of the commissioner of the Department of Human Resources, formally chosen by a board (all of whose members are gubernatorial appointees), but informally always the choice of the governor. The same holds true for the administrator of the Alcoholic Beverage Control Board.[4]

Thus, because of the governor's formal or informal appointive powers, such important functions as the supervision of the state's financial affairs; the location, construction, and maintenance of state highways and bridges; the disposition and use of National Guard and state law-enforcement personnel (the Highway Patrol Division in the Department of Public Safety); the performance of welfare services; and the operation of a business with a net income level of more than $100 million annually (the alcoholic beverage marketing system) are carried on under the immediate supervision of the governor.[5] In the case of 44 of 201 agency executive authorities counted in the survey made in the 1970s, the governor was given specific removal power. When a method of removal is not specified, the most common interpretation is that the official may be replaced by the governor. This, of course, adds appreciably to gubernatorial control of the administrative branch.

As to the elective officials, there are presently sixteen of them, in addition to the governor and the lieutenant governor. They include the attorney general, the secretary of state, the state treasurer, the state auditor, the commissioner of agriculture and industries, the three members of the Public Service Commission, and the eight members of the Board of Education. For a long time the state superintendent of education was listed among the state's elective administrative officers. Since the adoption of a constitutional amendment in 1969, however, the superintendent has been appointed by a now-elective State Board of Education.

In summary, the executive branch of Alabama's state government is characterized by a dilution of executive power; frequent use of boards whose members serve long, overlapping terms as the heads of agencies; separate accountability of some state executive officers to the public through popular election; considerable influence of interest groups in the staffing of agencies, particularly the many boards and commissions that regulate entry into occupations and professions; and yet, despite all this, numerous formal and informal opportunities for the exercise of gubernatorial influence.

OTHER EXECUTIVE OFFICIALS

Aside from the governor and the lieutenant governor, the attorney general is politically the most important elected state officer. The principal function of the person holding the office is to serve as the state's chief legal officer. The attorney general and numerous assistant attorneys general do routine legal work and represent the state when it has an interest in a court case. The governor may also appoint counsel for the state, and in some instances of litigation the governor has exercised this authority. This seems especially likely to be done when the governor and the attorney general are not on close political terms.

Most critical to the smooth operation of the state government, though, is the attorney general's role as legal adviser to state and local officials. Public officials often have questions about the legal aspects of their powers and duties. The concerned officials pose their questions to the attorney general's office, and the responses provide the necessary guidance.

In recent decades attorneys general have sought to capitalize on their visibility by using the job as a launching pad for a successful gubernatorial campaign. However, only John Patterson (governor from 1959 to 1963) was successful. In contrast, the positions of secretary of state, state treasurer, and state auditor have not ordinarily been perceived as powerful bases from which to launch a campaign for higher office. Before the constitution was changed to allow executive succession, a sort of round-robin was often played in which these three positions would be alternated among the same people.

The secretary of state heads an office responsible for the performance of a variety of activities, many of which relate to keeping and attesting to the authenticity of such public documents as the acts of the legislature, the governors' proclamations, records of incorporation, land titles, and the like. In addition, the office is responsible for the performance of a number of duties concerning the conduct of elections and the canvassing of election returns. The Secretary of State's Office, as headed by Don Siegelman (1979–87), undertook a major effort to reform the election laws, many of which this office is charged with administering.

The state treasurer is responsible for the custody and management of state funds and securities. A specific duty, for example, involves payment of the principal and interest on the state's bonded indebtedness. The treasurer's office pays out funds from the state treasury on the basis of authorizations ("warrants") issued by the state comptroller, the chief accounting officer in the Department of Finance.

Formerly the position of state auditor was one of considerable significance in the state government. However, financial reorganizations (especially that of 1939) have resulted in the transfer of major functions from the Auditor's Office to the Department of Finance and the Department of Examiners of Public Accounts.[6]

POLICY AREAS

Several key policy areas define the major contours of contemporary policies. Perhaps more important, their formulation and implementation, and the controversies they arouse, show how administrative roles actually are performed in the several phases of the policy cycle.[7]

Education

Education is, of course, one of the most important functions of state government.[8] The state education organization was turned upside down as a result of the constitutional amendment adopted in 1969. Now the elective State Board of Education appoints the state superintendent, who administers through the State Department of Education the educational policies formulated by the legislature and the board.

The board is composed of the governor as ex officio president and eight elective members, one representing each of eight districts. Recently the district lines have been redrawn to make them racially more representative of the Alabama population. In broad functional terms, the board exercises general control and supervision over the public schools and other educational institutions of the state, except for those institutions (universities, for example) that have independent status and that are governed by their own boards of trustees. It supervises elementary and secondary schools through the superintendent of education and the Department of Education, and the junior colleges and technical schools through a Department of Postsecond-ary Education. The actual provision and administration of public elementary and secondary education, however, is traditionally a function of the local school systems. In Alabama the local educational organization consists of sixty-seven county and more than sixty city independent school systems, each functioning under the general supervision of a local board of education.

Ordinarily, five members sit on local boards of education. As a general rule, the members of city boards are appointed by the municipal governing bodies, while the members of county boards are elected. Both types of boards have local superintendents of education to serve as their executive officers and to oversee the implementation of school laws and policies prescribed by the state and local boards. Each local board (with the assistance of the local superintendent) determines local educational policies, subject to frequently comprehensive state (and in more than a few instances federal) guidelines, and employs the principals, teachers, and other personnel necessary to operate the school system.[9] There has been a gradual centralizing of responsibility for educational policy-making to higher authorities. Not only does most of the money spent for local public education in Alabama come from the state, but in addition, most of the substantive school policies originate with the state. State authorities regulate the qualifications of teachers, the length of the school day and of class periods within the day, curriculum content, and such policies as those pertaining to the salaries of employees, deductions for union political contributions, initial textbook selection, and the like.

This is not to say that the local role in public education in Alabama is unimportant. Teachers are officially the employees of county and city school systems. Important school policymakers—the county and city boards and superintendents—are selected locally, either by election or appointment. City superintendents and some county superintendents are appointed by their local board of education. Most of the county superintendents are elected, generally for four-year terms.

The most notable fact concerning the financing of public education in Alabama is that the preponderance of funds received by local schools is supplied from state revenue sources. In 1986 Alabama localities raised only about 16 cents of every dollar available for the support of public elementary and secondary schools. In contrast, the state raised more than 67 cents out of every dollar available for local schools, with the remainder supplied by federal appropriations. In the nation as a whole, the average local contribution for the support of local schools was about half of every dollar (43 cents in 1986).[10] Aid for local schools amounted to about 80 percent of all state aid provided to Alabama localities in the early 1980s.[11]

One of the most important functions of the State Department of Education is to administer the Minimum School Program, under which state grants are made to local systems to pay the difference between the estimated cost of the minimum program and the capacity of each local system to finance such a program. The purpose of the Minimum School Program is to effect a redistribution of revenue and thereby to promote program equalization among the school districts. Because of differences in local resources, program disparities still exist, however. In view of the decision by the U.S. Supreme Court in the case of *Rodriguez* v. *San Antonio School District,* in which the Court declined to require the equalization of funding among school districts, such disparities will undoubtedly continue, at least into the near future.[12]

State grants for the public schools are made primarily from the Alabama Special Educational Trust Fund (ASETF). This fund is composed of the proceeds of some fifteen earmarked taxes, including such major sources of revenue as the income, sales, tobacco, and use taxes. In 1985 the income tax generated approximately $909 million in educational funds; the sales tax, approximately $820 million. Since these two taxes are such robust producers of state revenue, state expenditures in support of local schools assume impressive proportions.

Even though revenue for schools is designated, heated political controversies rage as the legislature slices the education pie and elementary and secondary schools compete with higher and technical education for their pieces of it. Some attempts to implement rational models of decisionmaking are reflected in the application of formulas to indicate the funding needs of the various institutions of higher education. Education funding seems to be determined largely, however, on the basis of a free-for-all among the state teachers' association (the Alabama Education Association, or AEA) and other organizations (such as colleges and universities) that are interested in various segments of the educational program. While the AEA may not always emerge victorious, for several reasons (including the number of legislators who are members of the AEA or who were elected with critical AEA backing) it is a potent force in the determination of education policy. It has the reputation of being one of the most powerful interest groups in the state. The AEA's campaign arm, the A-Vote organization, has in recent years probably been more successful in its efforts to elect favorable state legislators than any other single political action group. Traditionally, such groups as the AEA have been involved in the education policy-making process, but now groups other than the traditional ones have entered the field—for example, citizens' groups interested in monitoring the content of the textbooks used in Alabama schools.

Obviously, the greatest trauma for Alabama public schools in modern times has been that of desegregation and the accompanying flight of white students from tax-supported schools to private schools. In many situations a genuinely integrated educational setting has not been achieved. Thus in 1980 (the most recent year for which statistics are available), when there were about 228,000 black students in the public schools, over half of them (59 percent) attended schools that were 90 percent or more black. Between the mid-1960s and the mid-1970s, public secondary school enrollment declined by about a third. In the same period, enrollment in nonpublic secondary schools rose more than 80 percent. In the mid-1970s there were 239,000 students of both races enrolled in grades nine through twelve of the public schools. By 1984 this figure had declined to 199,000, about a 17 percent decrease. Losses in enrollments in public schools are, of course, not attributable entirely to continued resistance to integration. Lower birth rates are also a factor, as is the rise of the new religious conservatism, which has produced an increasing number of Protestant parents who want their children to be schooled in a religious rather than a secular setting.[13] Then too, many parents believe their children will receive a better education in private schools than in the public schools. What contributes to the racial imbalance in the schools, of course, is that the private "academies" are overwhelmingly white.

Highways

The construction and maintenance of highways and bridges is a second major activity of Alabama state government. The constitution had to be amended in 1908 so that the state could engage in this kind of work. Since then, the state's highway network has expanded enormously, so that the state is currently responsible for the maintenance of almost 11,000 miles of highways, including about 800 miles of interstate highways. Before 1979 the State Highway Department also was responsible for the roads in ten counties (popularly called "captive counties") in which the state had assumed responsibility for construction and maintenance of local roads. In 1979, however, the state divested itself of this responsibility and returned local road programs to the county governments. Taking care of local roads was an added expense the financially strapped Highway Department did not wish to bear any longer.

The State Highway Department is headed by a highway director, who is appointed by and directly responsible to the governor.[14] The director designates the road projects to be undertaken at state expense and supervises the Highway Department's many operations. Decisions related to road building frequently are political decisions. Where an opportunity for the exercise of discretion exists, it is likely that areas that have supported the incumbent governor may see more road-building activity than those that have not. It is frequently charged, for example, that the reason interstate work in the Birmingham area proceeded so slowly was because Wallace's support was relatively weak there. Highway activities are financed by several revenue sources, the most important of which in 1985 was federal aid, which accounted for 59 percent of all highway revenues. Other major sources were gasoline and motor fuel taxes (27 percent) and motor vehicle and carrier taxes and fees (8 percent). There were no highway bond issues in 1985. By virtue of a constitutional amendment adopted in 1951, state taxes levied on motor vehicles and fuels are for all practical purposes earmarked solely for highways. In 1985, Highway Department revenues totaled about $481 million, of which federal aid for all categories of road construction accounted for about $285 million.

Highways, heavily supported as they are by the motorists who use them, have not been a highly polarizing issue in Alabama. Obviously the levying of taxes is controversial, but taxes for highways have generally been passed as needed, with only a moderate amount of difficulty. In the not-so-distant past, governors of Alabama were frequently elected in substantial part on the basis of their proposed policies for the development of highways in the state. Highway construction as a political issue has declined in salience in recent years, however, as more and more roads were paved and other issues competed successfully for public attention.

The administration of local roads and streets remains a primary activity of local governments. However, this function is now largely supported by state subventions. For example, portions of state gasoline tax proceeds are shared with counties and municipalities. One consequence of the reapportionment revolution of the 1960s was that the formulas by which gasoline tax revenues are distributed to local governments in Alabama were rewritten to be somewhat more responsive to urban needs. In 1985 local shares of the gasoline tax amounted to approximately $99 million for counties and $11 million for municipalities. In the early 1980s, the state's proportion of state and local expenditures from instate sources for highways in Alabama was 67.5 percent. The U.S. average was 61.3 percent.[15] State aid to Alabama local governments for highways in 1983 amounted to 12.9 percent of total state aid.[16]

Welfare, Health, and Hospitals

The administration of welfare programs and the provision of health and hospital services are other important activities of state government.[17] In Alabama these programs operate largely as locally administered but stringently state-supervised functions in which county organizations perform moderately important roles. In the state governmental structure, both functions are directed by boards, which exercise general powers of supervision and control over departmental organizations.

The disadvantaged have very little political strength in Alabama, and thus the amount of assistance available to the needy hinges primarily on decisions made in Washington, not in Montgomery. The federal role is overwhelming: close to two-thirds of the funds spent by the Alabama Department of Human Resources come from Washington. The welfare function is thus less genuinely intergovernmental in Alabama than the maintenance of highways. Federal officials, not state or local officials, supply most of the funds and write most of the policies applied in the administration of welfare programs.

In Alabama the provider groups (especially medical doctors) have been very influential in establishing health policy. The State Board of Health (which technically is the State Medical Association) operates primarily through the State Committee of Public Health, which is now composed of both physicians and the heads of several health-related councils on which nonphysicians hold membership. This widening of the circle of health policy leadership resulted from a political skirmish involving the amount of control over health policy exercised by doctors to the exclusion of other groups, particularly other professionals and consumers.

In the local communities, public and private interests are again merged, and the governing authority of the county medical association and the chairperson of the county commission serve as the county board of health. Although every county has a health organization, not every one of the state's sixty-seven counties has a full-time county health officer. Because many counties are financially unable to employ individual health officers, the state health department has recently been emphasizing the formation of multi-county districts, which would use the services of district health officers.

Financing state mental hospitals (such as Bryce Hospital and Partlow State School) has historically been a state function, as little federal aid was available for mental health programs. Beginning in the 1960s, however, federal funds became available on a broader scale and state tax revenues available for mental health programs increased. These new funds came none too soon. As recently as the early 1970s, conditions in Alabama mental hospitals were so poor that federal judge Frank Johnson ordered corrective action in these institutions. This instance of federal judicial intervention came in the well-known case of *Wyatt* v. *Stickney,* which has been cited as "the earliest and most famous case" demonstrating federal judicial activism in the area of mental health.[18] Jeffrey Straussman notes that before Judge Johnson acted, state services for mental patients were "extremely poor": "The food allowance per patient was about fifty cents per day; there were few doctors, and there were charges of physical abuse committed by some of the hospital staff."[19]

To remedy these conditions, Judge Johnson required the state to provide confined patients with (1) a wholesome physical and psychological environment, (2) a larger staff of properly trained mental health workers, and (3) a specific treatment plan for each hospital patient.[20] Johnson appointed a human rights committee to monitor state progress in implementing the federal court ruling and charged it with reporting any violations of patient rights.

Cities and counties have set up local hospital authorities to administer general hospitals, receive taxes levied to pay for them, and manage available federally funded construction programs. Hospital construction in Alabama increased sharply after the 1946 enactment of the Hill-Burton Hospital Act, which made federal grants available for local hospitals. This legislation was cosponsored by Alabama senator Lister Hill (1938–69), who became well known for his support of major health programs. Hill-Burton brought hospitals to many Alabama communities where there had been none before. Medicare and Medicaid were also a boon to hospital expansion programs in the mid-1960s.

Recently, though, the federal government has insisted that both public and private hospitals do a great deal more to contain costs. At federal insistence, states have established boards to approve actions that would further increase hospital facilities. In Alabama this function is performed by the State Health Planning and Development Agency, which must assent before hospitals can expand, buy expensive new equipment, or institute additional medical programs.[21] This requirement has introduced an interesting new dimension to Alabama politics: local hospitals now engage in political battles to gain the agency's approval for the operation of special facilities.

The local financial role in health is more important—from the perspective of the burden borne locally—than in any of the other policy areas we have examined. In 1981 the state proportion of state and local general expenditures for health and hospitals was only 42.6 percent in Alabama, while the national average was 52.0 percent.[22]

RECEIPTS AND EXPENDITURES

The importance of the functions just discussed—education, highways, welfare, and health and hospitals—is illustrated by the fact that expenditures in these policy areas make up the bulk of Alabama's total expenditures, as they do in the states generally. This is the main reason why we selected these particular functions for discussion in preference to others. For example, net spending in the fiscal year 1985 amounted to approximately $5.4 billion. Disbursements for education and related activities amounted to $2.1 billion, or 39 percent of the total. Following in order at a considerable distance were health and hospitals, with $707 million (13 percent); highways, with $568 million (11 percent); and social services, with $370 million (7 percent). All of the many other activities of the state government accounted for the remaining 30 percent of state outlays.

Tax and Nontax Revenues

Most of the major activities of the state government are supported by federal grants. In many instances the federal assistance is substantial—amounting, for example, to 61 percent of Pensions and Security (now Human Resources) receipts in 1985. As noted earlier, 59 percent of highway funds came from the federal government during the same year. Thirty-six percent of the funds spent for general and mental health came from the federal government. The significance of federal funds varies from activity to activity, but since Alabama is still one of the poorer states, aid from Washington is consequential, even critical, in all the key functions of state government. In 1985 federal funds coming into the state treasury totaled $1.3 billion and amounted to 13 percent of total receipts.[23] For years,

Alabama's state and local governments participated in the program of general revenue sharing initially enacted by Congress in 1972. Local governments received two-thirds of all these virtually unrestricted grant funds appropriated by Congress, however, and eventually state governments did not participate at all in this federal aid program. In 1986 even the local shares were dropped because of increasing pressure to cut the federal budget deficit.

Funds used by the state government to finance its many activities are classified into tax and nontax categories. Tax receipts in 1985 amounted to $3.0 billion, while nontax receipts (excluding federal funds) totaled $5.6 billion. Nontax receipts include such items as members' contributions to retirement systems, for example.

  State taxes such as sales, income, and gasoline taxes are collected by the various divisions of the State Revenue Department. County officials have primary responsibility for the administration of the general property (or ad valorem) tax, and most of the proceeds of the property tax are directed to the support of local activities, such as schools, libraries, roads, and hospitals.[24] Historically, the local valuations for the same type of property varied greatly from county to county. Assessments tended to be much less in rural than in urban counties, and urban dwellers ultimately sought relief in federal court. The result was that the state was placed under a court order to reappraise and fairly value all property subject to taxation.[25]

Landowners, especially large landowners, then launched a campaign to head off what they anticipated to be major increases in their property taxes. This particular battle was fought both in the legislature and in the electoral arena to secure the adoption of restrictive constitutional amendments. Following a federal district court decision that a new constitutional amendment permitting different assessment ratios among the counties was invalid, the legislature passed and the voters approved another constitutional amendment that became known as the Lid Bill because it was designed to place a lid, or cap, on property taxes.[26] The Lid Bill and similar actions have had a great effect on the property tax base in Alabama. The state government received only about $62 million (or somewhat over one-half of 1 percent of total receipts) from the property tax in 1985.

A few years ago it was not unusual to see bumper stickers proclaiming Alabama "The Tax-Happy State." The motorists were probably especially conscious of the tax burden because so much of it is in the form of consumer taxes. Actually, the per capita tax bill paid by Alabamians in 1983 totaled $806, or 9.4 percent of per capita income. Only three states collected less in taxes per capita than Alabama (Tennessee, Arkansas, and Mississippi).[27] The emphasis on consumer taxes does, however, tilt Alabama's tax structure toward the regressive side. That is, lower-income people pay out a larger proportion of their income in taxes than higher-income people.

THE STATE BUDGET

Budgetary policy-making is severely restricted in Alabama by the fact that a very high percentage (some estimate as high as 90 percent) of state revenues are earmarked for specific programs. Policy-making controversies as they relate to financing, therefore, tend mostly to occur at the time taxes are levied and subsequently within (rather than between) functional categories—for example, primary and secondary versus higher education, rather than education versus highways or welfare. One hundred percent of both personal and corporate income tax revenue is earmarked for education. About 90 percent of the state sales tax is also set aside for schools. The almost total earmarking of these three most important revenue sources occurs in no other state. Efforts to reduce or eliminate earmarking—for example, during the Fob James administration (1979–83)—have had little support and therefore little success. Most of the beneficiaries of earmarking are satisfied with the portions they are getting from state revenues and have been successful in thwarting the establishment of a more flexible budgetary system. Consequently, a recent publication on subnational finance pointed to Alabama as having "the smallest general fund in relation to total state spending."[28]

Preparing the state budget is the responsibility of the state budget officer, a division head within the Department of Finance. The budget officer is appointed by the director of finance with the approval of the governor. In preparing the budget, the budget officer estimates the revenues available for the operation of the state government and apportions these funds among the various state agencies in line with an expenditure plan that has the governor's approval. Of the two major funds into which tax receipts flow, the Alabama Special Educational Trust Fund (ASETF) is by far the larger. In fiscal 1985, receipts of the ASETF totaled $1.8 billion; receipts of the general fund, $586 million.

Since the legislature now meets annually, budgeting has been switched from a biennial to an annual basis. The period for which revenues and expenditures are budgeted is the fiscal year, which runs from October 1 through September 30. The budgetary process begins with the filing of needs estimates by the various agencies for the next fiscal year.[29] In an arrangement that gives the legislature a head start in its consideration of the budget, the agencies submit their funding requests not only to the Budget Office but also to the legislature at hearings held by a joint meeting of the legislative finance committees for a few weeks before the session begins. Meanwhile, revisions of agency estimates are made by the state budget officer to reconcile what the agencies would like to get with the estimate of the amount of revenue that is likely to come in.[30]

The purpose of the budget is to guide the legislature in appropriating funds for the operation of state programs. Therefore, the governor and the budget officer complete the budget and submit it to the legislature early in the regular session. The legislative measures needed to implement the budget are included in the document, and these bills are introduced in the legislature by administration leaders. Thereafter, appropriation measures follow much the same course through the legislature as other measures, except that under a recently adopted "budget-isolation" amendment to the constitution, the major appropriation bills were expected to take precedence in the legislature. But this has not happened, as illustrated by the fact that appropriation measures are still highly involved in the politics of legislation and are usually not taken up until late in the session.

Normally the legislature passes two major appropriation bills. One is the education budget, which funds schools and their administration from kindergarten through graduate programs. The other, the general fund budget, appropriates money for all remaining state agencies and programs. As we have indicated, legislative action on the budgets, particularly the education budget, is highly controversial, and usually much political maneuvering is necessary to secure their passage. Indeed, at times the legislators have been unable to agree on the budgets before they were compelled by law to quit work and go home. Special sessions were required to make the necessary appropriations.

Expenditure Controls

State agencies are not free to spend money entirely as they wish. For example, annual appropriations are not made available to the agencies in one lump sum but are released by the state budget officer in quarterly allotments. This process is designed, of course, to prevent the agencies from using up their appropriations before the end of the fiscal year. More important as a device for controlling expenditures, however, is the process known as proration. Under the financial system employed in Alabama, there can be no deficit spending. Whenever it appears that not enough revenues will be collected to cover the full appropriations made for the year, the budget officer informs the governor and the governor orders the amount of the apparent deficit prorated among the state agencies by a prescribed decrease in appropriations. A balance may thus be maintained between revenues and appropriations, and deficit spending is avoided.

Despite constitutional provisions that virtually prohibit the practice, Alabama (through constitutional amendments and the use of public corporations) does borrow money for capital expenditures, and in 1985 the total state debt amounted to almost $4 billion. Most indebtedness is assumed when bonds are issued to pay for schools, highways, prisons, and other public facilities. Public debt in Alabama amounts to about 5 percent of per capita income, about a percentage point higher than the average for the southeastern states.[31]

Checking expenditures is mainly the job of the State Department of Examiners of Public Accounts, whose function is to postaudit (or audit after the transactions have occurred) the accounts of all state and county agencies and officers.[32] If the agency's examiners find any irregularities during an audit and the chief examiner (the agency head) later determines that officers have improperly handled public funds under their control, the sums in question may be "charged back" (billed to the official concerned) and the examiners will seek to collect the funds from the officers concerned.

In their general textbook on state government, Press and VerBurg point out that informal controls (such as news media criticism) may also influence the way public officials use the resources at their disposal.[33] A good example of the way these informal controls work occurred in 1985. Publicity and the possibility of a taxpayers' suit brought a quick response from Governor Wallace when it was found that some officials in the state government were apparently trying to disguise their use of state cars by putting private license tags on them.

PERSONNEL ADMINISTRATION

The people who fill the positions in Alabama state government are selected in a variety of ways. Some are, of course, elected. A large number of agency heads and their political assistants are appointed by or with the approval of the governor. These people are usually called the administration. As noted previously, some administrative officers are selected by boards or commissions. Most employees are selected, however, under the state merit system. In 1985, out of a total of 32,000 workers whose agencies were subject to merit-system law, 85 percent were designated as classified (merit system) employees.[34]

The merit system in Alabama is administered by a State Personnel Department, which functions under the general supervision of the five-member State Personnel Board. The State Personnel Board appoints the personnel director, who serves on an indefinite basis as the administrator in active charge of the department's affairs. In its administration of the state merit system, Personnel Department specialists prepare and administer the merit system examinations for the various positions in which vacancies exist, make up the lists of applicants who have passed the tests and are eligible for appointment, and forward the names of qualified applicants to appointing officers in the line agencies.

In the mid-1980s, the state work force was more reflective of the state population than it used to be. This was due mainly to the greater presence of blacks in state government. The opening up of opportunities for blacks in state administration stemmed largely from federal legislation and court orders requiring the state to eliminate discrimination, but state officials also took steps to achieve a greater representation for blacks in the state bureaucracy. Moreover, state administration also appears to have become more professionalized in recent years. Largely for this reason, public administrators in Alabama seem increasingly able to work with their Washington counterparts and administer the more complex programs now in place in virtually all aspects of government activity.[35]

ADMINISTRATIVE REORGANIZATION

Alabama's present administrative structure is to an appreciable extent a product of a major reorganization of the state government that took place in 1939. In the reorganization concerns it had during that period, Alabama was only one of many states where sentiment was strong that administrative reform would produce a more efficient, economical, and responsible government in place of an inefficient, wasteful, and fragmented government dominated by spoils politics. These goals were to be attained in large measure by giving the governor more powers of control over the administrative branch. Some scholars date the state reorganization movement's beginnings to 1917, when Illinois approved the first comprehensive plan of administrative reform. By 1938 twenty-six states had restructured their administrative systems to some degree. Other states, including Alabama, were publicly debating which, if any, of the suggested reforms they ought to adopt.

Arthur E. Buck, the leading academic in the reform movement, identified several recommended reforms that, he contended, had achieved a status far above that of unproven theories; instead, they were grounded in solid experience in many governmental jurisdictions. These principles were as follows:

1. Responsibility should be concentrated in the governor for the direction of administrative affairs. To accomplish this, the ballot should be shortened as most other previously elective executives became the governor's appointees and administrative functions were consolidated into a small number of departments, each guided by a single officer appointed and removable by the governor.

2. Previously existing offices, boards, commissions, and other agencies of administration should be consolidated and their activities integrated into a few departments, each of which should be organized on the basis of the major function performed.

3. Due to division of authority and persistent absence of initiative and responsibility, boards are impractical for purely administrative work. They should be replaced by single executives. Boards ought to be used only for advisory, quasi-legislative, and quasi-judicial functions.

4. Staff services—principally budgeting, accounting and reporting, purchasing, and personnel—should be brought together in a single staff department. Personnel should be administered on the basis of the merit system. Legal advice should be available from an attorney general not elected but appointed by the governor.

5. The legislature should have an officer—an auditor independent of the executive—to serve as its checking and investigating agent to look into the financial operations of executive agencies.

6. The cabinet concept should be employed by the governor in the same manner as in the national government.[36]

Not all of these objectives were involved in the Alabama reform movement of the late 1930s. The first point, so far as it included the short ballot, was not advocated by the leader of the movement, Governor Frank Dixon. When he ran unsuccessfully for governor in 1934, Dixon argued that only the governor and the lieutenant governor should be elected by the people; all other principal executive officers should be appointed by the governor. The reaction to the short ballot among Alabamians was so unfavorable, however, that when Dixon ran again in 1938, this time successfully, he dropped the concept and focused on objectives with greater political feasibility. As governor, Dixon was in fact able to achieve progress in administrative consolidation.[37] A survey of administrative agencies on the eve of reform showed 133 agencies; in 1942, in contrast, at the end of Dixon's term, there were 106. This is only a modest decline, to be sure, but it is the only period, certainly to the mid-1980s, in which there was such a reduction in the number of state agencies.[38] With regard to the second objective of the administrative reorganization movement, some smaller agencies were consolidated into larger departments. For example, five agencies in the area of conservation were supplanted by a consolidated Department of Conservation. Three business-related agencies were merged into a single Department of Commerce.

As to the third recommendation, which expressed a negative attitude toward agencies headed by boards, an effort was made in the reorganization movement to abandon the board or commission as an agency of administration insofar as practicable. For example, the Department of Revenue was substituted for the Tax Commission, the Highway Department for the Highway Commission, and the Department of State Docks and Terminals for the Docks Commission. Each of the new agencies was single- rather than multiheaded.

Substantial accomplishment of the fourth objective, bringing key staff services together in one place, has been perhaps the most enduring aspect of the administrative reforms of the late 1930s. As Governor Dixon saw it, the key agency in the state administrative system should be a consolidated Department of Finance, which would manage and control most of the state's financial operations. Its director would be the premier member of the governor's cabinet. Most of the expectations regarding the role of the Department of Finance have been realized. It continues as the department in state government with the most pervasive influence. Its director probably is second in power only to the governor. When former governor James took office in 1979, he served for a time as acting finance director to demonstrate his urgent concern about the financial activities of the other state agencies.

An auditing agency accountable directly to the legislature was not established as part of the 1939 reform program. The Department of Examiners of Public Accounts, whose activities we have briefly discussed, was created as a legislative auditing agency in 1947. Before this time the postaudit was performed by examiners working out of a division of the Department of Finance.

Recent illustrations of a concern with administrative reform include the Governor's Cost Control Survey, a study by loaned business managers of state government management practices and operating techniques that was authorized by an executive order issued in 1971, and the Governor's Committee on State Government Reorganization, created in 1975 with the aim of identifying those administrative options that seemed to hold the greatest promise for strengthening the leadership of the state's chief executive. Business interests have been heavily involved in the recent administrative reform movements, and their efforts have been directed mainly toward efficiency and economy, narrowly defined. Ultimately, Governor George Wallace, as a result of the administrative surveys performed during his third administration (1975–79), recommended to the legislature that it reorganize state government into fifteen major departments. However, the legislature never adopted this recommendation or any of the other proposals for sweeping administrative change presented to it during the 1970s. Wallace, however, did not push quite as hard for reorganization as he did for his other concerns as governor. Thus the 1939 reorganization still stands as the last major reform of the Alabama administrative system.

Alabama was, however, the second state in the Union (following Colorado) to adopt the form of legislative oversight of administrative agencies popularly called sunset legislation. Under an act passed in 1976 the legislature must vote on whether administrative units affected by the law should continue in existence. In practice, primarily because of the legislature's limited staffing, the device has not proved to be a very effective way of evaluating agency performance. Few agencies have been terminated.[39]

Another recent example of a program of legislative oversight of administration is the creation of the Joint Committee on Administrative Regulatory Review within the Alabama Legislature. This committee's approval is required for major administrative rules changes to take effect. In 1985, for example, changes in the Alcoholic Beverage Control Board rules banning "happy hour" specials required committee approval before they would be applicable to liquor retailers within the state.[40]

So far, efforts to reorganize Alabama's administrative structure have been only partially successful. The structure is far from a neat little pyramid on an organization chart, with heavy black lines of authority flowing down from the Governor's Office, as the advocates of the standard reorganization proposals would have it. On the other hand, there are those who might say that the present structure is not necessarily a bad state of affairs. Some scholars think that the public interest is served quite well by a large number of governmental institutions having the freedom to respond to citizen needs as communicated to them by many different constituencies. Beyond that, there is the question of accountability. The governorship in Alabama is much more powerful than it appears on the surface. If the governor's control over the bureaucracy is to be strengthened to the point of being the sole guardian of the public welfare, then (to ask an age-old question) who will guard the guardian? In Alabama, until such potential guards as legislators and political parties mature in this role, those who advocate a cautious approach to reorganization may have a point.[41]

CHAPTER SEVEN

The Judiciary

A system of courts makes up the third branch of Alabama's state government. It consists of several categories of trial and appellate courts that function on various jurisdictional bases within the state. Inferior courts, or local courts of limited or special jurisdiction, form a broad foundation for the system. Next above the inferior courts are the general trial courts, where the more important cases usually begin. In some states the apex of the judicial structure, the court of final appeal, is next higher; but in Alabama a set of intermediate appellate courts has been placed between the general trial courts and the highest appellate court.

In 1973, when the judicial article mentioned in chapter 3 was adopted, Alabama's inferior courts included probate courts, county courts, juvenile courts, special courts, and municipal courts. Circuit courts served on a county or regional basis as the trial courts of general jurisdiction. Two intermediate appellate courts having statewide jurisdiction were designated the Court of Civil Appeals and the Court of Criminal Appeals. The state Supreme Court was the court of final appeal.

Having formerly operated on a highly decentralized basis, all of Alabama's courts were affected by the adoption of the new constitutional amendment. They were merged into the unified state court system that it established. Changes in organization, however, took place only in the bottom tier of courts, where variation had become a severe problem. Probate courts were continued and municipalities could choose to retain their own courts, but otherwise (except for juvenile jurisdiction in some counties) the existing inferior courts were replaced by a new set of district courts.

UNREFORMED LOCAL COURTS

County courts were minor criminal courts originally established by general state law but found in their intended form only in some Alabama counties. In many counties this particular court had been abolished by local acts of the legislature. Where the county court existed, the judge of probate was ex officio county court judge. Because it was an inferior criminal court, only "bench trials" took place in the county court—that is, cases were tried by the judge alone, without the use of a jury. If defendants in the county court wanted a jury trial, they could appeal their cases to the circuit court.

Probate courts doubled as juvenile courts except in counties having conventional juvenile courts established by local laws. Before 1972, Alabama's court system also included justices of the peace. These courts had trial jurisdiction over minor civil and criminal cases and preliminary jurisdiction over more serious criminal cases. (Preliminary jurisdiction refers to the power of an inferior court to determine whether an accused person should be "bound over" to the grand jury or held for proceedings in the circuit court.)

Frequently, legislation applying only to particular counties lopped off the justices' statutory criminal jurisdiction and limited them to their constitutional civil jurisdiction. The law ordinarily gave the jurisdiction of justices of the peace to a special court created for the county. The dissatisfaction with justices of the peace that these laws reflect peaked in 1972 with the adoption of a constitutional amendment that abolished the office.[1] Doing away with these courts was not strongly contested, because they had long had bad reputations due to the amateurishness of "JP justice" and their association with speed traps and marriage mills.

Special courts of the sort just mentioned were established by local acts of the legislature in many Alabama counties. The name and jurisdiction of each special court, its procedures, and whether the county court was abolished were all determined by local legislation applicable to particular counties. Since the content of this legislation varied greatly, the courts operating in the counties bore little resemblance to one another. This, of course, seriously hampered the ability of outside attorneys to practice law in local courts.

The municipal court was called the recorder's court. A recorder could be appointed by the municipal governing body, but when this was not done the mayor served as the recorder. Most municipalities appointed a recorder. Probably many of them did so in the early 1970s following the decision of the U.S. Supreme Court in the *Ward* case (1972) that a mayor was not an impartial judge.[2] The recorder's court had jurisdiction over minor criminal cases that arose within the municipality or its police jurisdiction (the area just outside the city limits).

REORGANIZED LOCAL COURTS

Problems resulting from the extreme diversity among local courts led the Constitutional Commission (in its proposed constitution of 1973) to recommend the establishment of district courts with uniform jurisdiction and procedures throughout the state.[3] As seen by the commission, the district courts would replace all existing inferior courts except probate courts. When considered by the legislature, however, the Constitutional Commission's proposed judicial article was amended in such a way as to allow municipalities an option: they could either keep their municipal courts or come under the jurisdiction of the district courts.[4] Their success in getting the judicial article amended so that city courts could be retained if desired demonstrates the municipal officials' considerable political clout.

Under the 1973 article, municipal judges must be lawyers, and the procedures of all municipal courts must be uniform. Their jurisdiction is limited to cases involving municipal ordinances. Judges must be appointed, which is a requirement that eliminated the constitutionally questionable mayor's court. Whenever the governing body wishes, it may abolish its municipal court and have its jurisdiction transferred to the appropriate district court. These transfers sometimes happen. Two occurred during 1983, making a total of sixty-one municipalities using district courts to perform their judicial function.

District courts have exclusive jurisdiction over civil cases involving no more than $500 and share jurisdiction with the circuit court when the sum involved does not exceed $5,000. Cases of the former type are placed on a small-claims docket for trial under simplified procedures. This is supposed to make it easier for ordinary people to take their grievances to court without the expense of heavy legal fees. In criminal matters, district courts have original trial jurisdiction over misdemeanors, including traffic violations. Regarding felonies, district courts conduct preliminary proceedings and, concurrently with the circuit courts, receive guilty pleas in cases not involving the death penalty.

The district court's jurisdiction over guilty pleas graphically illustrates the importance of this plea as a means of settling criminal cases. The great bulk of them never come to trial. As in the rest of the country, guilty pleas in Alabama frequently result from a process of negotiation (known as "plea bargaining") in which the defense lawyer and the prosecutor reach an understanding about the sentence to be imposed if the defendant pleads guilty. The defendant's objective, of course, is to lessen the severity of the sentence in return for saving the prosecution the time and expense of a trial. The practice is widely condemned, but plea bargaining also has its supporters and at least one redeeming feature: it does enable the courts to accommodate their huge criminal caseload. Parenthetically, neither are most civil cases actually tried. These, too, are mainly settled out of court, without a full trial.[5]

When the legislature passed a law in 1975 to implement the judicial article, it generally provided for one district court, with one judge, for each county. Exceptions to this pattern were made then and later, however. A number of the more heavily populated counties have more than one district judge (one county had as many as eleven district judges in 1983), and in two instances, counties were combined to form larger districts. Thousands of cases are filed in the district courts—nearly 475,000 in 1983.[6] As figure 4 shows, 42 percent of them were traffic cases.

Except for jurisdictional changes made during the reorganization, probate courts function much as they have in the past. These courts were—and remain—important components of the state's judicial machinery. Because their jurisdiction is limited and special, we have classified them as inferior courts. Even so, probate courts handle some highly important matters, such as the administration of wills and estates, the commitment of the mentally ill, and cases involving adoptions and guardianships, except when these cases fall within the jurisdiction of the juvenile court.

There is a probate court in each county. Judges of these courts need not be lawyers, although before 1973 they could possibly be judges of three courts within the county. Ordinarily they are very important local officials in Alabama, because in most counties their duties range well beyond those concerning the probate court. In about half the counties, the probate judge chairs the county commission—the county governing body—and is thus an especially important official in those counties.

CIRCUIT COURTS

Under the judicial article adopted in 1973, the legislature continues to determine the number and boundaries of judicial circuits and districts and the number of judges for each court. However, the legislature must now take

Figure 4. District Court Filings, Fiscal Year 1983 (Total Filings: 474, 596). (*Source:* Alabama Administrative Office of Courts, *Alabama Judicial System Annual Report, Fiscal Year 1983; October 1, 1982, to September 30, 1983,* p. 11)

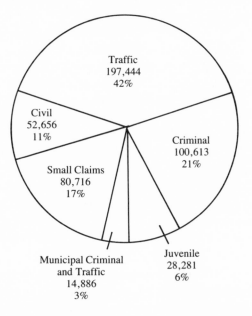

into consideration guidelines established by the state Supreme Court as well as the recommendations of the Supreme Court in regard to the specific changes suggested by proposed legislation. The legislature is apparently free either to follow these guidelines and recommendations or ignore them. What seems to be required is that it give the state Supreme Court an opportunity to comment on the proposals. As of 1983, the state was divided into thirty-nine circuits, with 114 circuit judges.[7] Generally, the larger counties make up separate circuits, while smaller counties are grouped to form circuits. Many circuits have one or two judges, but the more populous have additional judges—ranging up to twenty or more in the Tenth Judicial Circuit (Jefferson County).

The 1973 judicial article continued the circuit courts as the general trial courts, with original jurisdiction over both law and equity cases and with appellate jurisdiction over cases heard in the minor courts. Here, then, is where the more serious cases are brought: felony prosecutions and civil cases involving large sums of money. Figure 5 indicates that 126,218 cases were filed in circuit courts during 1983.

Figure 5. Circuit Court Filings, Fiscal Year 1983 (Total Filings: 126,218). (*Source:* Alabama Administrative Office of Courts, *Alabama Judicial System Annual Report, Fiscal Year 1983; October 1, 1982, to September 30, 1983,* p. 10)

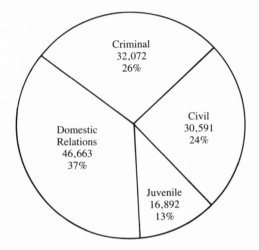

Criminal cases in the circuit court are based on indictments made by a grand jury and are prosecuted by the district attorney, formerly known as the circuit solicitor.[8] Alabama's constitution calls for the popular election of a district attorney in each judicial circuit. The district attorney must be a lawyer and serves for a term of six years. District attorneys appoint a varying number of assistants to help carry out such responsibilities as working with grand juries, drafting indictments, and prosecuting defendants in criminal trials.

Traditionally, district attorneys have been important political figures in their communities. Because of their high visibility, particularly in the trial of criminal cases, they develop considerable name recognition and may be able to use the publicity they receive to win promotion to higher political office. Charles Graddick, for example, developed a reputation as a tough prosecutor in Mobile before his election as state attorney general in 1978.

Defendants in criminal cases who are unable to pay for their defense are represented under an indigent defense system that may involve use of either court-appointed counsel or public defenders. Most counties, including Jefferson (the most populous county), use the appointment system. Only a handful of counties, such as Tuscaloosa, for example, use public defenders.

Members of the grand and petit (trial) juries used in the circuit courts are drawn from a master list of prospective jurors prepared in each county by a county jury commission.[9] The jury list is based on such lists of county residents as lists of registered voters, those holding driver's licenses, and the like. The computerized list of drivers maintained by the Department of Public Safety seems to be a frequent source of names, especially in counties not having a computerized list of voters.

From time to time, as the need for jurors arises, the jury commission selects at random from the master list the names of a sufficient number of prospective jurors to meet the needs of the court for the immediate future. Their eligibility to serve as jurors (whether they are citizens, residents, and can speak English, for example) is determined on the basis of a form ordinarily processed by mail. Some of the individuals summoned for jury duty are slated for service on the eighteen-member grand jury. They serve for a matter of months (the term varies depending on local conditions) and meet periodically to consider indictments in the cases that the district attorney refers to them. Twelve members of the grand jury must agree to indict a person. The other prospective jurors summoned for service make up the panels from which petit juries are formed. They may or may not actually serve on a jury, though. Actual service depends upon whether they are struck from the panel by the attorneys involved in the cases scheduled for trial.

At one time the jury list in some counties was so small as to amount, almost, to a set of "professional" jurors. Exemption from jury service was granted to a wide range of occupational classes, blacks hardly ever served on juries, and women were ineligible. In more recent years, however, largely because of the federal courts' insistence on more representative juries, women and blacks have regularly been included on juries. Further-more, the legislature decided in 1978 to end the policy of granting automatic exemptions to select groups.[10] Now individuals called for jury service may be excused by a judge but only for such reasons as undue hardship or public necessity. Postponements are granted with reasonable leniency; outright excuses, though, seem rather hard to come by. As a result of these develop-ments, juries are now much more representative of the community than they once were.

Although the legal system assigns an important decision-making role to the "citizen jury" in the trial of cases, comparatively few jury trials actually take place. During fiscal 1983, for example, the circuit court in Tuscaloosa County held only 141 jury trials, yet it disposed of 1,908 criminal cases and 1,003 civil cases, or a total of about 2,900 cases.[11] In the state as a whole, about 3,000 jury trials took place. These figures illustrate our earlier comment that most cases are settled out of court, but we should note, too, that many kinds of cases (divorces, for example) do not require a jury.

APPELLATE COURTS

As a general rule, the person losing a trial may (but usually does not) appeal to a higher court, asking the appellate court to decide that a fault in the proceedings justifies overturning the decision in the trial court. As indicated at the beginning of the chapter, there exists in Alabama an intermediate appellate rung in the judicial ladder. This kind of court decides appeals in cases of lesser importance, while the state Supreme Court considers the more important appeals. Ever since a reorganization conducted in 1969, when (among other changes) the old three-judge Court of Appeals was abolished, Alabama has had two intermediate appellate courts—a Court of Criminal Appeals and a Court of Civil Appeals.[12] The Court of Criminal Appeals has five judges, the Court of Civil Appeals only three—a difference that indicates to some extent the relative caseloads of the two courts (1,452 new criminal cases filed in 1983 compared to 562 new civil filings). The Court of Criminal Appeals has appellate jurisdiction over the criminal cases decided by the trial courts. The civil court's docket consists of cases involving (1) no more than $10,000, (2) appeals from most administrative agencies, (3) worker's compensation, or (4) domestic relations.[13]

As another result of the 1969 reorganization of Alabama's appellate courts, the state Supreme Court has a good deal of leeway in determining the cases it hears. Cases decided by the courts of appeals may be taken to the Supreme Court only by petition for a writ of certiorari, a process of review that is almost entirely at the discretion of the Supreme Court. Only when a case involves the death penalty is the grant of certiorari considered a right.

The Alabama Supreme Court presently consists of the chief justice and eight associate justices.[14] In an arrangement that preserves continuity of experience (and minimizes the likelihood of drastic policy changes), their terms are staggered so that only a part of the membership is elected at each general election. Before 1975 the court's membership consisted only of white males. In that year, however, Justice Janie L. Shores was elected as the first female member of the court, while Justice Oscar W. Adams, Jr., the first black to serve, was appointed by Governor James to fill a vacancy in 1980.[15] Adams was subsequently elected for a full term.

A few kinds of cases are heard originally in the Supreme Court—for example, impeachment proceedings against some state and local officials. As the highest court of review in state cases, its jurisdiction is essentially appellate. Some appeals to the Supreme Court come directly from the trial courts, but under the certiorari requirement, all of its criminal and many civil cases come to the Supreme Court from the courts of appeals.[16] As table 6 shows, the court disposed of 1,245 cases during fiscal 1983. It issued written opinions in 633 cases, or an average of about 70 opinions per justice. Of the total workload of almost 2,000 cases, 713 were carried over to the next year.

As in the U.S. Supreme Court, regular terms of the Alabama Supreme Court begin on the first Monday in October of each year and continue through the following June. It may hold special sessions when necessary.

In Alabama the Supreme Court's power of judicial review has been carried a step further than in some jurisdictions. The Alabama Supreme Court can give advisory opinions on constitutional questions. Whenever a major constitutional question arises, the governor or either house of the legislature may ask the justices of the Alabama Supreme Court for their opinion about the question. Because advisory opinions do not involve actual cases in controversy (in which the adversarial context in which the legal system operates assures that the issues in a case will be fully explored), these opinions are not considered as weighty as judgments in real cases. Advisory opinions of the justices are nevertheless important. Following the justices' advice could prevent a lawsuit from arising later.

An interesting organizational feature of the Alabama Supreme Court is that it operates on the basis of two sections. Each is composed of four justices, with the chief justice a member of both groups. Each section can hear oral argument and decide cases for the court, since the vote of five justices is usually all that is necessary for a decision. Thus a unanimous vote in a case settles the issue. That is why, in news accounts of Supreme Court activity, one often sees reports of cases decided on the basis of 5–0 votes, even though the court consists of nine members. If there is a dissent within a section, however, the question is considered by the court as a whole. The entire court makes decisions in a few other instances as well. For example, previous decisions of the court cannot be overruled or modified unless reviewed by the whole court. Petitions for certiorari in cases involving the death penalty are also considered by the entire court.[17] The court decides most cases without oral argument on the part of the lawyers involved. Trial records and the arguments submitted by the lawyers in their written briefs are used to settle most issues.

Table 6: Alabama Supreme Court, Cases Docketed and Disposed,
October 1, 1982–September 30, 1983

Cases Docketed:	
New Cases	
Appeals and Extraordinary Writs	723
Petitions for Writ of Certiorari	464
Miscellaneous Docket	110
Certified Questions	4
Advisory Opinions	3
Total New Cases	1,304
Cases Carried Over from Previous Year	654
Total Cases Docketed	1,958
Cases Disposed	
Appeals	495
Petitions for Certiorari	114
Extraordinary Writs, Certified Questions	
and Advisory Opinions	24
Petitions for Writ of Certiorari Denied	284
Dispositions by Court of Miscellaneous Docket	
and Disposition by Clerk's Office	328
Total Cases Disposed	1,245
Cases Docketed but not Submitted	713

Source: Alabama Administrative Office of Courts, *Alabama Judicial System Annual Report, Fiscal Year 1983; October 1, 1982, to September 30, 1983,* p. 8.

Cases accepted by the Supreme Court are assigned by the clerk of the court to the various justices on a rotation basis for the purpose of writing the opinion that explains the court's decision. Before the 1970s the justices voted on a case after the opinion had been written, when it was read in conference.[18] Robert J. Frye commented on this procedure as follows:

Once an assignment has been made, there is very little communication between a justice and his associates concerning the case; the operating assumption is that the case is the particular justice's "baby." It is he who bears the responsibility for reading the briefs and transcript in the case (the transcript record itself does not circulate), for conducting the independent research, and drafting the opinion. It is unfortunate, but true, that Alabama's system is basically the "one-man decision" system which is consistently deplored in the literature on judicial processes.[19]

Professor Herbert Jacob has observed that in state supreme courts, in contrast to the U.S. Supreme Court, decisions are more likely to be made on the basis of traditional legal theory and are less likely to reflect intracourt divisions.[20] According to Frye's research, both of these characteristics were especially applicable to the pre-1970 Alabama Supreme Court. For example, Frye said in regard to the court's traditionalist perception of its role:

> There seems little doubt that the legal philosophy underlying the work of the Court is that of analytical jurisprudence, a philosophy that the function of an appellate court is to "declare" the law. . . . Thus, the Court has professed its function to be that of applying a relatively fixed body of law to particular factual situations. In the process the Court has emphasized that its role is one of giving expression to policies enunciated by other branches of government, especially the Legislature. . . . Consistent with this general philosophy is the strong orientation which the Court has toward resolving conflicts almost exclusively on the basis of precedent. . . . Through its careful adherence to precedent, and its corresponding reluctance to depart from precedent, the Court has expressed in effect the view that responsibility for effecting social change lies elsewhere within the political system.[21]

Frye also found that the court's members conducted their business without a great deal of disagreement. In examining 161 cases decided between the fall of 1966 and the spring of 1967, Frye found only 8 cases in which a justice dissented from the majority opinion—a dissent rate of about 5 percent. Six of the eight dissents, moreover, were filed by only one justice.[22] According to Frye, three factors accounted for the high level of agreement in the court: the role perception prevailing among its membership, its heavy workload, and the system of operating procedures it used to cope with its workload.[23]

The appellate reorganization of 1969 seems, however, to have had a marked effect on the operation of the Alabama Supreme Court. Increasing the intermediate courts' authority and establishing the discretionary writ of certiorari as a way of routing cases to the Supreme Court (along with a concerted effort during the early 1970s to deal with its backlog of undecided cases) went a long way toward reducing the court's workload to a more manageable level. Enlarging the Supreme Court's size from seven to nine provided two more members to help with the work.

Unanimity in the Alabama Supreme Court seems less prevalent now than before the reorganization, and the justices appear to have become more inclined to address the policy questions raised by important cases. Good examples of these tendencies include the 1975 set of decisions discontinuing the immunity of local governments from damage suits, the 1978 decision announcing a less permissive policy toward Alabama's constitutional limitations on local legislation, and the 1983 decision that the legislature could not propose a new constitution as a single amendment.[24] Justices filed strong dissents in all of these cases.

JUDGES

Originally judges in Alabama were elected by a joint vote of both houses of the General Assembly. They held office for good behavior and could be removed either by impeachment or by the governor, after a two-thirds vote in each house of the General Assembly, for offenses not justifying impeachment. By 1868, however, constitutional changes had produced a judiciary composed of judges chosen by popular election for six-year terms.

Elective judges are chosen in partisan elections and still serve for terms of six years. Some recent judicial elections have been sharply contested, but they are usually low-key affairs. Incumbent judges frequently run unopposed for reelection, and sometimes there is little apparent public interest in who fills which judicial slot. Municipal judges are appointed by the municipal governing bodies for terms of either two or four years, depending upon the part- or full-time nature of their employment. All judges other than probate judges and municipal judges receive salaries paid by the state. In some instances, though, counties supplement the salaries of circuit and district judges, a practice that obviously enhances the attractiveness of these positions.[25] The judges' salaries cannot be reduced during their term of office. Vacancies in elective judgeships are filled by appointment by the governor. A high proportion of appointees are subsequently elected to the position.[26]

JUDICIAL REORGANIZATION

By the 1960s it had become apparent that Alabama's judicial machinery was badly in need of repair. Court calendars were congested with a backlog of cases, and criticism of the local courts intensified. A study of state court systems reported by two political scientists ranked Alabama among the lowest in the nation in terms of legal professionalism.[27]

A citizens' conference on the state's judiciary held in 1966 issued a highly critical report and made many recommendations for the improvement of Alabama's courts. Its recommendations amounted to a complete revision of the court system.[28] Probably the conference's most controversial recommendation dealt with judicial selection and tenure. It proposed the "merit system," or Missouri Plan, of judicial selection.[29] Although there are differences in the operation of the plan in the states that have adopted it, the Missouri Plan essentially involves the use of a nominating commission to compile a list of nominees for judgeships and appointment from the list of people to fill the positions. The appointed judges are periodically subject to elections as their terms expire. They are not opposed by other candidates at the elections. The question is whether the voters want the judge to continue in office for another term. If the vote is negative, the judge's tenure in office ends and the original selection process (nomination and appointment) is started over again. The plan's supporters argue that it produces a more highly qualified corps of judges. Opponents of the Missouri Plan argue that it really does not take judges out of politics, as its supporters frequently claim, but simply gives more political power to the organized bar, which plays the most important continuing role in the process of judicial selection.

The citizens' conference concluded that Alabama's judicial system required significant improvement for it to operate efficiently. The legislature had created the Judicial Conference in 1961 in an attempt to give the state a means of continuously studying and revising the judicial organization and procedures, and followed this up in 1971 with the creation of the Permanent Study Commission on Alabama's Judicial System, which supplemented the Judicial Conference. These efforts to generate helpful changes were supplemented by the establishment, also in 1971, of a Department of Court Management, which would both assist the chief justice in carrying out the responsibilities of the office as administrative head of the judicial system and also assist the Judicial Conference. Among other duties, this department (now the Administrative Office of Courts) performs important financial functions, such as budget preparation and purchasing; collects information about the courts and their workloads; and conducts various kinds of studies and projects bearing on the administration of justice and its improvement in Alabama—for example, studies of juror selection procedures and information management systems.[30]

The establishment of the agencies concerned with judicial administration, the reorganization of the appellate courts, the establishment of an independent commission having responsibility for the discipline and removal of judges (as a substitute for impeachment), and the abolition of justice of the peace courts, were all among the goals of the citizens' conference that had been achieved by the early 1970s. Other recommendations included a uniform set of local inferior courts and a formal retirement system for the state's judges. These changes were among the major revisions enacted in 1973 with the adoption of the new constitutional provisions dealing with the state judiciary. Alabama then joined the list of states in which judicial reform was pursued by the process of court unification.[31]

Under the 1973 article, the state judicial power is vested in a unified judicial system (figure 6) consisting of the Supreme Court, the Court of Criminal Appeals, the Court of Civil Appeals, the circuit courts, the district courts, the probate courts, and the municipal courts. The unification of the judicial system was accomplished through several key features of the new article. First, the article created a state court system. Thus the trial courts, formerly identified with local government, became a part of the state governmental structure, and all the courts were financed by the state except for the probate and municipal courts. A second element of the unification process involved the establishment of trial courts of uniform jurisdiction operating under standardized rules adopted by the state Supreme Court.

In addition, the 1973 judicial article formally established the chief justice as the administrative head of the state judiciary. Previously lacking the staff necessary to perform this function effectively, the new article made specific provision for the appointment of an administrative director of courts and other needed personnel to assist the chief justice in handling these administrative tasks.

Further, Alabama's judges are now under the rules of conduct and ethics, disciplinary provisions, administrative regulations, and judicial retirement system authorized by the 1973 article. Except for probate and municipal judges, judicial salaries are fixed on the basis of recommendations made by a judicial compensation commission. The commission submits its recommendations regarding salary levels to the legislature, and they become effective unless the legislature rejects them, as sometimes happens. For example, the legislature in its 1979 regular session rejected proposed increases for all judges except circuit judges.

In the Constitutional Commission's opinion, considerations of due process required two agencies to handle judicial disciplinary problems rather than the one tenure commission that was created in 1972. Consequently, under the 1973 judicial article, the investigation of complaints concerning judges is performed by the Judicial Inquiry Commission, while trials of charges made against judges are conducted by the Court of the Judiciary. This court may order the removal, suspension, or retirement of a judge, or it may censure a judge for misconduct. The range of options available to the Court of the Judiciary is generally seen as making this disciplinary process

Figure 6. The Unified Judicial System. (*Source:* Hugh Maddox, James H. Faulk-ner, and William C. Younger, eds., *Alabama Appellate Courts, 1981* [Montgom-ery, 1981])

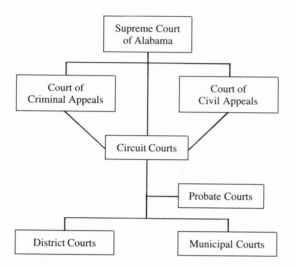

more effective than impeachment. The court may more nearly "fit the punishment to the crime," which was not always possible under the all-or-nothing impeachment process.[32] A judge may appeal an adverse decision by the Court of the Judiciary to the Alabama Supreme Court.

Although the judicial disciplinary system has been in effect for a rela-tively brief time, the procedure has been used on several occasions. In 1983, for example, the Alabama Supreme Court upheld an order suspending a judge for the last few weeks of his term. As a news report of the incident put it,

The Alabama Supreme Court, in a stern ruling Friday, upheld the disciplinary action against a white judge who recommended a black man get a sterilization operation. "Such conduct harks back to an attitude which we have made substantial progress in eliminating. It cannot be tolerated in our courts of justice," the Supreme Court said in an unsigned 8–0 ruling.[33]

The recent judicial reform movement in Alabama has seen the imple-mentation of most of the important recommendations made by the 1966 citizens' conference on the state judiciary. Changing the method of judicial selection is virtually the only major recommendation that has not been implemented. The reorganization has produced a unified set of courts that by and large has lived up to expectations for improvement. Certainly conditions today are a far cry from the way they were in the old days when, as Alabama's chief justice once remarked, for many a fledgling lawyer "finding the proper procedure for filing a particular motion was as much a cause for celebration as actually winning the case."[34]

CHAPTER EIGHT

Parties
and Interest
Groups

Political parties are organized in Alabama in about the same way as in most other states. The Alabama law regulating party organization says that each party may establish an executive committee for the state as a whole and also one for each county and municipality. The legislature has not described these committees; it has only authorized their existence. Consequently, each party determines the precise composition of its committee structure. In practice, both the Republican and the Democratic parties have organized state and county committees, but neither party uses city committees.

Over the years, the state Democratic committee has played an important role in Alabama politics. For this reason, control of the committee has often been one of the key battlegrounds for factions supporting and opposing close ties with the national Democratic party. Beginning in the 1940s the former came to be called "Loyalists," while the latter were identified as "States Righters" or "Dixiecrats."[1] Until the 1960s these two factions battled each other on fairly even terms for control of the state committee. Most of the time the Loyalists won, however, and today conflict within the committee mainly reflects nonideological struggles for power among competitors for important party nominations. National party loyalty has become the norm, and the Democratic state committee typically works in harmony with national party guidelines, including those designed to ensure that participation in party activities is open to all interested persons, particularly such groups as blacks, women, and youths.

The parties may select their committees in either primaries, conventions, or mass meetings. For years, Republican county committees were generally chosen in mass meetings or county conventions, but recently in the larger counties they have been selected in primaries. Republican state committee members were named at the state convention. At present, most members are selected in county-based primaries. A few are still chosen in local conventions or mass meetings.

Earlier, Republican candidates were usually picked in mass meetings or in county or state conventions, but since the early 1970s, Republican primaries have been held both for the election of party committee members and for the nomination of candidates. Given the strong prospects for Democratic victory, however, the Republican primary ballot may contain only a few names of aspirants for public office. Either no Republicans offer themselves or only one candidate for the nomination emerges, thereby eliminating the need for primary balloting. Recruiting candidates is an important concern of the Republican organization.

The Democratic party in Alabama does not hold conventions. Members of the state and county Democratic committees are selected in primaries, as are the Democratic candidates for public office. The fact that conventions are not used means that the Democratic party as such takes virtually no policy positions and that nomination struggles mostly involve individual candidate organizations, with little participation by the party leadership.

As is true of most state party organizations at present, both the Alabama Democratic and Republican parties have full-time executive directors and headquarters staffs. The conclusions of John F. Bibby and his coauthors regarding state parties generally seem applicable to Alabama: in recent years both parties have become "more sophisticated organizations that have developed a capacity for substantial fund-raising, gathering and processing of data, and provision of campaign services"—the kinds of activities performed by the state party organizations.[2]

PATTERNS OF PARTISANSHIP

Until relatively recent times, electoral victories for candidates on the Democratic ticket were assured. Now Democratic success, while still probable in state and local elections, has become improbable in presidential elections. In each of the presidential elections held in 1948, 1956, 1960, 1964, 1968, 1972, 1980, and 1984 individuals other than those nominated at national Democratic conventions won one or more (and in the last five instances, all) of Alabama's presidential electoral votes.[3] In contrast, in 1936 Franklin D. Roosevelt won 86 percent of the popular presidential vote in Alabama. Democratic candidates received all of Alabama's electoral votes in every presidential election from 1876 through 1944, when national Democratic support for civil rights began to erode the party's base in the southern states.

Scholars have made a considerable effort in recent years to construct a classification of states based on the relative strength of the Democratic and Republican parties. Alabama was, of course (as we have just illustrated), one of the states in the traditionally Democratic Solid South, formed in the aftermath of the Civil War. In a study of state politics Austin Ranney points out that each of the seven states classified as one-party Democratic was a member of the Confederacy and was subject to Republican Reconstruction policies following the Civil War. Each of the four states Ranney classified as modified Democratic one-party states had also seceded from the Union. The group of seven modified Republican one-party states (there were no plain one-party Republican states) consisted of two states that had fought on the Union side and five others that had been settled principally by families from Union states.[4]

Jewell and Olson classified the states on the basis of control of the governorship and the legislature between 1961 and 1982. In this classification system Alabama was listed (along with Arkansas, Georgia, Louisiana, Mississippi, South Carolina, and Texas) as a "dominant" Democratic state.[5] Bibby and his associates reported that in the years 1974 to 1980 Alabama was the most Democratic state of the eight so classified during these years. Its score exceeded that of Georgia, Louisiana, Mississippi, Arkansas, North Carolina, Maryland, and Rhode Island, the other one-party Democratic states identified in the study. Among the remaining southern states, South Carolina, Texas, Florida, and Tennessee were now put in the modified one-party Democratic category. No southern states could yet be grouped into the two-party category.[6] These classifications were based only on campaigns for state offices, but because Republicans have done well in races for the U.S. House and Senate in recent years, as well as for the presidency, Alabama can be cited as one of a number of southern states that seem to have a "two-tiered electoral system." That is, elections are competitive for federal offices in Alabama, but much less so in state and local races.[7]

Professor Paul C. David's index of Democratic strength for Alabama (a combination of gubernatorial and congressional votes) has been consistently higher than the Democratic presidential vote in Alabama over the past several decades. Half a century ago these two voting lines were virtually the same. The sharpest divergences occurred in 1948 and 1964, when the name of the Democratic presidential nominee was not even represented on the

Alabama ballot. But at other times as well there has been a substantial difference between the two lines, with the presidential line significantly lower.[8] Republican presidential candidates have recently run well in Alabama. In the 1984 presidential election Republican Ronald Reagan won 60.5 percent of the Alabama popular vote, Democrat Walter Mondale only 38.2 percent.

Another statistic that points to Democratic dominance in state politics is the fact that in the period 1946–1980 Alabama was one of only three states (the others were her eastern and western neighbors, Georgia and Mississippi) that had no experience with divided government; that is, where the executive and legislative branches were at least at some point controlled by different political parties.[9] This distinction did not come to an end until 1986.

Just as Alabama's traditional Democratic orientation stems primarily from the Civil War experience, so too does its most persistent strain of Republicanism, that in the half-dozen or so northern counties where there has been, through the years, a relatively high degree of Republicanism. These counties (of which Winston is the best example) were centers of Unionist sentiment in Alabama during the Civil War, and after the war many of the inhabitants became Republicans. The north Alabama Republicans enjoyed some success in local politics but, more important, they were essentially the Republican party in Alabama until the middle decades of the twentieth century.[10]

In the 1960s new leadership arose in the Republican party, and the pace of its activities quickened significantly. One of the most successful leaders was a young Birmingham attorney, John Grenier, who, after his service as chairman of the Alabama Republican party, was selected by Senator Barry Goldwater, the party's 1964 standard-bearer, as executive director of the Republican National Committee. Republicans continued to gain strength, especially in the metropolitan areas of Alabama, and had their greatest success in the 1964 elections, when they won the state's presidential electoral vote for Goldwater, five of the then eight seats in the U.S. House of Representatives, and a good many local offices as well. Along with the rise in Republican voting strength came a heavy emphasis on the party's organizational activities.[11]

Republican gains since the 1960s have been inconsistent, and few serious inroads on the Democratic dominance of state and local politics were made until Guy Hunt's election as governor in 1986. Even so, the state government remains mostly the preserve of Democrats, except for a relative handful of Republicans in the legislature and in some local offices. In 1984, for example, only fourteen of Alabama's sixty-seven counties had Republican officeholders. (As noted in chapter 11, municipal elections are conducted on a nonpartisan basis.) Republican party officials conclude that a minimum of 37 percent of Alabama voters can be counted on to vote for any Republican candidate who contends seriously for a state or federal office.[12] With this base of support, Republican victories are by no means inconceivable, especially when there is dissension in the Democratic ranks, as in 1986.

Alabama, however, is a state whose party system is usually classified as noncompetitive. Some scholars see the presence or absence of party competition as closely related to socioeconomic conditions in the states. Thomas Dye, for example, observes that "party competition is greater in those urban, industrial states in which separate socioeconomic groups reside." In contrast, "rural agricultural states with homogeneous populations do not provide enough social division to support well-organized, disciplined and competitive parties."[13] Dye also finds that compared to one-party states like Alabama, two-party states tend to be more highly urbanized and wealthier and to have a higher median educational level. On the whole, two-party states also tend to have smaller proportions of blacks than one-party states.

In the past, some critics of Alabama's political system have expressed the view that a strong two-party system was essential to the state's full development. Aside from any intrinsic value to the two-party model, however, modern scholarship casts doubt on the implications for public policy outputs of the level of party competition. To Dye, "available evidence suggests that interparty competition does not play a really influential role in determining public policies."[14] The content of public policies in such areas as education, welfare, taxation, and highways, for example, seems to be more closely related to socioeconomic factors than to the extent of party competition.[15] Dye believes that the absence of party competition may have serious implications, however, in that it "can seriously affect the degree of popular control over state government and the ability of individuals to hold public officials responsible for the state of public affairs." Also, he observes, the lack of party competition may limit voter involvement in state politics, since one party is practically guaranteed victory.[16] We agree with Dye's point of view.

The image of an Alabama legislature with a significant minority bloc capable of keeping the majority party in line has a strong attraction. Yet, even in two-party states the degree to which legislators divide along party lines varies significantly. While party-line voting is pronounced in New York, for instance, it is low in Oregon. Ohio and Washington State (and Congress) are in a middle range. Where divisions in state legislatures based on party label do occur, they tend to focus on a relatively few issues.[17] Nevertheless, it bears repeating that important institutionalized functions may be performed in two-party states that are not performed by unstable factions in one-party (that is, no-party) states such as Alabama.

Dye has also said that with increasing frequency in the South's urban areas, "the Democratic and Republican parties are coming to represent . . . separate socioeconomic constituencies."[18] This seems to be the case in Alabama, where in the Birmingham metropolitan area, for example, the central city contains higher proportions of low-income groups and minorities and is heavily Democratic, while the suburbs, predominantly middle income and white, are much more likely to support the Republican ticket, particularly in presidential elections. Moreover, Charles Press and Kenneth VerBurg see "a 'nationalization' of the supporters of each party." Accordingly, as a general pattern, "within each state the interest groups and voters show the same distinctive tendencies—the 'have nots' are more often Democrats, the 'haves' are more often Republicans. . . . It is a pattern that encourages centralization as members of each party are becoming more united in outlook."[19]

An examination of the characteristics of partisan supporters indicates that this observation also seems applicable to Alabama, where national-state party harmony has been the recent tendency. Over a period of years, the Capstone Poll has asked a sample of the adult Alabama population about its partisan orientation from both national and state perspectives. In terms of national party identification (table 7), in 1985 about 44 percent identified themselves as Democrats, 28 percent as independents, and 28 percent as Republicans. From the state and local standpoint (table 8), 51 percent labeled themselves as Democrats, 31 percent as independents, and only 18 percent as Republicans.[20] Alabama has no party registration system with which to check these survey responses. Another problem is that survey data relating to party allegiance are available for only the very recent past. Nevertheless, it does seem that any movement away from the traditional Democratic party identification that may be taking place is occurring at a relatively slow pace. This observation is more applicable to state and local than to national politics, however. As election statistics indicate, more Alabamians relate to the Republican party in national than in state politics. Too, the party identification statistics seem to offer, on the whole, little tempta-

Table 7: National Party Identification of a Sample
of the Adult Alabama Population, 1982–1985

	Fall 1982	*Fall 1983*	*Fall 1984*	*Fall 1985*
Republican	17%	20%	31%	28%
Independent	29	30	24	28
Democrat	54	50	45	44
Total	100	100	100	100
N	448	441	448	455

Source: University of Alabama, Capstone Poll.
Note: The data are from responses to the question "When it comes to national politics, do you consider yourself a Republican, a Democrat, an Independent, or what?"

Table 8: State and Local Party Identification of a Sample
of the Adult Alabama Population, 1982–1985

	Fall 1982	*Fall 1983*	*Fall 1984*	*Fall 1985*
Republican	13%	15%	19%	18%
Independent	29	33	29	31
Democrat	58	52	52	51
Total	100	100	100	100
N	449	428	446	445

Source: University of Alabama, Capstone Poll.
Note: The data are from responses to the question "When it comes to local or state politics, do you consider yourself a Republican, a Democrat, an Independent, or what?"

tion to aspiring officeholders to switch from the Democratic party to the Republican. But party identification no longer has the influence on voting behavior that it had during the day of the Solid South. As Donald Strong put it, "Alabamians apparently know how to split a ticket."[21] Consequently, some candidates do make the switch, especially in the metropolitan areas, where the Republicans' strength tends to concentrate. A good example is H. L. "Sonny" Callahan, who switched from the Democratic to the Republican party and won the race in Mobile in 1984 to succeed veteran Republican congressman Jack Edwards.

As they do nationally, black voters make up an important component of the Alabama Democratic party. In the 1984 presidential election, all but one of the black-majority counties (Alabama has ten such counties) voted for Walter Mondale. Throughout the state Mondale received an estimated 90 percent of the black votes cast; Reagan, no more than 10 percent.[22] A distinct cleavage between black and white voters is suggested by the estimate that only 22 percent of white voters supported Mondale, while 78 percent supported Reagan. Figure 7 shows that Mondale won in Alabama's Black Belt but that Reagan did considerably better than Mondale in most other parts of the state. In the 1980 election, 38 percent of whites are estimated to have supported Carter, while 58 percent voted for Reagan.[23] In the 1982 gubernatorial election, black voters overwhelmingly supported Governor Wallace against Emory Folmar, his Republican opponent. White Alabama Democratic leaders seem fully conscious of the significance of black support for the party and have, in recent years, made major revisions in the composition of the state Democratic executive committee to allow for greater black representation. It is estimated that blacks, most of whom regularly vote Democratic (table 9), amount to about a fourth of Alabama's registered voters.[24]

In a 1985 Capstone Poll, a third of the white respondents identified themselves as Republicans (table 9). White voters obviously are not attracted across the board to Republicanism. As is the case elsewhere, the higher the income, the greater the likelihood of a Republican identification. A 1980 study found that 23 percent of white Alabamians earning over $20,000 a year accepted the Republican label, compared to 16 percent of those earning less than $10,000. Neither of these figures is very large. Sixty-one percent of Alabamians earning under $10,000 in 1980 identified with the Democratic party, as did 45 percent of those making more than $20,000.[25] The combined total of Republican and independent identifiers for the more-than-$20,000 group, however, was 55 percent.

Age is also related to party preference. In 1980, for example, 63 percent of Alabama whites in the 18–40 age group had voted Republican, while only 43 percent of all voters sixty-one and over had. The Democratic presidential nominee in 1980, Jimmy Carter, won only 31 percent of the votes of all voters in the 18–40 age group but 56 percent of those in the sixty-one and over group. Perhaps a story told about a Republican candidate has something to it. A few years ago, the story goes, a would-be state legislator in southeast Alabama met an elderly gentleman and attempted to get his vote. The candidate got a favorable reception, but only until he told the old man he was a Republican. At that point the old man's vote was lost; he walked away crying "No, no, no." Baffled, the candidate followed the

Figure 7. Alabama 1984 Presidential Vote, by County. (*Source: The 1984 Presidential Election in the South*, edited by Robert P. Steed, Laurence W. Moreland, and Tod A. Baker. Copyright © 1986 by Praeger Publishers. Reprinted by permission of Praeger Publishers, a division of Greenwood Press, Inc.)

Table 9: National Party Identification of a Sample
of the Adult Alabama Population, by Race, 1982–1985

	Fall 1982	Fall 1983	Fall 1984	Fall 1985
Percent Republican				
White	21%	24%	37%	33%
Black	2	5	7	11
Percent Democratic				
White	46	41	36	37
Black	86	87	84	73
N	448	441	448	455

Source: University of Alabama, Capstone Poll.
Note: The data are from responses to the question stated in Table 7.

man and asked for an explanation. It was short and to the point: "Hoover," the old man answered.[26]

A backward glance to 1982 helps us summarize the characteristics of Alabama's major political parties. The Democratic victory in George Wallace's last bid for the governorship has been credited to a black-white coalition that drew heavily on rural and labor votes. Republicans competed for the office with a coalition consisting mainly of young, white, more prosperous voters plus many adherents of the new religious right. Lamis reminds us, too, that Republicans are a more compact, ideologically consistent group than Democrats.[27] Union members, black and white, are particularly vital to the welfare of the Democratic party. In 1984 about a third of those who voted in the Democratic presidential primary came from union households.

Adult Alabamians seem to have reasonably accurate perceptions of the Democratic and Republican party policy stances. Capstone Poll surveys have shown, for example, that a majority believe the Democratic party favors the federal government's having the primary responsibility for helping people who are poor, assisting citizens in paying for medical care, protecting the civil rights of minorities, and providing income for people who are retired. In none of these areas did a majority of the respondents say that the Republican party believed the federal government ought to have the principal responsibility for addressing citizen needs. More stress, instead, was placed on the role of state and local governments, and of organizations outside of government.[28]

On the basis of what we have said so far in this chapter, it seems likely that Democrats will, for the foreseeable future, continue to win most of the contests for state and local offices in Alabama. Nevertheless, in the 1986 elections the Republicans held onto their two congressional seats, elected twenty state legislators, and although they lost the U.S. Senate seat they had won in 1980, enjoyed a big win in the governor's race. Figure 8 shows where the winning Republican gubernatorial candidate, Guy Hunt, enjoyed his greatest popularity. Republicans will undoubtedly continue to enjoy such successes. Over the long haul, both parties probably will operate in fairly close harmony with the national parties; and the same kinds of issues that concern Americans generally and that promote or inhibit partisan development nationally will increasingly come to determine the fortunes of political parties in Alabama.

INTEREST GROUPS

Michael Engel has defined interest groups as "organizations of citizens which are formed to promote a particular political interest held in common." "They may exist," Engel observes, "to advance economic interests, promote particular ideologies, provide public information, or pursue a single issue."[29] In contrast to political parties, they do not run candidates for office. Their goal is essentially to influence those actors (including legislators, administrators, and voters) whose decisions are important in the policy-making process. Because their interests sometimes clash, their relationship to one another is frequently antagonistic, with groups who want something opposing those who are reluctant to give it up.

Groups that observers usually describe as the more influential in Alabama include the Farm Bureau, the utilities, the highway interests, the Associated Industries of Alabama (now merged with the state Chamber of Commerce to form the Business Council of Alabama), the Alabama Education Association, organized labor, and the Alabama Democratic Conference (a predominantly black group within the Democratic party). A professional group consisting of plaintiffs' trial lawyers, and a second predominantly black group, the New South Coalition, have also come into prominence recently.[30]

Alabama is usually identified as a state in which political interest groups have a strong influence on public policy.[31] In part this is due to its being a weak-party state in which the parties, including the dominant Democratic party, do not give much direction to politicians in office or mobilize voters in support of the party's positions on issues if, indeed, they take a position at

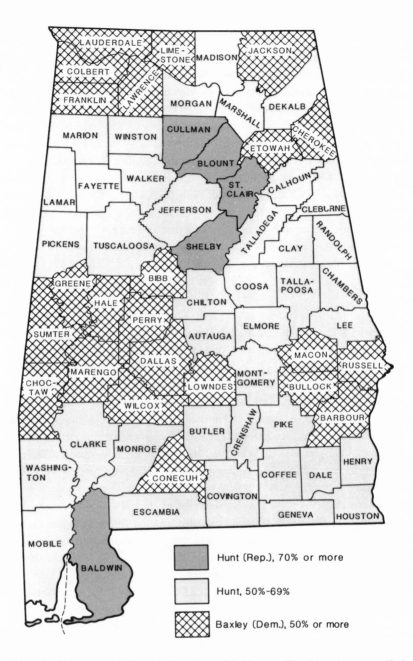

Figure 8. Gubernatorial Election Results, 1986. (*Source:* Election returns supplied by the Office of the Secretary of State, State of Alabama)

all. Alabama shares other conditions associated with states having strong interest groups, including less industrialization and relatively large gaps between the rich and the poor.[32] Further, Harmon Zeigler, the principal developer of state classifications based on interest group strength, notes that "the strong interest group [states] typically do not have complex economies." It is the "absence of complexity" that, he believes, "provides greater opportunities for the exercise of interest group power."[33]

Another characteristic of strong interest group states relates to our discussion, particularly in chapter 6, of the centralization of taxing and spending in Alabama, which is another variable positively associated with strong interest group influence. Zeigler has found that states where interest group influence is not as great as it is in states such as Alabama generally do not have financial systems as centralized as Alabama's. The explanation for the correlation is that interest groups focus on the arena where the money and resources are, which in Alabama is the state government.[34]

The primary instruments of interest group influence in the legislature are the lobbyists. Recently, most of the groups represented by professional lobbyists in Alabama have been trade associations.[35] Thus the Alabama situation conforms to Ziegler's hypothesis that "we should expect that state legislatures are more likely to encounter, especially on a sustained basis, lobbyists for businesses or professional associations" than lobbyists for other kinds of groups.[36] Zeigler found that in "strong lobby states" such as Alabama, 75 percent of the groups classified as powerful are business groups.[37] There are more than twice as many lobbyists as legislators. A recent tally showed that 335 persons had complied with state law and formally identified themselves as lobbyists, compared to 140 senators and representatives.[38]

Due to inadequacies in legislative staffing, a point we have made before but which merits reemphasis, legislators in Alabama depend on lobbyists for much of the information needed for lawmaking. One lobbyist Pool interviewed said that he had

learned fast that as a lobbyist, I am also semi-staff to individual legislators. That puts us in a unique position—one that requires honesty in presenting facts and figures. Our integrity is built on our reputation for giving both sides of an issue and persuading the legislator to our side.[39]

Observers such as Zeigler, though, see "a clear relationship between the extent of professionalism in the legislature and the strength of the groups." The dependency on interest groups, Zeigler points out, "is not necessary when legislators can learn all they need from their own staffs."[40]

Groups establish and maintain their legislative contacts in various ways. The Alabama Dental Association, for example, attempts to gain access to legislators through a legislative contact system in which there are a minimum of two dentists for each senator and representative. The group refers to these members as "contact dentists." Generally, "contact dentists" are selected in consultation with the legislators with whom they are supposed to work.[41] Another professional group, the Alabama Medical Association, can make its presence known through its "physician of the day" program, whereby a doctor is on call throughout the day in case any legislator needs some sort of medical attention.

Another technique that a group may use is that of building coalitions with other organizations. Wayne McMahan, the lobbyist for an association in the health field, for example, stresses the importance of "good rapport with other health organizations." In order to heighten the chances of success in the effort to secure legislative enactment of policies favored by his group, McMahan stresses that there needs to be "a loosely knit coalition involving other health related organizations."[42] Business groups have used the same technique.

A grass-roots campaign designed to sway public opinion and through the public indirectly to influence legislators and other officials involves higher costs than a strictly legislative lobbying effort. Nevertheless, groups frequently use this approach. But if not the general public, then a group may at least seek to persuade its members to write their legislators and urge them to take the group's position on matters coming before the legislature. They may also urge their members to write letters to the editor of their local newspapers, and it may not be left completely to the members' discretion as to what should be said in such letters. Instead, the group leadership may suggest the most appropriate thoughts. Feedback on the letter-writing campaign is provided when blind copies are sent to the association's headquarters. One lobbyist pointed to the effectiveness of this approach: "Not only has the 'homework' been assigned, but someone is going to check it."[43] Group leaders thus assume that individual letters to legislators are beneficial in that it becomes easier to convince these officials that it is not merely the group's designated lobbyist who is asking for help but also rank-and-file members of the group within the legislator's constituency back home.[44] If the group or coalition is affluent enough, it can also air TV and radio commercials, run newspaper advertisements, and issue press releases. These kinds of techniques were used in 1983, for example, in connection with a bill that would have required major oil companies to divest themselves of the service stations they operated directly in Alabama. The legislation was defeated.

Outside the legislative arena, groups have additional strategies they may employ to achieve organizational objectives. Most noticeably, they may work in political campaigns. The state education association, for example, has recently supplied a great deal of labor for political campaigns in Alabama, from state legislative elections on up through the presidential election. In 1984 the Alabama Education Association—like its parent, the National Education Association—strongly endorsed Walter Mondale for president and operated telephone banks with the (unfulfilled) hope of getting out a large Mondale vote.

As in other parts of the nation, the organizations' political action committees (PACs) have become important participants in election campaigns in Alabama. PACs were active in the 1982 state elections on an unprecedented scale, and there is no sign of a decrease in their use.[45] The primary impact of PACs is felt in campaign finance. A 1982 survey showed that the biggest spenders in the governor's and lieutenant governor's races were building contractors, trial lawyers, agribusiness people, physicians, labor union representatives, and nursing home administrators. In all, twenty-eight PACs reported that they had donated $5,000 or more to candidates contending for the state's two top offices. Candidate support can take other forms, of course, than campaign contributions. In the 1984 Democratic presidential primary the Alabama Labor Council, like the Alabama Education Association, used many telephone lines to call union members with the message that they should support Walter Mondale.[46] This effort continued, though much less successfully, in the general election campaign, when most union members apparently supported President Reagan.

An example of a locally based, election-oriented group is Birmingham's Citizens Coalition, led by Mayor Richard Arrington, the city's first black mayor. This group endorses and provides campaign workers for candidates in city through national races. In 1984 the Citizens Coalition endorsed Walter Mondale over Rev. Jesse Jackson in the presidential primary. The Coalition took major credit for Mondale's 59 to 37 percent win over Jackson in the Birmingham area, even as Jackson was winning over Mondale in the Black Belt and Mobile.[47]

Groups usually identified as "moral issue groups" have become a factor in Alabama politics. Religious groups have, of course, been active in Alabama politics for many years. Both chapter 1 and chapter 11 refer to struggles over the legalization of alcoholic beverage sales, for example, in which coalitions of church congregations and individual church members have been central participants. The new religious right, though, has made its appearance in Alabama just as it has in the rest of the nation. Groups of religious conservatives were initially most conspicuous in the 1980 congressional primary battle between Birmingham's incumbent Republican U.S. representative John Buchanan and Albert Lee Smith, who had the support of the Alabama affiliate of the Moral Majority. Smith won but was defeated for reelection two years later. The rising volume of appeals to authorize prayer in the public schools and to purge "secular humanism" from textbooks provides further evidence of the increasing visibility of the new religious right in Alabama politics. The Eagle Forum, for example, has been active in struggles related to textbook content and at one time had several of its members serving on the state Textbook Selection Committee.[48]

CHAPTER NINE

Campaigns
and
Elections

To many people there is nothing more exciting than a hotly contested election campaign. Behind the excitement and drama, however, there are formal and informal rules that condition the terms of the contest. This is the subject we now take up.

VOTING

The individual's part in the political process mostly involves voting. Traditionally the states had the predominant role in deciding who could vote, but primarily as a reaction to racial discrimination in the southern states, the national government has assumed many constitutional and statutory guarantees of the right to vote. Under the U.S. Constitution, states are forbidden to deprive anyone of the ballot on account of race, sex, failure to pay a poll tax, or age (provided the prospective voter is at least eighteen). The principal statutory guarantees are contained in the 1965 Voting Rights Act, which we will examine later in the chapter.

In order to vote in Alabama, a person must first register with his or her county board of registrars.[1] Except for a few groups who can register by mail (members of the military and college students, for example), people interested in voting must go in person to register, and the boards of registrars hold frequent meetings to register new voters. In fact, voter registration is now practically continuous. To make registration more convenient, new voters are registered at high schools, college and university campuses, shopping centers, and other such places, in addition to the county courthouse. People who are legal residents of the area in which they wish to vote (without any specified prior period of residence), at least eighteen years of age, and United States citizens should experience little difficulty in registering.

Alabama's voting qualifications were formerly much more proscriptive than they are now, but relatively recent actions taken by the federal government have liberalized these requirements considerably. Such actions include passage of the Twenty-fourth and Twenty-sixth amendments to the U.S. Constitution, the Voting Rights Act of 1965, and judicial decisions that, for example, invalidated the requirement of a year's prior residence in the state and shorter periods in the county and election district before a person could register and that curtailed the long list of crimes that disqualified people from voting.[2] Perhaps because of the feeling that it would be a waste of effort to protest, but also because of the significance to white politicians of a growing black electorate, a marked change in attitude on the part of many public officials regarding black voting has occurred along with these federal actions. Blacks today do not have the difficulty in registering that they once had.

Until the Twenty-fourth Amendment and judicial decisions forbade the use of poll taxes, because they were part of a network of measures designed to disfranchise blacks, Alabama required payment of poll taxes by prospective voters. As originally adopted in the constitution of 1901, the poll tax provision was notoriously burdensome. It was only $1.50 a year, but payment was required months before any election, and liability for payment of the tax extended, on a cumulative basis, to each year of a person's life between the ages of twenty-one and forty-five. Before being scrapped altogether because of federal initiatives in this area, Alabamians themselves liberalized the poll tax considerably through constitutional amendments (such as those providing exemptions for veterans), and in its final form included liability for payment of the tax for only the two years preceding the election in which a person would begin to vote. Because liability ended after age forty-five, this meant that people over the age of forty-seven were no longer subject to the poll tax requirement. Many Alabamians then sought to register as voters.

As a result of the adoption of the Twenty-fourth Amendment to the U.S. Constitution, the use of a poll tax was invalidated in elections for federal officers. For a time, the state retained its poll tax as a qualification for voting in state elections. This was discontinued, however, following decisions by the federal courts in 1966 that such a practice was a violation of the U.S. Constitution.[3]

The poll tax was not, in fact, the primary disfranchising tactic it is frequently thought to have been. Other discriminatory devices were much more effective instruments of white supremacy. Prominent among these devices were constitutional amendments adopted in 1946 and 1951. Basically, the 1946 amendment added an understanding requirement to the 1901 literacy test, under which voters had to "read and write any article of the Constitution of the United States in the English Language," while dropping a property-owning alternative. Finding that the amendment was racially discriminatory (it was adopted shortly after the demise of the "white primary," in which only white voters could participate), a federal court invalidated it in 1949 as a violation of the Fifteenth Amendment.

The amendment adopted in 1951 was essentially a refinement of the earlier amendment. It contained the requirements that voters must be able to read and write in the English language any article of the U.S. Constitution, must have good character, and must embrace the duties and obligations of citizenship under both the U.S. Constitution and the Constitution of Alabama.[4] Further, the prospective voter had to complete a written questionnaire that was supposed to supply the information on which the registrars might make a decision regarding the person's eligibility to vote. The board, however, had virtually unlimited discretion as to whether an individual met the qualifications and should be registered. This feature of the registration system obviously enabled it to be administered in a discriminatory fashion, and it often was. Registration practices varied widely within the state, but in those days few blacks were permitted to register as voters. It was estimated in 1955, for example, that the number of black registrants was only about 55,000 out of a total black population that approached a million.

Although the 1951 amendment was later repealed, registration officials continued to use the questionnaire until the mid-1960s. At that time the Voting Rights Act of 1965 suspended all such requirements in states or political subdivisions in which less than 50 percent of the voting-age population was registered to vote in November 1964 or did not actually vote in the Goldwater-Johnson presidential election, and which required literacy, understanding, or good-character tests as voting prerequisites. Federal examiners could be used to register otherwise qualified voters if local registration officials showed a reluctance to do so. When the Voting Rights Act was applied to Alabama, federal examiners were appointed for some counties, and the use of questionnaires and supplementary literacy requirements was discontinued throughout the state. Congress has extended the act from time to time, and even today Alabama remains under its provisions. Currently the main requirement is that changes in the state's election laws be approved by federal authorities (usually the Department of Justice) before the legislation can become effective. Approval is withheld if the changes would have a racially discriminatory effect.

Following the elimination of the poll tax, the voter qualification questionnaire, and the durational residence requirements, the voters' rolls increased substantially, with much of the increase among black registrants. In 1964, for instance, only 19.4 percent of black Alabamians eligible to vote by age and residence were registered as voters. In 1966, after the Voting Rights Act had been in effect for only one year, the estimated proportion of Alabama blacks registered had risen to 51.5 percent.[5] The number of white registrants, however, also rose in the years following passage of the Voting Rights Act, probably in large part as a reaction against increased black political activism.

THE MECHANICS OF ELECTIONS

The voters usually fill elective offices from the candidates presented by the parties listed on the general election ballot. Thus nomination by a political party is normally required for a person to run in the general election, although there are, as we shall see, other procedures that may be used to vote for individuals who have not received a party nomination.

Nomination by direct primary is the most common method nationally, and Alabama has used the primary for many years. Indeed, in the past, winning the Democratic primary in this and other southern states was usually described as being "tantamount" to election. That is to say, the nominees in the Democratic primary were certain to take office; given the minority status of the Republican party, the general election was simply a formality.

Until the mid-1970s, Alabama primary elections to nominate candidates for public office were held in May. Since Democrats were certain to win most public offices, this meant that about eight months elapsed between the time a candidate "won" an office and the time the office was actually occupied. In more recent years, as interparty competition grew somewhat more intense, the feeling developed that campaigns were too long. Many candidates would announce in January of the election year, and probably before then informally, and this ensured a campaign spanning nearly an entire year in cases in which there was general election competition. To deal with the problem, the state experimented during the period 1978–1984 with September primaries. In time, though, two things were found to be wrong with that schedule. First, some politicians argued that it left too little time to settle charges of irregularities in contested elections. Second, and probably more important, Democrats began to feel that there was now too little time for them to heal their wounds and unite against the Republicans when there was serious opposition in the general election. Whether for these reasons or not, in 1985 the Democratic legislature moved the primary date to June.

The traditional runoff feature of Alabama primaries is still used. If no candidate receives a majority of the votes cast for an office in the first primary, a runoff primary is held three weeks later between the top two candidates. Recently, however, the practice of using runoffs has come under increasing criticism, particularly from blacks, many of whom believe that the majority-vote requirement decreases opportunities for blacks to be elected when the typically larger group of white voters coalesces behind white candidates in runoff contests.

Alabama's presidential primary, a means by which party members may indicate their preferred candidate for president as they choose delegates to the national nominating conventions, is held on the second Tuesday in March of presidential election years. The state held its first preferential primary in 1980. The 1984 primary received a substantial amount of national attention when former vice-president Walter Mondale's victory in the primary enabled him to overcome a challenge from Senator Gary Hart, who had beaten him in four primary contests in the preceding three weeks. Also, Senator John Glenn withdrew from the presidential race when he fared poorly in the Alabama primary.

In recent years, Alabama Democratic party rules have held that only individuals "who have been Democrats for at least 14 days in advance of the primary, who are qualified electors in this state, who believe in the principles of the Democratic Party and who . . . pledge to abide by the results" of the primary and "to aid and support all the nominees thereof in the ensuing general election" are eligible to participate in the primary.[6] But these rules have had only a minimal impact, since voters in Alabama are not required to register their party affiliation, and only the official lists of qualified voters (not designated by party) are used to identify the people seeking to vote in primary elections. Usually any person whose name appears on the official list of voters is allowed to cast a ballot in the Democratic primary. Thus it operates (in effect, if not in design) as an open primary, or one in which anyone may vote, regardless of party affiliation.

That Alabamians seem to confuse the Democratic primary with the general election simply reflects a fact of political life in Alabama. Since for years it has been "tantamount" to that, participation by voters of all persuasions created few problems. By 1978, however, Republican strength had grown to the point that Democratic party officials began to perceive Republican participation in the Democratic primary as a factor that could possibly influence the result in an undesired way. In 1979 they therefore adopted a rule to the effect that no one who had voted in the Republican first primary could vote in the Democratic runoff primary. It was this rule that was at issue in the Baxley-Graddick election dispute of 1986. Graddick's failure to enforce it led the Democratic party committee to rescind his electoral victory and give the gubernatorial nomination to Lieutenant Governor Baxley.

Alabama Republicans, a smaller group, do not attempt to achieve exclusiveness in Republican primaries by the use of a test of allegiance, and they have opposed the statement that by law must appear at the bottom of both primary ballots, which reads: "By casting this ballot I do pledge myself to abide by the results of this primary and to aid and support all the nominees thereof in the ensuing general election."[7] The Republican party once labeled the loyalty oath "discriminatory, unconstitutional, and unenforceable."[8] The last criticism is the most valid. The oath is clearly unenforceable, given the secret ballot.

So far most of our discussion has related to state and county elections, but municipal officials must also be elected to staff the city governments. Municipal elections are held under statutory provisions similar to those regulating general elections but with the important exceptions that usually they are nonpartisan, they are held at different times, and they are administered by municipal officers. Most municipal elections are held in July of the year in which the president of the United States is elected, which is an "off year" with respect to the election of most state officers. Alabama also requires a majority vote to elect a municipal officer, so runoff elections may be held after the regular election. As a general rule, new municipal officials take office in October.

As noted earlier, political parties usually nominate in their primaries the candidates who have ballot position in the general election, but provision exists for nominations by mass meetings, for independents, and for write-in votes. Prospective independent candidates, whether for state, district, or county office, must file petitions signed by at least 1 percent of the registered voters in the area concerned. Except in municipal elections, voters wanting to cast a vote for a person who has not been officially nominated are permitted to do so. Where paper ballots are used, the voter may write the person's name in the blank column included on the ballot. Voting machines contain a supply of paper that may be used for write-in votes. The election of write-in candidates, though, even in county and district elections, is extremely rare.

New political parties may be formed to offer candidates for public office if these groups meet certain requirements. In order to be eligible for ballot position, such groups need to give evidence through petitions filed with the secretary of state that they have at least 5,000 members. In order to retain ballot position, parties must regularly nominate candidates. If a party skips two or more consecutive general election contests for state offices, it is required to file new petitions. Rules like these, which are fairly common in the states, make it difficult, of course, for minor parties to challenge the well-established Democratic and Republican parties.

CAMPAIGNS

Getting on the ballot, however, is only part of the story; candidates must still campaign to win the election for the position they are seeking. Political campaigns in Alabama have traditionally been among the most colorful in the country. In what was until recently a mostly rural society, people looked to politics not only to fill public offices but also for entertainment.

One of the most attention-getting campaigners was James E. "Big Jim" or "Kissin' Jim" Folsom, who was governor from 1947 to 1951 and from 1955 to 1959. Folsom's belief was that, "People enjoy their politics in Alabama," and his campaigns over a period of two decades were based on this assumption.[9] The reaction of *Life* magazine to Folsom's style of campaigning was that apparently "American vaudeville never died," it "merely went into politics."[10]

One of Folsom's innovations was bringing music to Alabama gubernatorial campaigns. In his first successful race, in 1946, Folsom toured the state's rural hamlets with a "string band" he called the "Strawberry Pickers." The name was related to Folsom's home county, Cullman, which was known at that time for its production of strawberries. A newswriter in 1970 credited—or charged—Folsom with "introducing the frivolity of the country music band in the serious world of politics."[11] For at least the next quarter century, the policy of attracting crowds with country and western music was an integral part of virtually all successful Alabama gubernatorial campaigns. In his 1954 race for a second term, Folsom used the song "Y'all Come" as his campaign song. In his last major campaign, in 1962, Folsom called his band the "Meat Grinders," so labeled because of Folsom's pledge to "bring up the ham [state funds] and save the gravy [the good things of life] for you."[12]

Folsom also used campaign props to attract attention. In his 1946 race the principal artifacts were an "old cornshuck mop and [an] old sudsbucket."[13] He solicited campaign contributions by passing the "sudsbucket," exhorting, "You folks furnish the suds and Old Big Jim'll do the mopping."[14] By mopping, Folsom meant that he would rid the state capitol of the "Big Mules"—usually identified as large industries and utilities—which, he argued, were wielding excessive power in state politics. During his campaigns Folsom spoke at length about four times every day except Sunday, and in his speeches he attacked the most powerful of the mass media of his day, the daily newspapers, which he labeled collectively as "them lyin' daily newspapers."[15]

Other candidates relied on other kinds of campaign gimmickry. For example, John Patterson (1959–63) used a color comic book telling of his life and accomplishments, and it attracted considerable voter interest. At times candidates organized motorcades to tour the state with them to demonstrate the depth of their support. George Wallace was best known, of course, for the flamboyance of his oratory, particularly for his denunciations of "carpetbaggin', scalawaggin', integratin' " federal judges.[16] Until 1986, debates between the candidates were not a part of gubernatorial campaigns in Alabama, although in recent years the candidates have appeared in the same forums, and the state's public television network has organized interview and call-in programs in which the candidates appear in close succession. Debates have occurred from time to time between candidates for other offices.

In the absence of strong political parties, candidates must themselves construct the organizations with which they hope to forge electoral success. Journalist Neil Davis reported that in Folsom's first successful campaign he "had no county campaign committees or campaign chairmen."[17] He did have these in subsequent races, however, and observers often tell us that George Wallace learned about the construction of campaign organizations when he served as south Alabama manager for Folsom in the latter's 1954 campaign. In the case of statewide candidates, organizations would be composed of politically active people from throughout the state who offered their support on the basis of their personal motives.[18] For Wallace, and for a few other candidates as well, these organizations continued in existence from election to election. According to Donald Strong, the Wallace organization was more highly structured than most, however, with a chief coordinator in each county. The leaders of the Wallace organization met not only during election campaigns but also when mutual concerns arose after the election.

Nowadays the mass media, especially television in the case of statewide candidates, play more important roles than cornshuck mops and sudsbuckets. Of course, the mass media play very important roles in political campaigns today in every state. However, Margaret Latimer argues persuasively that the media, like the candidates' personal organizations, are likely to be especially important in states like Alabama where the role of political parties is weak.[19] As would be expected, Latimer found that well-known officeholders like George Wallace, with their high levels of name recognition and solid organizations, were less dependent on the media than unfamiliar, nonincumbent candidates. Latimer discovered that in the Alabama legislative districts she studied (those outside the largest metropolitan areas), state Senate aspirants in contested races in 1982 paid out an average of about $4,000 in mass-media expenses, amounting to approximately 40 percent of their total expenses.[20] State legislative candidates made greater use of newspapers and radio than they did television because almost any television station's signal would go into many districts and thus would not be cost efficient.[21] In contrast, radio stations today generally have formats that appeal to smaller and more sharply defined audiences. Thus in 1982 the Wallace campaign prepared special commercials that aired only on radio outlets oriented mainly toward black listeners. For most candidates, radio's main impact is apparently to boost name recognition, not to convey specific information about the candidate.[22]

Latimer's study also showed that many candidates were fairly serious about reaching the voters in their campaigns for office. Fourteen professional in-state and possibly as many as four out-of-state campaign consulting firms operated in Alabama during the 1982 elections. The activity of these firms was not confined to statewide contests but included local legislative races as well.[23]

The principal conclusion of the Latimer study was that effective spending on the media along with the use of advice from professional political consultants rivaled incumbency as variables positively associated with candidate success. One important illustration of how influential the combined use of media and professional campaign organizations can be in a state election came in 1978, when virtual political unknown Fob James was elected governor. James relied heavily on a mass-media campaign directed by an out-of-state consulting firm. In substate elections Latimer found media impact in Alabama to be inversely correlated with population density and education and income levels.[24]

VOTER PARTICIPATION

Election outcomes in Alabama are determined by an electorate (the people eligible to vote) that is in large measure a product of the Voting Rights Act of 1965. This federal law has been described by social scientists as well as politicians as one of the most effective pieces of legislation ever enacted by Congress. The effectiveness of the act in Alabama can be shown not only by the increase in registration among blacks mentioned above but also by their subsequent election to important political positions: county and city offices, legislative seats, and judgeships (including a position as a justice of the state Supreme Court). At the same time, the number of blacks in both appointive and classified civil service positions in state and local government also has risen substantially.

In sharp contrast with the time when the Alabama electorate was almost lily white, Cohen, Cotter, and Coulter found that in 1981 there was "little racial difference in participation."[25] Their findings were supported by Alabama's experience in 1984, when virtually the same percentages of registered blacks and whites voted in the presidential election (61.6 percent and 61.3 percent, respectively).[26] As these writers put it, what the parity in black-white turnout meant was that "a revolution in southern black political behavior ha[d] occurred over the past two decades."[27] Victims of discriminatory voting practices for years, blacks were apparently now voting at the same rate as white Alabamians.

Overall voter turnout in Alabama, however, is not very high. In the period 1974–1980, according to the findings of one study, the mean percentage of the Alabama voting-age population actually going to the polls in major federal and state elections (presidential, congressional, and gubernatorial) was 33.6 percent. This percentage was higher only than that of Georgia, with 30.9 percent. In presidential elections in this period the mean percentage was 47.4. The percentage of the voting-age population nationally that participated in the 1976 presidential election was 54.4; in 1980, 52.6. Thus Alabama's participation rates are lower but do not differ drastically from national norms in presidential elections. In gubernatorial elections, however, the mean percentage of 27.0 was found to be higher than that of only two other states (Texas and Georgia). For U.S. senator and representative, the mean Alabama turnout for 1974–1980 was 30.1 percent, higher than only Louisiana and Georgia.[28] Table 10 presents responses of white and black voters themselves (rather than analyses of election statistics) when asked about the frequency with which they have participated in the major types of elections. As is common, voters tend to recall balloting in

Table 10: Degree of Participation in Elections by
a Sample of the Alabama Population, 1981

	All	Most	Some	None	Total	N
	Proportion of Elections *in Which Respondent Voted*					
Whites						
Presidential elections	51%	24%	14%	11%	100%	423
General election for governor	45	27	14	14	100	422
Primary election for governor	38	28	16	17	99	420
Local elections	35	30	17	18	100	422
Blacks						
Presidential elections	50	20	24	6	100	98
General election for governor	34	21	33	12	100	98
Primary election for governor	36	15	30	19	100	96
Local elections	35	16	26	22	99	99

Source: University of Alabama, Capstone Poll.
Note: The data are from responses to the question ''Would you say that you have voted in all, most, some, or none of the following types of elections since you have been old enough to vote?''

more elections than election returns indicate. It is interesting to note, however, that white and black survey data show their participation rates to be about the same for many types of elections.

One factor that determines the size of the electorate, of course, is the size of the voting-age population. In 1981 Alabama's total voting-age population was estimated at 2,812,000. Of this number, 644,000 (or 22.9 percent) were estimated to be black. The black percentage of the Alabama voting-age population was fifth highest in the nation, behind four other southern states—Mississippi (31.0), South Carolina (27.3), Louisiana (26.6), and Georgia (24.3).[29] In midyear 1984, Alabama was reported as having 2,268,515 registered voters. Of this total, 1,757,870 were identified as whites and 510,645 as blacks.[30]

CAMPAIGN FINANCE REGULATION

Like other states, Alabama has laws that regulate the use of money in political campaigns. Alabama's principal legislation governing the disclosure of campaign contributions was enacted in the 1920s. The law is officially known as the Corrupt Practices Act. Although a Democratic party rule does require such reports, the law does not require the revelation of sources of campaign funds before an election. Instead, it calls for candidates to file their disclosure statements "within 15 days after a primary election and within 30 days after any other election."[31] Funds received before official qualification as a candidate are exempt from the reporting requirement. Qualification must be made at least sixty days before the first primary. Obviously, serious candidates would accumulate substantial funds long before qualification, when the voting would be scarcely two months off.

Candidates for state and local offices file reports with the Secretary of State's Office on their sources of campaign funds and objects of expenditure. Latimer, who examined these reports, found that they varied "from clear and exact to vague and confused."[32] It is common knowledge that the state's campaign finance legislation is inadequate. The statutory requirement, for example, that expense reports be filed after the election means that voters may not be able to base their candidate choices on the sources of financial support for particular aspirants. We have not, however, detected a great deal of sentiment for change in the state's campaign finance legislation. For this reason, comprehensive reform seems to us a difficult goal to accomplish, at least in the near term.

CHAPTER TEN

State-Local
Relations

From the beginning the American states have established subunits to perform governmental functions in local communities. In Alabama the most important local governments are those for counties and municipalities. Under the system that prevails in Alabama, the legislature, unless it is limited by the constitution, has complete authority over the local governments. There are, though, many ways in which the framers of Alabama's constitution sought to control the legislature's power to regulate the counties and municipalities. Debt and property tax limitations are obvious illustrations of these restrictions. Changes in county boundaries are subject to several limitations, including the requirement of a two-thirds vote in the legislature. Section 104 of the constitution, for another example, forbids the legislature to incorporate cities and towns or to change their charters by local legislation, that is, legislation affecting named local communities. In practice, though, the legislature has generally applied its authority over the local governments through legislation having specific local effect, and much of this legislation concerned municipalities, despite the constitutional language just mentioned.[1]

The state-local relationship in force in Alabama is founded on the legal doctrine known as Dillon's Rule. According to this doctrine, local communities have no right to govern themselves; they have only those powers that they receive from the state, and these powers are strictly construed by the courts.[2] It is important to recognize that the legislature has granted a significant measure of authority to local governments, especially to municipalities. Nevertheless, the dominant legislative policy is one of close supervision over local governments and over their power to manage local affairs.[3]

Although a decision of the Alabama Supreme Court has restricted the legislature's power to enact laws having specific local application, its members have continued to display an interest in the details of local governmental policy.[4]

In their general relations with local governments, Alabama's state legislators have been relatively generous. But even in this context they sometimes show their overriding concern with the details of local policy. The Lid Bill, adopted in 1978 as a constitutional amendment, is a good illustration of state legislative interest in the way the local governments use their powers. Among many other provisions that regulate property taxation, this legislation authorizes local governments to make certain increases in their property tax rates. This seemingly generous grant of authority is checked, however, by other provisions, including the stipulation that no increase may become effective unless it is approved by an act of the legislature.

HOME RULE

As an alternative to the practice of close legislative supervision, those who study state-local relations in the United States often advocate the devolution of substantial powers of self-government (or "home rule") on local governing authorities. For example, the Committee for Economic Development (a national business-oriented organization) has recommended the adoption of home rule as a means of strengthening subnational government in the United States. It describes the advantages of home rule as follows:

> It would strengthen state governments by freeing legislatures from a multitude of special local bills and the accompanying log-rolling. It would eliminate the one-man rule which exists when a single legislator from a county can, in practice, veto the decisions of a multi-member county board—as in Maryland, South Carolina, and many other states. And it would prevent local officials from evading responsibility by blaming the legislature.[5]

Most states have granted some measure of autonomy to their local governments, more commonly to cities than to counties.[6] Interest in home rule arose in Alabama in association with the movement for constitutional revision in the 1970s. Reflecting this interest, the Alabama Constitutional Commission proposed the extension of home rule to the state's cities and counties.[7] The commission's recommendation was much like the procedure suggested by the Committee for Economic Development: the state would grant broad powers of home rule only to localities that had reorganized their governmental structures. According to the commission's proposals, the restructuring of local governments could be accomplished either under optional plans prescribed by the legislature or by the adoption of home-rule charters through local proceedings. It was the commission's opinion that few of Alabama's local governments would adopt a home-rule charter; most, if they made any change at all, would accomplish the increase in their local powers through the adoption of a plan of government prescribed by the legislature. The commission's suggestions, however, did not receive a warm welcome in the real world of Alabama politics.

The new constitution Governor James proposed to the legislature in 1979 was based largely on the document produced by the Constitutional Commission.[8] As introduced into the legislature, however, the proposed constitution made no provision for the local adoption of municipal charters, an omission that apparently reflected the municipalities' satisfaction with their authority and the existing procedures. While the necessity of frequently turning to the legislature for permission to do some rather trifling things may at times be frustrating, the absence of home rule does allow local officials to deflect citizen complaints about local services with the response that the community government is not empowered to do whatever the citizen wishes to see done. For whatever reason, devolution of power had so little support in the legislature that it eventually deleted James's constitutional language providing for the local adoption of county home-rule charters.[9]

Despite the interest in enlarging the powers of local self-government that is expressed from time to time, the proposal's fate in 1979 raised considerable doubt about the prospects for home rule, at least in the near term. Probably because of the limited interest by that time in home rule, the proposed 1983 constitution simply authorized optional forms of county and municipal government. Home rule is thus an alternative that has been proposed for Alabama but never adopted.

STATE-LOCAL LEGISLATIVE RELATIONS

Alabama's legislature has traditionally regulated the local governments through laws having specific local effect. In contrast to general legislation, local legislation does not apply to the entire state or to an entire class of persons or things within the state; it deals with specific political subdivisions. This kind of legislation can be a useful means of accommodating local needs that require special consideration.[10] Through local legislation the legislature can, for example, give needed authority to local governments that have special problems not common to the rest of the state.

During the latter half of the nineteenth century, Alabamians discovered, however, that local legislation was not an unmitigated blessing. As Professor Hallie Farmer noted, the ability to pass this kind of legislation gave members of the General Assembly opportunities to intervene strongly in local affairs. Besides, the pressure of local demands could distract the legislators' attention from problems of general concern to the state. Consequently, the framers of the constitutions of 1861 and 1875 sought to limit the power of the legislature to enact local legislation. Indeed, the framers of the 1875 constitution seem to have thought that they had ended the abuse of special legislation, whether applicable to localities or to private interests. In reality, though, their efforts were not as definitive as they had imagined. Farmer points out that only a few years after the 1875 document was adopted, "a decision of the Supreme Court of Alabama effectually destroyed the provisions so carefully written into the Constitution."[11] In this decision, the court announced virtually a hands-off policy as far as the legislature and its passage of special legislation were concerned. Consequently, Farmer continues, "the constitutional provisions relating to local and private legislation became ineffective, and there was practically no restraint on the passage of such legislation."[12]

Because of the large volume of special legislation subsequently enacted in the latter part of the nineteenth century, the framers of the 1901 constitution went to great lengths to control the passage of local and private legislation. A prime example of such a provision is Section 104 of the Alabama Constitution. It lists a number of specific subjects on which the legislature may not enact special legislation. Section 105 is another example. This section says that no local or special law may be enacted in any case provided for by general law or when the necessary relief can be obtained from the courts. Section 106 bans the passage of any permissible special legislation unless notice of the intention to introduce the bill (along with the substance of the proposed measure) has first been advertised in the county concerned.

Again, however, the courts construed the provisions regarding local legislation so liberally that they were practically read out of the constitution. The effect of Section 105, for example, was reduced through judicial approval of local laws that had some differences from general laws on the same subject. More important, Alabama's courts described the concept of general legislation in such a way as to permit the passage of laws applicable to particular local governments when the legislation involved the principle of classification. Almost all of them were population classifications and were so narrow in practice as to apply only to a single city or county. This kind of measure, which obviously violated the spirit of constitutional rules on the subject, was euphemistically known as a "general bill with local application." It was clearly a local law, but the legislator introduced it as if it were a general law in an effort to evade such constitutional limitations on local legislation as the list of prohibited subjects or the publication requirement, for example.

Despite criticism of the practice, the body of general legislation with local application was for years a major part of the legislative product. In 1978, however, the state Supreme Court reversed its stand and announced a new policy of strict adherence to the constitutional limits on local legislation. With respect to general bills of local application, the court put it plainly: "A population classification cannot be utilized in the future to avoid the definition of a local act." As to any legislation having specific local effect, the court continued, "Henceforth when at its enactment legislation is local in its application it will be a local act and subject to all of the constitutional qualifications applicable to it."[13]

The Court's new policy reduced the volume of local legislation markedly and virtually eliminated "general bills of local application." As one result of the decision, the legislature must now deal with cities under a more substantial system of population classifications. The legislature continues, however, to regulate county affairs through the enactment of local legislation. Indeed, much of the legislative product still consists of these local laws. May a local official employ additional personnel or receive an expense allowance? In numerous instances of this sort, not to mention such important actions as levying new taxes, for example, local legislation provides the necessary authorization.

To understand local-legislative relations in Alabama, one must understand that local legislation is treated differently from other measures.[14] As Farmer states, "In theory such legislation is handled like any other. . . . In practice the process by which a local or private bill becomes law is far different."[15] To put it briefly, the legislature treats local bills having the unanimous support of the local legislative delegation under a form of "legislative courtesy" that virtually guarantees their passage as a matter of course. This affects legislative decision making in several ways. In all probability, for example, it contributes greatly to the high percentage of bills reported favorably by committees. But, as Farmer points out, this approach to local legislation has implications for individual legislators as well:

The legislator, willingly or otherwise, becomes the arbiter of the affairs of his county. At the worst he may emerge as a petty tyrant, with no recourse open to his constituents before the next quadrennial election. At best he is pulled and hauled between local political factions, forced to give more time and attention to local affairs than he can possibly give to the State as a whole; for advancement of local interests must be his major political concern if he wishes to remain in the Legislature. Local legislation, furthermore, frequently becomes the issue for quarrels between senators and representatives which impair the full measure of their cooperation.[16]

Local legislation is not inherently wrong. As a report by the Brookings Institution stated, "Local legislation within reasonable limits is necessary and proper; and it should not be wholly prohibited by the Constitution. It is quite true that conditions and requirements of the different counties are not alike."[17] Farmer identified the problem as being one of excessive local legislation, a problem that was, she thought, of "pressing importance in Alabama," and one easy to identify but difficult to resolve.[18]

In a sense, Alabama does have a form of home rule, since the legislature enacts virtually any local legislation that the local delegations support. Obviously, however, this is not home rule as described in the textbooks and advocated by those who want to grant more authority to local governments.

LOCAL POLITICAL INFLUENCE

Alabama's traditional political culture has not supported as much grass-roots citizen participation as may be characteristic of other states.[19] The South generally has not seen the establishment, for example, of such devices as the New England town meeting. There has been a substantial centralization of authority in the state, and thus Dillon's Rule has been quite compatible with the cultural and political traditions of Alabama. The tradition has been one of deference to legal authority, coupled with a distrust of the consequences of democracy, particularly in the sense that such consequences could have jeopardized existing patterns of race relations. Nevertheless, localities are not mere passive participants in state politics.

Alabama municipal elections are mainly nonpartisan contests. However, most local officials in the state—municipal as well as county officials—are publicly identifiable as Democrats. This provides a possible source of local political influence, but partisanship does not seem to have a great impact on intergovernmental relations in Alabama. If there were a genuine two-party system, party ties might make a greater difference. As things stand now, though, party is no more important in state intergovernmental relations than it is in the overwhelmingly Democratic state legislature. The Democratic party has traditionally been a broad umbrella organization covering many diverse factions. It has not provided a basis in Alabama for teamwork in state intergovernmental relations (or in many other policy-making contexts, for that matter).

Local governments do maintain, however, active lobbying associations to press for favorable consideration of their interests by state legislators and administrators. In Alabama the two principal groups of local officials are the League of Municipalities and the Association of County Commissions. There are additional specialized subgroups of officials within, or paralleling, these broad associations—for example, probate judges, sheriffs, city clerks, revenue officers, planners, and city managers. These groups also participate in the affairs of their national associations (such as the National League of Cities, the U.S. Conference of Mayors, the International City Management Association, and the National Association of Counties), and they maintain active contacts with Alabama's congressional delegation, hoping to secure favorable federal policies.

The local governmental organizations have political clout. For example, when the Alabama Constitutional Commission's report was being debated in the legislature in 1973, the League of Municipalities was able to get the judicial article amended to provide for the continuation of municipal courts with some independence from the new district court system.[20] Municipal officials probably could have blocked legislative passage of the entire article if its advocates had not been willing to compromise.

In addition to lobbying, the municipal and county associations provide considerable technical assistance to member governments—for example, in the administration of workers' compensation programs—which augments their managerial capabilities. These associations also encourage cooperation among localities to achieve particular administrative or political objectives. Both the League of Municipalities and the Association of County Commissions, for example, regularly formulate legislative programs that they seek to have accepted by the legislature. Interestingly, George Wallace, while a member of the Alabama House, was at one time in effect a legislative floor leader for the League of Municipalities.

Local officials often lose, however, in their encounters with state officials. Adoption of the Lid Bill and other measures that eroded the property tax base, for example, attests to that. State-local relationships in Alabama, then, have developed along the lines suggested by Frederick M. Wirt, who has observed that "The world of urban decision [is] penetrated by centralizing forces which shape local policy agendas, set the rules of local policy making and implementation, and effectively dominate the policy outcomes for citizens. The result is the transfer of decisional space to outsiders."[21]

Our discussion so far has concentrated on the amount of "decisional space" that the legislature allows to local governments or that they are able to assert through their political influence in the legislature. Thomas A. Henderson and F. Glenn Abney, however, suggest that "increasingly the state bureaucracy has replaced the legislature as the center of control" in state-local relations.[22] Charles Adrian agrees, noting that the exceedingly complex character of government in America has meant that state legislators have been "somewhat reluctantly but inexorably forced to transfer increasing amounts of supervision over local government to the professional bureaucracies of the administrative branch of the government."[23] Observations like these reflect the significance of bureaucratic relationships in modern systems of government. To give due consideration to this dimension of our subject, we turn at this point to an examination of state-local administrative interaction in Alabama.

STATE-LOCAL ADMINISTRATIVE RELATIONS

There are at least seven major types of administrative contacts occurring between the state and the local governments. These are (1) state review of locally administered programs, (2) state services for localities to upgrade their administrative capabilities, (3) state regulation, (4) state substitute administration, (5) state mandates, (6) state grants, and (7) state coordination of state-local administrative contacts.[24]

One example of the first area of contact, state review, is that in Alabama the local tax officials' property tax assessments are reviewed by the Revenue Department.[25] The commissioner of the department is supposed to check the work of local tax officials and attest to the accuracy of the tax assessment books. The Revenue Department has been under federal court order in recent years to supervise a statewide property tax reassessment program. This has contributed to a heavy state involvement in local tax procedures. In chapter 6 we discussed some of the functions of the Department of Examiners of Public Accounts, which audits the accounts and the records of all county and state offices and other agencies. The chief examiner of public accounts is responsible for putting into effect a uniform accounting system to make the audits easier to conduct.

The second type of state-local administrative action involves a more cooperative relationship. State agencies indirectly supervise local communities by providing services for localities that will help them perform administrative functions more professionally. For example, state community colleges conduct classes to help prepare operators of municipal water and wastewater treatment plants for the certification tests they are required by state law to take and pass. The Alabama Peace Officers' Standards and Training Commission sets minimum standards for the recruitment and training of local and state law enforcement officers. A third training program is administered by the Firefighters' Personnel Standards and Education Commission. State law says that a city can employ only firefighters who have met age, educational, and physical requirements and have successfully completed a training program in an approved school.

In terms of a more traditional transfer of knowledge, the attorney general, as we saw in chapter 6, is a legal adviser to all county and municipal departments and agencies. Further, the State Board of Health advises all county boards of health, health officers, and designated quarantine officers with respect to the technical performance of their jobs. The State Textbook Committee recommends textbooks for local elementary and secondary schools to the Department of Education, which in turn prepares book lists that local schools must use to make their textbook selections.

Other state administrative agencies also provide various kinds of assistance to local governments. For example, the Department of Revenue collects locally levied sales taxes, for which it charges a relatively small fee. The State Personnel Department contracts with municipalities to furnish them with many of the same personnel services provided to state agencies. County, municipal, and other public or quasi-public organizations may choose to have their members covered by the Employees' Retirement System of Alabama.

In the Department of Public Safety the Highway Patrol Division enforces laws regulating the use of motor vehicles on both county and state roads. This unit also investigates all rural traffic accidents. The Alabama Bureau of Investigation aids local law enforcement agencies in their efforts to solve major crimes. Further, the Office of Prosecution Services aids local district attorneys in their efforts to fight crime through successful prosecution of lawbreakers.

A third and generally less benign form of state-local administrative interaction involves state agency supervision of local communities through regulation. The ethics laws, for example, apply to many county and municipal as well as state officials who have to make decisions regarding the use of public funds in performing their duties. The basic requirement is that these officials file statements with the State Ethics Commission disclosing their personal financial interests.

Other instances of state agency regulation may be found in such areas as education and public health. The State Department of Education has standardized the grading of public schools and prescribes minimum course content within the grades. With regard to school buildings, the department has made rules to ensure proper construction and sanitation. In 1982 the Division of Solid Waste and Vector Control in the Alabama Department of Public Health began a more vigorous program to investigate, and order any necessary corrective action against, locally managed open dump sites within the state. Private child-care facilities must file notice of intent to operate such facilities with their local fire and health departments so that they can be inspected to see that they conform to state as well as local fire and environmental health regulations.

A small state agency, the County Records Commission, surveys county documents and issues regulations for classifying them. Basically, these regulations prescribe which county records must be preserved, in what form, and for how long. No county official may dispose of any county public record unless the commission gives its consent.

We pointed out in an earlier chapter that the rules and regulations issued by state agencies have become an important source of public policy. Seeing its role in policy-making as primary, Alabama's legislature has sought to control the agencies' rule-making power. Under the Administrative Procedure Act, approved by the legislature in 1981, for example, the Legislative Reference Service was made the depository for the rules and regulations issued by these and many other agencies. It also publishes the *Alabama Administrative Monthly,* which informs people about agency rules and rules changes. By executive order, a forty-five-day notice must be given to the League of Municipalities and the Association of County Commissions before administrative regulations affecting municipalities and counties can be implemented. This notification requirement is another indication of the political strength of local government interest groups.

The most extreme form of state administrative control over local governments occurs when the state suspends performance of some or all functions by local officials and puts the functions in the hands of state officials. This is generally known as substitute administration. There are few examples available to illustrate the outright state assumption of local authority in recent Alabama administrative experience. We did note in chapter 5, however, that in 1954 the governor of Alabama declared martial law in Phenix

City when some local officials were suspected of involvement in the assassination of a nominee for state attorney general. Substitute state administration continued until Phenix City was, in the eyes of state officials, "cleaned up." Less dramatically, particular departments may formally or informally take control of their local counterparts if they find the performance of local officials unsatisfactory. This is most likely to occur in health-related areas.

Perhaps the newest form of state administrative control is through the mandate. Joseph F. Zimmerman observes that "from the point of view of local government officials one of the principal irritants in state-local relations is the 'state mandate.' "[26] He defines a state mandate as "a legal requirement . . . that a local government must undertake a specified activity or provide a service meeting state standards."[27] In Alabama a fiscal note estimating costs must be attached to any measure having an impact on city or county revenues before it can be enacted by the legislature. This is a recent concession the legislators have made to local resentment of state mandates—for example, a mandate to house state prisoners in county jails. In the late 1970s, however, Alabama was reported to have fewer mandates than any other state except West Virginia, which had 8 to Alabama's 11. In contrast, California had 52, New York 60, Minnesota 51, and Wisconsin 50.[28] The fact that local governments in Alabama are subject to relatively few state mandates is probably attributable both to lower levels of social and economic development and to a cultural tradition that continues to be unsympathetic to many kinds of government regulation. The training programs identified earlier in the chapter provide additional examples of mandates imposed by the State of Alabama upon its local governments.[29]

In chapter 6 we noted the importance of state grants for the support of locally administered programs. These grants constitute a sixth, and arguably the most important, avenue for state interaction with and possible control over local administrative activities. In 1981 state aid to local governments in Alabama amounted to almost 30 percent of total state general spending. Nationally, state aid was less significant in twenty states and more significant in twenty-eight.[30]

The formulas governing the distribution of state funds to localities in Alabama have been a source of complaints, especially in the areas of revenues from motor and aviation fuel and alcoholic beverage taxes. The more populous cities and counties have long felt that rural sections received more than their fair share of the state grant funds. In recent years about one-fourth of the total local revenues in Alabama have come from the state.

However, discontent remains among the state's larger cities and counties, where there is sentiment that despite reapportionment they are still too frequently slighted by the legislature. In a 1985 special legislative session, for example, the Wallace administration proposed to give local governments fixed shares from the state's oil and gas trust fund. However, legislators from the large counties resisted the notion that about half of the money should be distributed on the basis of county equality and half on a population standard. No agreement could be reached on the distribution of the funds, so no state oil and gas revenue-sharing program was adopted at that time. A legislative leader was reported to have accused the big counties of being greedy and of trying to "rape the small counties."[31]

Some examples of grant programs, in addition to those cited in chapter 6, include the Aeronautics Department's provision of state funds for the construction of airports, the Public Library Service's grants to local libraries, and the awarding of proceeds from the sale of bonds issued by the State Industrial Development Authority to counties, municipalities, or local industrial development boards for purposes of economic development. Emergency welfare services for communities hit by natural or other disasters and administration of the individual and family grant programs for presidentially declared disasters are functions of the Department of Human Resources.

In regard to grants from federal revenues, there has been an emphasis in the Reagan administration on block grant programs rather than more specific (single-purpose) categorical grants. Under this approach, the states assume an important role in channeling more limited federal funds to local areas. For example, the Job Training Partnership Act of 1982 represents a major shift to the states of functions previously performed by the U.S. Department of Labor. This program calls for a joint federal-state-local and private-sector partnership to deal with unemployment problems.

It is apparent that most state-local administrative interaction takes place within a functional context. There is a final form of state-local interaction that relates to the coordination of these functional relationships. Alabama has no agency with this specific responsibility. However, there is one agency, the Alabama Department of Economic and Community Affairs (ADECA), that aids local governments by offering comprehensive technical assistance. From one perspective ADECA serves as an information clearinghouse. But in addition, the agency administers the Alabama Community Development System, which is supposed to help strengthen the service delivery capabilities of local governments. The department's contacts are primarily with counties, municipalities, and regional agencies. But it has no real authority that it can use to order these units to implement its recommendations.

We have mentioned that localities are able to maintain some autonomy despite the network of controls identified in the preceding pages. This is partly due to the political muscle they are able to bring to bear through their lobbying groups and the attention that they get from state legislators, who are frequently eager to act as spokespersons for local governments. In any event, local governments in Alabama seem reasonably satisfied with their authority. There is no great outcry for constitutional home rule. Neither municipalities nor counties have been in the forefront of what limited movements have occurred recently in behalf of constitutional revision in Alabama. They may complain about specific restrictions, they may chafe at disliked mandates or at what seem to them to be unnecessary or even harmful regulations, but on balance they appear to be more satisfied than dissatisfied with the niche they occupy in the government of Alabama.

CHAPTER ELEVEN

Community Government and Politics

Many governmental functions are administered through local government. In fact, most contacts that people have with government are probably with employees of local governments: the people who pick up the garbage, patrol the streets, license cars, and operate parks and playgrounds, for example. The legislature creates, or authorizes the creation of, local subunits either for general governmental purposes or for such special purposes as schools, public housing, soil and water conservation, public health and hospitals, utility services, and fire protection. We concentrate our discussion here on Alabama's system of general-purpose local governments, the counties and municipalities.

COUNTY GOVERNMENT

Alabama is divided into sixty-seven counties, the same number as in Florida, for example, but far less than in Georgia, where there are 159. The government of an Alabama county consists of a relatively small elective commission, which serves as a general governing body, and sundry other officials and agencies responsible for carrying out more specific county programs.[1] The official name of the governing body once varied a great deal, but since 1970 it has been uniformly called the county commission.[2] Differences persist among the counties in the make-up of the county commission, which ranges from three to seven members, but it is most frequently composed of the judge of the probate court and four commissioners, as described in the general law on county government. The voters elect the judge of probate on a countywide basis to a six-year term. The commissioners usually represent districts within the county, although an at-large feature has frequently been added to the district residence arrangement. At-large elections are rapidly decreasing in number, however, as they are currently under vigorous attack for unconstitutionally diluting black voting power. In general, commissioners' terms are four years; in several counties, however, the term is six years.[3]

The commission has a good deal of authority over the county's property and finances, and over some specific activities, such as solid waste disposal in rural areas, election administration, and, especially, county roads and bridges. Its financial powers include the authority to adopt the county budget, to make appropriations as set out in the budget, to approve claims against the county (bills that the county pays), to levy county taxes, and to manage the county's indebtedness. The commission's financial powers are severely constrained, however, by provisions of state law (both constitutional and statutory) that require elections on bond issues and specify permissible amounts and purposes of taxation, expenditures, and indebtedness. In addition to its other powers and duties, the commission may designate a county depository of funds in the treasury and may appoint a county attorney, the county road crews, a county engineer, and members of a variety of boards and other organizational units.[4]

When the judge of probate is a member of the county commission, he or she serves as its chair. In addition to presiding over commission meetings and related duties, the judge is primarily responsible for preparing the county's budget and paying its bills. The legislature, however, by means of local legislation, has removed the judge of probate from the governing body in almost half of Alabama's counties. In this event, an elective chair is usually (but not always) provided for, and that person takes over the functions regarding the commission that otherwise would have been handled by the judge of probate.[5]

One of the counties' chief complaints these days is that the state places too many mandated (compulsory) activities upon them without providing the necessary funding. Nevertheless, county operations are financed to a considerable extent by state money. The state grants large sums to counties for the support of county educational, highway, and health activities. Major state revenues shared with counties include the proceeds from such sources as revenues from the gasoline tax and the motor vehicle license tax, receipts from national forests, and various forms of income collected by the Alcoholic Beverage Control Board. Local sources of revenue include fines, fees, and county taxes. The property tax is the largest producer of county tax income, but because of such factors as an unrelenting need for revenue and the unpopularity of property taxes among their more affluent constituents, county officials have recently been driven to an emphasis on other kinds of taxes.

The tendency of county commissioners (with state legislative authorization) to turn to such excise taxes as those on beer, gasoline, tobacco, and general retail sales has meant a decline, of course, in the historic role of the property tax as the cornerstone of the county revenue structure. On the other hand, federal fiscal assistance, especially when it included revenue sharing, has been a significant source of county income.[6]

As observed previously, the internal organization of the county government includes many more officials and agencies than the commissioners and the judge of probate. They include the sheriff, the tax assessor, the tax collector, the treasurer (or depository), the coroner, the board and the superintendent of education, the county health unit, the county department of human resources, the board of equalization (of property valuations for tax purposes), the library board, the hospital board, the jury commission, the board of registrars (for voting), the park and recreation board, the civil defense unit, the board of supervisors (for election administration), and perhaps others.

The commission has only limited authority over the other parts of the county government. Many of the more important county offices are elective, so such activities as schools, law enforcement, and tax administration are carried out on a relatively independent basis. In addition, the units of county government concerned with, for example, health, welfare, education, and libraries are subject in varying degrees to administrative controls imposed by departments of the state government. To some extent, these agencies are therefore beyond the reach of the county commission.[7]

As a general rule, county government in other states is as structurally unintegrated as it is in Alabama. The responsibility for performing county functions is spread among many relatively independent officers and agencies. Over the years, county government has received its share of criticism, much of it disparaging the county's effectiveness as a unit of government. Reorganization plans that have been offered to improve county government usually assume that the governing body should be strengthened in its relationships with the other county agencies. This is the basis for county manager or executive plans of organization, for example, which would establish the governing board or commission as a legislative policy-making unit and provide the county with a chief executive who would oversee administration.[8]

The policy statement of the Committee for Economic Development, *Modernizing Local Government,* illustrates these reorganization proposals:

> Policy-making mechanisms in many units are notably weak. . . . Lack of a chief executive officer is one of the most glaring deficiencies in the structure of most local governments. . . . We recommend that policy-making authority be entrusted to a small, popularly elected and adequately compensated body. A full-time chief executive should be empowered to manage and coordinate all administrative operations, including appointment and removal of department heads.[9]

Since the judge of probate chairs the county commission in many Alabama counties, he or she occupies a critical position in the county government and may become a real political leader, bringing unity and direction to the management of the county's affairs. In recent years, moreover, the position of commission clerk has become an increasingly important management position in Alabama county government.[10] But neither of these officials is the sort of chief executive, common in municipal government, that the reformers suggest for counties.

MUNICIPAL GOVERNMENT

With the exception of a growing number of administrative boards, such as those for the operation of airports, utilities, public housing, recreation, and so forth, the governments of municipalities are considerably more unified than those of counties. Under the rules that formerly prevailed, the legislature could charter cities by means of "general laws of local application," and it did so, in fact, in the case of most larger municipalities. As a result of the Peddycoart decision, however, the legislature must now enact municipal legislation under a less specific system of classification that includes eight broad classes.[11] Mainly, though, Alabama municipalities are governed under one or another of the optional plans of government authorized by general state legislation. These plans are the ones used elsewhere in the United States: the mayor-council, commission, and council-manager forms. Ordinarily, but not always, a city adopts a plan of government by means of a referendum on the question.[12]

There are approximately 435 incorporated municipalities in Alabama, and almost all of them are governed under the mayor-council form. As the plan's name suggests, it provides for a mayor and a city council, both elective. The mayor is the formal head of the municipal government and the chief executive officer; the council is the legislative policy-making body.

As chief executive, the mayor has broad powers of supervision over the administration of municipal programs. For example, the mayor appoints all city officials whose method of selection is not otherwise provided for and may fire any official appointed by the mayor alone. In the case of most other officials, the mayor has the right to make a temporary removal, an action that becomes permanent when the council approves it. The mayor usually has a strong influence on the preparation of the budget and thus on the municipality's spending policies.

As a legislative body, the council can adopt ordinances not in conflict with state law, provide for the safety of the municipality, and "preserve the health, promote the prosperity, [and] improve the morals, order, and convenience" of its inhabitants. Clearly the council has a lot of power with which to regulate the municipality's internal affairs.

The council also has a broad power of appointment. For example, it appoints the municipal clerk and, in the larger municipalities, a treasurer. The clerk generally serves as the municipal licensing officer and frequently as the treasurer and purchasing agent. In small cities the council selects the heads of the police and fire departments and also the municipal tax officials, unless the county tax assessor and tax collector are empowered to administer the municipal taxes.

There is a good deal of variation among Alabama municipalities with respect to relationships between the council and the mayor. In small towns (those of less than 12,000 population) the legislative functions are performed by the mayor and five council members. The mayor sits with the council, presides over its meetings, and has a discretionary vote in its proceedings, except in the event of a tie, when the mayor must vote. The mayor usually does not sit with the council or have a vote in council proceedings in cities having a population of 12,000 or more. Where mayors do not sit with the council, they usually have a veto over the ordinances passed by the council, and a two-thirds vote in the council is necessary to override the mayor's veto. The mayor does not have a veto in the smaller communities.

In municipalities of less than 12,000, the five council members may be elected either at large or from wards established by the council, but in practice they have generally been elected at large. In some large cities, the voters elect a president of the council from the city at large; in others the council members select a president from their membership. The larger cities elect a varying number of council members (ranging up to thirteen), either at large or from wards. For important political reasons, discussed later, the recent tendency is toward the use of wards for the election of council members.

City councils are organized into committees—on such subjects as finance, utilities, streets and parks, the police and fire departments, sanitation, recreation, and perhaps others—through which they conduct much of their work. Where the mayor sits with the council, the general pattern is for the mayor to make the committee assignments; otherwise, the council president makes these appointments.

Each committee has the responsibility for overseeing the municipal functions falling within its jurisdiction and makes policy recommendations to the council about these programs. Apparently the influence of committees is great not only within the council but also in the actual administration of municipal activities. The extent to which the council may participate in administration through its personnel powers and its committee structure obviously diminishes the mayor's role as chief executive. This has been identified as one cause contributing in years past to the extensive use of commission government in the state.[13]

For a long time, the largest cities (and many smaller ones as well) employed the commission form of municipal government. The chief characteristic of this plan is that it concentrates all the legislative and executive powers of the municipality into the hands of, in Alabama, three commissioners elected from the city as a whole. As a collective body, the commissioners act as a city council. Individually, each commissioner serves as the administrative head of one of the three departments into which the city's many activities are aggregated. Interestingly, Jefferson County follows a commission plan of organization but has recently switched to a five-member commission with the adoption of a district election system.

The commissioners usually have equal status, although one of them is the president or chair of the commission and the city's mayor. As a general rule, they group the various municipal activities into the departments of public safety and public health; streets, parks, and public property and improvements; and accounts, finances, and public affairs. Ordinarily, the powers and duties of the departments may be defined by the commissioners as they see fit.

Because the practice of electing commissioners from the city at large has recently come under attack as racially discriminatory, commission government has all but disappeared in Alabama. This trend has been accompanied by a rapid increase in mayor-council government, as may be illustrated by the examples of Birmingham, Montgomery, Mobile, Tuscaloosa, and elsewhere. However, the state still makes little use of council-manager government. The most notable and enduring example of a managerial system bearing some resemblance to textbook models is in Mountain Brook, a wealthy suburb of Birmingham.

In its customary form, the council-manager plan calls for an elective council to serve in a legislative capacity and a manager, employed by the council, to supervise administration. The plan includes a mayor, but the mayor's role is essentially that of ceremonial head of the city. The manager is the chief operating officer. Alabama's laws have long authorized any municipal governing body to appoint a manager. Managers must see that applicable laws and ordinances are enforced, and they have the power to appoint municipal employees (with some major exceptions), to remove the employees they appoint, and, subject to the approval of the council or commission, to fix the employees' compensation. They keep the governing body informed of the municipality's financial condition, and they prepare the budget. The manager may be appointed municipal clerk and must be appointed purchasing agent for the city. City managers serve indefinite terms. They may be removed by a two-thirds vote of the entire membership of the governing body.

The positions excepted from the manager's appointing power include the chief of police, the chief of the fire department, and the heads of municipal utilities. These exceptions limit the manager's control over major administrative departments to such an extent that some observers long ago questioned whether it is really a manager plan at all.[14]

For a number of years, only Anniston had the recommended system of council-manager government, as authorized by special legislation. More recently, similar laws permitted the adoption of genuine council-manager government in Dothan and Phenix City. Still later, however, the legislature passed the Council-Manager Act of 1982, which finally established an authentic council-manager plan as one of the optional forms of municipal government that the state permits its cities to adopt.[15] A few cities have taken advantage of the new legislation.

Municipalities finance their various activities through such sources of revenue as taxes; fines; fees; assessments against property owners to offset the cost of certain improvements (such as paving streets); charges for water, sewerage, garbage collection, and other services; and the operation of utilities. They also share in such state revenues as the gasoline tax and the profits from the state liquor stores. Federal grants provide additional funds.

The municipal tax structure is based mainly on property taxes and licenses. Compared to municipalities elsewhere, Alabama municipalities make relatively little use of property taxes, and for revenue they rely heavily on a broad power to license business activities. In addition to the licenses usually required of businesses, Alabama municipalities also use their licensing power to tax such items as alcoholic beverages, gasoline, tobacco, movie tickets, general retail sales, and even salaries and wages paid within the municipality.

INTERLOCAL RELATIONS

Much of Alabama's growth in urban population has been in the suburbs and in "fringe areas" around municipalities.[16] Some of these communities are incorporated and others are not. In either case, the presence of these satellite communities raises problems concerning the delivery of services and the coordination of activities within the entire urbanized area. These problems may not have been quite as serious in Alabama as in other states, however, because of the authority that Alabama municipalities could exercise beyond their corporate limits.

An Alabama municipality may enforce its police power—its power to provide for the public health, safety, morals, and convenience—within its "police jurisdiction," or an area three miles beyond its corporate limits in the case of cities having a population of at least 6,000, and one and one-half miles in the case of smaller municipalities. Cities ordinarily provide some services (fire protection, for example) to the residents of unincorporated fringe areas, and license taxes on businesses within the police jurisdiction may be used, along with service charges, to assist in financing these "extraterritorial" activities.[17]

At one time Alabama municipalities carried on planning and zoning and subdivision control well beyond their city limits.[18] In an important case decided in 1970, however, the state Supreme Court held that, although the powers of planning and subdivision control could be used beyond a municipality's corporate limits, state law did not allow the use of the municipal zoning power beyond these limits.[19] As a result of the decision, municipalities could establish plans and subdivision regulations for the rural planning area but could no longer enforce the plans and regulations through the extraterritorial use of their zoning power. Naturally, this construction of the law seriously weakened the ability of municipalities to control their own development through the regulation of property located along their corporate borders. Because counties generally had no zoning power, the problem of fringe-area regulation became one of much concern not only to Alabama's municipal governments but to the counties as well.[20] More recent decisions of the Alabama Supreme Court that, in general terms, require the fees and charges for extraterritorial services to be related more specifically to the cost of the services rendered further complicate the fringe-area problem.

Annexation of outlying territory is the most definitive method of dealing with the fringe area, but that procedure involves legal and political obstacles that may not be easily overcome. In Alabama annexation may be accomplished either by local proceedings involving an election on the question or by local legislation enacted by the legislature. Although municipal boundaries are frequently extended by local legislation, the effectiveness of the procedure, as Joseph C. Pilegge has observed, depends on the local legislative delegation's assumption of the political risks involved. Nationally, annexation has occurred on a significant scale in recent years, most notably elsewhere in the South and in the West, but in Alabama its utility as a device to enlarge municipal jurisdictions appears limited. In Pilegge's estimation, "Annexation of outlying territory has been a difficult process for most Alabama municipalities."[21] It has also become an important civil rights issue.

The urban-fringe problem illustrates the difficulties facing local governments in attempting to cope with issues that extend beyond the boundaries of individual jurisdictions. Students of local government are much concerned with this question, and they have suggested various approaches by which local boundaries and powers might be adapted to the requirements of these larger problems.[22] Examples include the transfer of functions to a larger jurisdiction, such as the county, a special district, or the state; annexation, or merger in the case of incorporated municipalities; other forms of merger, such as county or city-county consolidations; and local intergovernmental agreements. Each of these approaches has advantages and limitations.

Annexation is a useful device for extending the reach of cities, but difficulties of implementation limit its application. Transferring functions to larger jurisdictions raises funding questions and could exacerbate the problem of accountability. The voters might not understand who is responsible for what. Too, consolidations involving counties and cities have been successful only in isolated instances; by 1977, the number of city-county consolidations stood at twenty-five in the entire United States. Although municipal mergers sometimes occur, county consolidations are rare indeed.[23]

On the other hand, intergovernmental agreements, while their utility is limited, are nevertheless widely used for the joint or coordinated administration of local functions and for the delivery of services under contract with other jurisdictions. In California, to cite a notable example in a state where interlocal agreements have been used extensively, the community of Lakewood contracted for the provision of virtually all of its public services through Los Angeles County. Subsequently it became common practice for newly incorporated cities in the county to adopt the Lakewood Plan for the delivery of municipal services.[24] In Alabama, where the physical reorganization of local government is politically unfeasible, the further development of county powers and the wider use of intergovernmental agreements may be more acceptable ways of dealing with multijurisdictional problems.

POLITICS

How local political institutions are used as instruments of government depends very much on the competition for influence in the community that makes up its politics. A better understanding of local government requires, then, an appreciation of the political environment in which it operates, and we now turn to a discussion of the local political environment.

Candidates for elective office emerge essentially through a process of self-selection. Many of them are local businessmen, although an increasing number of women are seeking and winning local offices. In general, municipal elections are nonpartisan, while county elections are conducted (along with elections for state offices) under a system of partisan voting. Aspirants file their candidacies with the proper authorities and enter either the municipal election or, if their goal is county office, the party primary. In either case, the candidates must generally fight their own battles, because the party organizations have little to do with electing candidates to local office. This is understandable, of course, in the case of the nonpartisan municipal elections. The relative inactivity of the local party organizations in county elections stems largely from the still-peculiar nature of the Democratic primary.

Despite the growth of Republican voting in the state, Alabama remains basically one-party Democratic in party identification. Consequently, as

Donald Strong has pointed out, most of the state's officeholders are Democrats who "are elected [in effect] in the Democratic primary, which is still the chief political contest."[25] The Democratic party does not endorse candidates in primary elections; in general elections, the Democrats usually win with little organized opposition. Consequently, the partisan county elections ordinarily fail to generate much more in the way of interparty competition than the nonpartisan municipal elections. Because of the generally inactive role of the party organizations, local politics in Alabama operates essentially as a form of "candidate" politics, in which the candidates conduct personal (rather than partisan) campaigns for office.

Even so, Republicans are sometimes elected to local offices. Their traditional strength is in north Alabama. Ever since the Civil War there has been a prominent strain of "mountain" Republicanism in that part of the state. As A. B. Moore, the late Alabama historian, wrote in the heyday of the Solid South: "In a few of the hill counties [Republicans] have been able to control the local offices, and they usually manage to send one or two representatives to the legislature."[26] Mainly since the 1950s, however, Republican voting in the state has increased significantly, especially in presidential and congressional elections.[27] But the increase in Republican voting has been felt among local communities as well, so that now one finds Republican officeholders in communities outside the traditionally Republican counties of north Alabama.

Geographically, Alabama's new Republican voters are located for the most part in the metropolitan counties and, there, mainly in the suburbs.[28] In these areas, Republicans have been elected in increasing numbers to the state legislature, for example. During the 1960s, expanded Republican activity in local arenas produced some results, with 1964, the year of the Goldwater sweep, the year of the party's greatest success. Also, candidates identified as Republicans were elected in the 1960s to the city commission in Mobile and to the city council in Birmingham. In 1967 the Birmingham Republican council member (George Seibels) was elected mayor.[29] Although Republicans lost strength after 1964, it remains true that local office is no longer the sole preserve of the Democrats. Conspicuous examples of Republicans holding local office in the 1980s include Emory Folmar, the Montgomery mayor who was George Wallace's unsuccessful opponent in the gubernatorial election of 1982, and John Smith, one of the relatively few black Republicans in Alabama and the mayor of Prichard, a suburb of Mobile.[30]

Methods used to campaign for office vary, depending on such factors as the amount of money the candidate has raised to finance the campaign and the setting in which the contest takes place. Typically, though, candidates try to reach the voters through such standard techniques as advertisements in the mass media; signs posted along roads and streets; and talks at civic club meetings, union halls, and political rallies or forums. In her study of the 1982 Alabama Senate elections, Margaret Latimer points out that for most Alabamians the mass media are major sources of political information. Apparently realizing the effectiveness of media communications, candidates increasingly rely on professional consultants for campaign advice, especially for advice on the use of the mass media.[31] But the candidates want to meet personally as many voters as possible, so they sometimes undertake door-to-door canvasses of the constituency, and they would assuredly frequent the busy street corners and shopping centers, speaking to the passersby and handing out campaign cards. In general their efforts are directed, as Key said, to seeking out "all the centers of influence within the electorate" that they can attract in support of their candidacy.[32]

Because of the essentially personal nature of local politics, elections often seem bland and issueless. The candidates all want to "do what's best" for the community, and the main problem for the voter is to try to figure out who actually can. Obviously some campaign issues do arise. Race remains an issue, especially when blacks and whites are contending for the same offices. Conditions vary widely, but in some instances political conflict reflects a polarization of the races, while in others a black-white coalition emerges, seeking to stabilize community politics along lines acceptable to both races. Local elections may also involve a small-scale form of sectionalism. The location of paved roads and streets, drainage projects, and other public improvements, for example, can generate issues, and the question of whether to conduct the county road function on the basis of districts or the county-as-a-unit system comes up at times in county politics. In the 1985 council election in Birmingham, the primary issue seemed to be the power of the incumbent mayor, Richard Arrington, and his political organization, the Citizens Coalition, which endorsed a slate of four blacks and one white for council seats. Only one candidate viewed as unfriendly to the mayor's programs succeeded against Citizens Coalition disapproval.

A high percentage of the respondents in a 1981 Capstone Poll indicated that they voted in local elections at least some of the time.[33] News media reports usually describe voter turnout in municipal elections as light or moderate, however, with less than half the registered voters participating in the election. When the turnout is light, the kind of election that we have characterized as bland and issueless has simply failed to stimulate enough interest to send the voters to the polls.

In addition to campaign issues, controversy may also develop from time to time out of specific incidents that arise or conditions that prevail in the community. Naturally, these issues assume a wide variety of forms—ranging, for example, from shows featuring male dancers (not "strip joints") in Tuscaloosa to horse racing in Birmingham. What should the community do, for other examples, about spouse and child abuse, drunken driving, environmental protection, dog control, pornography, the use of alcohol and drugs by school children, or the police shooting policy? These kinds of issues can be highly controversial because, for one thing, they often raise questions about the community's moral values. When this is the case, religious groups are frequently involved in the controversy, perhaps aligned against business interests viewing the issue in economic terms.

Undoubtedly the moral issue that creates the most controversy is the "wet-dry" question that is rooted in the state's local-option system of alcoholic beverage control. As controversial as the issue is, it is likely to become even more so due to a 1984 law that permits wet-dry referendums in some cities in otherwise dry counties. Formerly these referendums were conducted on a countywide basis. A news account of an incident in Jasper shows how the issue evolved there:

A resolution opposing the legalization of liquor sales will go out in a bulletin distributed to some 900 people expected at First Baptist Church's Sunday services.

And religious leaders say that's just the beginning of their campaign against local business leaders who hope to place a wet-dry referendum on the city's November ballot.

The group of 11 business and community leaders, called the Jasper Progress Committee, says legalization of liquor sales [ultimately approved] would bring Jasper some $100,000 a year in additional revenue.[34]

An issue of major importance throughout the state concerns the nature of the governmental structure. At one time, the organization of county government was highly unstable, being frequently changed by local laws for no apparent reason except the personal or political. Indeed, the Brookings Institution, in its 1932 study of county government in Alabama, described county organization as "the football of factionalism."[35] Recently, though, the question of changing the form of government, or the method of electing the local governing body, has been most likely to arise as a civil rights issue.

The best example of the issue in a municipal context is the 1962 election on the question of whether to replace Birmingham's city commission with the mayor-council form of government. The election became in essence a referendum on the racial policies of the incumbent commissioners, among whom was the controversial police commissioner Eugene "Bull" Connor. Donald Strong has said of the election: "This was really no mere technical change in the form of city government. It was part of a scheme to change both the personnel and policies."[36] The effort to make the change was successful.

As Latimer has said, "The first order of business for black citizens . . . was to claim the right to vote; the barriers to black office-holding were severe."[37] But after the passage of the Voting Rights Act of 1965, growth in black political strength eventually produced a substantial number of locally elected black officials, especially in the cities and in the rural counties of the Black Belt. Municipal offices held by blacks included council positions in such cities as Birmingham, Montgomery, and Selma, as well as many others, and the position of mayor in Birmingham, Prichard, and Tuskegee, for example. In some counties, blacks were elected to such offices as probate judge, sheriff, district judge, tax assessor, tax collector, and county commissioner. In Greene and Macon counties, political power shifted entirely to the black majority.[38]

Yet the number of black elected officials remained relatively small. In 1982, for instance, the U.S. Commission on Civil Rights studied racial conditions in selected Alabama counties, including, for purposes of an overview, the Black Belt counties. The commission concluded:

Despite these political gains, blacks have not been successful in gaining political office in many of the counties in the 16-county study area. For example, as late as 1982, there was no black representation on the county commissions of 7 of the 16 counties; 4 of these 7 counties had majority-black populations.[39]

Later in 1982 blacks were elected in Sumter County.[40] Obviously, though, this did little to increase the overall representation of blacks in local political offices.

During the 1970s, civil rights supporters began to focus their attention on the method of electing local governing bodies (including county school boards) as a major reason for black underrepresentation.[41] At-large election systems came under particular attack, on the ground that they tended to diminish the capacity of blacks to participate effectively in the political process. Because the commission form of municipal government used in Alabama called for at-large elections, that form of government became a special target. The goal was to replace at-large systems with district systems, which were expected to produce black representatives on locally elected governmental bodies.

Although changes to district systems (and in district systems) frequently occurred by other means, such as negotiated settlements of district lines, blacks pursued their quest for representation largely through the process of litigation. They filed numerous cases in federal courts challenging city and county election systems as racially discriminatory. Undoubtedly the best known of these cases was *Bolden* v. *Mobile*—the case in which the U.S. District Court for the Southern District of Alabama ordered a mayor-council government for the city (with the council elected from single-member districts) in place of the city commission. The U.S. Supreme Court reversed the decision on appeal because purposeful discrimination had not been demonstrated, but a change to a district system seemed inevitable. Eventually the city adopted the mayor-council plan. There were differences, of course, but the *Bolden* case nevertheless became something of a model for future litigation. In fact, the tendency of the courts to substitute district for at-large election systems was so pronounced that, when a suit was filed in 1984 challenging the legality of Tuscaloosa's commission form of government, the commissioners announced that they would not contest the suit but would work with the legislative delegation to obtain a suitable district system—again, as it usually turned out, a mayor-council system.[42]

A related issue that arose from the existence of all-white municipal governments concerned the annexation of unincorporated territory. Here the configuration of the municipality's corporate limits was identified as the problem, and the annexation of outlying black neighborhoods became the issue. The controversy raised the question of racially discriminatory boundary lines, and in this respect it was similar to the Tuskegee boundary incident involved in the famous 1960 U.S. Supreme Court case of *Gomillion* v. *Lightfoot*. To illustrate the later problem, the Alabama Democratic Conference (a predominantly black political organization) issued a report in 1984 in which it identified specific municipalities "where the census data suggest that there might be a number of black people living just outside the city limits who could be 'Annexed' to increase the black population." As the report suggested, annexation of these areas would heighten "the potential for electing more black municipal officials."[43]

Believing that in unity there is strength, the participants in political controversies tend to organize their efforts and form groups. Community politics is thus in large measure group politics, but with well-placed individuals also involved in the action.[44] In a Dillon's Rule state such as Alabama (that is, one without a policy of home rule), the ability of local governments to deal with local problems frequently depends on actions by the state legislature. Because of the importance of the connection between the legislature and local government in Alabama, we include legislators among the influential people most involved in community politics. With respect to groups, some are formed on an ad hoc, temporary basis, reflecting the transitory nature of the issue with which they are concerned. Others have more continuous concerns; some indicate support for such national movements as those involving civil rights, women's rights, prohibition, labor (including public employee organization), religious conservatism, and efforts to curtail drunken driving.

Groups involved in community politics sometimes attempt to influence the outcome of elections; they lobby public officials, try to generate supportive public opinion, use litigation, or perhaps picket or hold demonstrations. But whatever means they employ, political activists seek community policies with which they are comfortable, and it is the lot of the politician to work out some accommodation of their often-conflicting demands. For a number of reasons (economic and social as well as political), prominent business people in Alabama, as elsewhere, will probably always have influence in determining the course of community affairs. How an issue is ultimately settled, however, depends very largely on how the politicians view the pattern of public support on the issue. At bottom, the forces of politics determine the policy decisions of those who occupy the offices in the governmental structure and even the characteristics of the structure itself.

CHAPTER TWELVE

Conclusions
and
Observations

We have not attempted in our study to examine Alabama state and local government from a primarily historical perspective. We have made no effort to set the facts and judgments of the preceding pages in a precisely chronological order. We have noted, however, important milestones in the development of the state and have given attention to the impact of Alabama's cultural heritage on its political evolution. These developments have produced an Alabama of today that is in important respects different from the Alabama of even a few decades ago.

SOCIAL CHANGES

Growth and movement in Alabama's population during the past couple of decades have not been dramatic. Alabama's population expansion has been at about the national average in recent years—and at less than the rate of most of the other states in the Sun Belt. During the 1960s and 1970s, Alabama lost two U.S. representatives (down to seven) but held its own after the 1980 census. Thus specifically growth-induced changes could hardly have been of a revolutionary character. In some respects Alabama has more in common with older industrial states in the North than with its sister Sun Belt states. Nevertheless, due to rising educational and political participation levels within a basically settled population, we find now in Alabama an increasingly pluralistic society—that is, a society possessed of a greater range of values that must be considered in the public policy-making process. It may, therefore, be more difficult to secure consensus than it has been in the past. We think, too, that blacks and women will become increasingly active in Alabama politics, although both groups, especially blacks, are already very involved politically.

Mainly because of the sweeping social changes that occurred in the two intervening decades, state policies in 1986 were different from those that prevailed in 1966. Resolutions of an obviously racial character, for example, were no longer passed by the Alabama legislature. Defiant attitudes of resistance with respect to changes in race relations were no longer expressed openly by politicians of any consequence. On the other hand, the state has not changed so much that we see the legislature giving a great deal of aid and comfort specifically to blacks as a group, either. More generally, the legislature still does not assign urban-oriented legislation a very high place on its policy agenda.

When we reflect, however, on the fact that as recently as the 1960s there were Alabama counties with large black populations but with no or only a handful of black voters, we are reminded of just how much change has occurred in the short span of two decades since the passage of the Voting Rights Act of 1965. There are still sharp cleavages between blacks and whites, as evidenced, for example, in the overwhelming white support received by Ronald Reagan and the even heavier backing Walter Mondale received from blacks in the 1984 presidential election. Nevertheless, blacks and whites, particularly within the framework of the Democratic party, work together in ways unknown in the past. Blacks, in Alabama as nationally, are among the most loyal supporters of the Democratic party. In return for this support, blacks are able to bargain for somewhat more sympathetic policy and personnel considerations than they would otherwise be likely to get from many white Democratic officeholders.

Analysts of contemporary American politics frequently point to the increasing role religious movements play in national politics. As we have seen, religion has traditionally been important in Alabama. However, Alabamians do not seem as religiously and socially conservative now. For example, many places of business now remain open on Sunday. Although there is widespread concern over drunken driving, alcoholic beverages are nevertheless more widely available now than in the past. Horse racing with pari-mutuel betting began in Birmingham in 1987, and three dog tracks where gambling was permitted have been established in Alabama.

Yet, certain manifestations of a culturally conservative state remain. Women continue to be less politically active than men. The number of women legislators, for example, has been well below the national average. Conservative religious denominations are the fastest growing in Alabama.[1]

Students at Alabama colleges and universities are generally considered more conservative than their counterparts elsewhere.[2] Protests and other deviations from societal norms are usually unwelcome in most small Alabama towns. X-rated-movie theaters and "adult" bookstores are found only in the state's largest cities, and even there they are likely to lead a precarious existence. And, despite all we have said about change, church activities probably still constitute the reason for the expenditure of more nonwork time for Alabamians than is the case in some of the other states. Furthermore, religious leaders remain important participants in the public policy-making process.

ECONOMIC CHANGES

In recent years Alabama has had one of the highest unemployment rates in the nation. This has been due in large measure to the dominance of basic industry in the state's economy. Presumably a more diversified economy would have been less affected by recent recessions. Because the rate of growth in the Alabama economy can be expected to remain moderate at best, unemployment will probably continue into the foreseeable future as an important public policy problem.[3] Economic development has thus become a major state goal.

Recently the state employed a consulting firm to identify assets and liabilities pertinent to attracting new industry capable of providing additional jobs.[4] The firm reported that Alabama's natural resources, for example, attracted industry, but on the negative side it cited such factors as the state's reputation for having inferior public schools, a "redneck" mentality, and a bad "legislative climate" as discouraging to economic growth. Nevertheless, industries continue to locate, and to expand, in Alabama. Although facilities based on modern technology are found elsewhere in the state, it seems likely that economic growth will not be concentrated in "high-tech" industries, except at such obvious sites as Birmingham and Huntsville. Most development will probably occur in manufacturing, service, and the traditionally important basic industries, or outgrowths of these industries, such as steel and extractive industries, especially timber, oil and gas, and strip-mined coal. But whatever development Alabama experiences could be expected to lead to further urbanization and social differentiation. This, in turn, could have important political implications.

More Alabamians are enjoying the good life today than ever before, but many, also, are abjectly poor. There is a rising urban professional class in

Alabama, but there is also an underclass in poverty which is not benefiting from the general rise in the standard of living. Again, we see the salience of economic development—improving economic opportunities in the state—as a major public-policy concern.

Alabama's agricultural economy has also changed over the years. Agriculture is no longer the dominant industry, and cotton is no longer "king." Cotton remains an important crop, but it does not dominate the agricultural economy as it once did. Instead of worrying about boll weevils, Alabama's farmers have grown increasingly concerned about the price of beef, pork, and soybeans. Today, only a small fraction of Alabama workers make their living in agriculture. Many rural people have gravitated to the cities, to northern cities as well as those in Alabama and other southern states, in search of work as Alabama's farms have increasingly developed into highly mechanized operations geared toward large markets. Selling Alabama-grown agricultural commodities in foreign markets, for example, has become a major source of farm income.

The Tennessee-Tombigbee Waterway is now open, the culmination of a long, highly politicized struggle. This mammoth canal connects the Tennessee River on the north with the Gulf of Mexico on the south. It provides a slack-water route for vessels going north and was thus conceived as an attractive channel for barge traffic. Some observers have speculated that the waterway will revolutionize the economies of areas adjacent to it. A more restrained view is probably in order. Nevertheless, the waterway may be expected to provide good industrial sites along its banks. Thus incremental economic development may be encouraged in the Tenn-Tom Corridor.

Energy policy is obviously a key element in the future development of the Alabama economy. Alabama is well-off in coal resources and also has substantial oil and natural gas reserves. The traditional culture of Alabama does not seem to promote, however, any great consciousness of the need to conserve energy. Ideas for saving energy, as through recycling, carpooling, bicycling, and the like, are not as warmly received as they are elsewhere, so the market can be expected to serve as the primary influence on the extent to which Alabamians conserve energy. Since the energy crisis has eased, we find very few organized efforts in Alabama to promote a policy of energy conservation.

From the perspective of energy utilization, Alabama seems most responsive to demands to develop its energy resources. Ethical and environmental considerations do not appear to figure as prominently as economic interests in decisions about these resources, although at times voices are raised in protest against proposals that have environmentally damaging implications. There is no great inclination to experiment with the more esoteric energy sources. However, Alabama does have a number of nuclear power plants, and there has been no widespread opposition to the use of nuclear power in Alabama. The main obstacle to its further use would probably be cost inefficiency.

POLITICAL CHANGES

The drift of political power and leadership to urban and suburban areas has not been as dramatic as other recent changes, largely because of the long-continuing political role of George C. Wallace, the archetypal southern politician whose appeal was to essentially rural interests. In his last bid for the governorship, in 1982, Wallace was strongly challenged in the Democratic primary by a young urban politician, former lieutenant governor George McMillan. Urbanization came relatively late to Alabama, so there are many urban residents who still have one foot in the soil. But as urbanization intensifies, it seems likely that the urban political influence reflected in McMillan's try for office will continue to grow, not only in elections for the governorship but in those for other offices as well.

Reapportionment has been most responsible for whatever movement there has been so far in shifting the center of political power and leadership to urban areas. It has permitted urban political influence to be more strongly institutionalized. The Alabama legislature, for example, is no longer dominated by conservative Black Belt politicians in the way that it once was. With blacks voting and gaining office in larger numbers, blacks themselves are able to serve the Black Belt (and inner-city areas) in the legislature. We think it unlikely, though, that Alabama's politics will, in the foreseeable future, have a "big city" flavor, for the simple reason that, aside from Birmingham, the state has no cities with even a quarter of a million population. Even so, there is more of an urban orientation to state politics now than in the past. Political campaign efforts, for example, are largely focused on urban areas, where the most votes are.

A coalition of planters and "Big Mules" no longer dominates the public policy process in Alabama. In its place there is now a more varied set of interest-group constituencies. Some groups that are powerful now had scarcely any political muscle only a few years ago. Good examples are the predominantly black groups and the militant teachers lobby, the Alabama Education Association. Trial lawyers have also emerged as a political force to be reckoned with, and labor unions have more access to decision-making structures now than they did, say, in 1953, when the state's "right to work" law was passed. Even if they do not have the votes to secure passage of many supportive bills, unions sometimes do have enough influence to block legislation they feel is antilabor. In the main, the groups that have become more active and influential recently seem more responsive to middle- and lower-middle-class political values than to elite values. This may signal a major change in the state's traditional political culture. However, there has not been such a drastic change in actual policies that the more affluent groups in the population have been made uncomfortable.

Because the interest-group configuration has become more varied, it is more difficult now to construct coalitions to enact public policies. It was obviously easier to push through new policies when only a small set of actors—the planters and the "Big Mules"—had to reach an agreement. We would place the interest-group pattern in Alabama, however, at the moderate level, not yet as diverse as it is in the more highly urbanized and industrialized states.

Even so, Alabama has lost some of its distinctiveness and has become more like the rest of the nation. Cultural forces that tend to standardize our society (national economic and communications networks, for example) have been "powerful nationalizing influences" in Alabama, as in the rest of the nation.[5] One result, at least in terms of national politics, is that Alabama can now be described as a two-party state. Alabama is on the beaten path of presidential candidates in modern elections, and it has even been called a key state in the South.

We anticipate, however, no realization in Alabama of any sort of "ideal" two-party model in the foreseeable future. Because political conservatism enjoys a broad base of support in the state, it is likely that the Republican candidate for president will carry Alabama much of the time, and Republicans will probably hold onto the congressional seats they now occupy—and perhaps even gain one or two from time to time. But the Alabama Democratic party will probably continue as the partisan framework within which political struggles mainly go on, certainly until a firmer basis for partisan differentiation develops in the state. The Republican party in Alabama has been unable to broaden its appeal to include working-class people. Ideological appeals have been insufficient to overcome heritage and tradition, and thus the Republicans have remained distinctly a minority party. So we expect Democrats to win a heavy majority of state and local elections in the future, much as they have in the past. In the rapidly growing urban areas, however, Republicans are able to mount serious and often successful challenges for state legislative and local offices.

We have in earlier chapters discussed at considerable length efforts to replace Alabama's frequently amended 1901 constitution with a new one, but as long as the present low level of interest continues, it is unlikely that a new constitution will be adopted. Perhaps constitutional reform will revive as a political issue if it becomes an item on the agenda of a future Alabama governor. Even then, however, entrenched interests can be expected strongly to resist efforts for comprehensive constitutional reform. In the meantime, Alabama's political leaders will probably give priority to immediate, tangible, and substantive problems over the long-term, abstract, and seemingly academic subject of constitutional reform.

Sweeping governmental reorganization would probably be easier to achieve than a new constitution. However, both administrative reorganization and constitutional reform seem to depend primarily on gubernatorial leadership, and neither was a long-term interest of Governor Wallace or any other governor since Frank M. Dixon's reorganization of 1939. For one thing, the payoff in terms of voter support seems unlikely to be worth the effort required to achieve either objective. A management-minded governor in the post-Wallace era might be able to effect substantial reorganization, though, especially if it were offered more in the context of economy than political accountability. In recent years structural changes have been much more significant in local government than in state government. As noted in chapter 11, there are movements in many cities from at-large to district systems for electing city councils. This change is also taking place in the counties. Both movements have occurred mainly in response to federally supported demands of blacks for more opportunities to participate in local decision-making structures.

In chapter 2 and elsewhere we noted the various instances of federal intervention into Alabama's political institutions, processes, and policies. We have the feeling, though, that with the greater professionalization of Alabama's state and local governments, along with the attitudinal change that we have mentioned, such intervention may not occur as often as it has in the past. Also, with a current federal policy of cutbacks in assistance (expressed as slashes in the rate of growth in appropriations or in total appropriations or both) there may be less opportunity for federal direction of state and local affairs. In any event, there is a rising mood in the state to make the "Alabama" and the "punting" syndromes obsolete as terms explaining state politics and policies. Alabamians today are likely to believe that these behavior patterns—both of which involved a contumacious atti-tude toward disliked federal policies, combined with an unwillingness to exert state leadership—damaged the state's national image.

Education is an important policy area in both state and local forums. In expenditures, it is the most important policy area. Moreover, an effort to improve the quality of public education now ranks as perhaps the highest item on the state's governmental agenda, being linked with economic development as the means to develop a more prosperous polity. Highways, welfare, and health and hospitals—the other activities on which Alabama spends large sums of money—will undoubtedly generate important policy questions, as will programs on which lesser sums are spent, such as prisons and mental health. Indeed, we anticipate no dearth of problems. But, if for no other reason than its cost, we expect education to remain perhaps the most prominent of the policy concerns facing Alabamians and their govern-ments over the next few years.

The exodus of white students from the public schools to private schools has severely lessened white taxpayer support for local public education. More generally, city and county systems throughout the state are continuing to lean heavily on state support of education. It is not necessarily bad that the state has assumed so important a responsibility for funding locally administered elementary and secondary education programs. It is in fact reformist to the extent that it amounts to the state's taking tax revenues from where they are most abundant and effecting a mild redistribution of these funds to areas where they are most needed. Still, many children in Alabama schools receive a lot less than a quality education because of the weak tax base of the communities in which their schools are located. For various reasons, most of them political, local property taxes remain low. So long as the local areas that could raise more school funds fail to do so, state funds are necessarily denied to the poorer school districts and to the colleges and universities. Thus the state is confronted with the continuing problem of having to provide more and more resources for education to advance on all fronts. Many other problems will probably be settled before this one is.

CONCLUSION

In the preceding pages we have presented information and opinions about many topics of concern to those interested in Alabama politics and public policy. One of our main points is that social, economic, and political forces of relatively recent origin have been important factors in shaping the state's present character. Any listing of the more important of these developments would include the civil rights movement and the economic growth that has occurred since World War II. The civil rights movement has produced what can only be termed a revolution in race relations. Economic development moved Alabama first into the Industrial Age and now into the era of high technology, along with the rest of the country. The general increase in prosperity accompanying economic growth is especially noticeable in rural areas, where, as J. S. Reed remarks about the South in general, "Many of the more picturesque derivatives of rural poverty and isolation have vanished, to the point where undergraduates look puzzled at the mention of pellagra or soil erosion."[6] These days, brick houses and tractors (and satellite TV receivers) are common sights in rural Alabama.

Not all have prospered, however. A relatively large proportion of Alabama's population lives below the poverty level, many if not most in rural areas. Generally the black population fares much worse than the white population. And a per capita income that persists at about 80 percent of the national figure gives further insight into why political campaigners place such great stress on jobs for Alabamians.[7]

All things considered, though, recent social change has moved Alabama into a closer relationship with the other states. In time, the state will probably move even further into the mainstream of American public life. Experience with divided government will add a new dimension to Alabama politics. But we do not think that Alabama's political institutions will soon lose their distinctively Alabama flavor. In their major contours, we suspect that Alabama government and politics will remain for some time to come much as we have described them here.

Suggestions
for
Further Reading

The ongoing study of Alabama government and politics can be informative and at times even amusing, particularly as the reader is introduced to or becomes better acquainted with colorful political figures in Alabama's history. The reader's attention will also be drawn to the drama of historic political campaigns and movements, the sometimes turbulent role of the state in national politics, and the increasingly important role of black people in the development of Alabama.

Readers may be pleasantly surprised by both the quantity and the quality of the materials now available for the serious study of Alabama's political institutions and processes. Most of the citations that follow relate specifically to Alabama government and politics. Historical, comparative, and cultural studies, however, provide a context for the consideration of governmental processes, so we also include a sampling of them. We must stress that our citations are only illustrative, not exhaustive, and are not judgmental about works we have omitted. Our intention is to suggest places and ways for the further study of Alabama politics. Readers who pursue these works will inevitably be led to other sources.[1]

GENERAL

Libraries

The principal libraries are the Alabama State Department of Archives and History (DOAH) Library and the libraries of the two largest state universities, Auburn University and the University of Alabama. Other colleges and universities may have quite large collections of materials pertaining to their particular sections of the state. The same holds true for local public libraries. The Network of Alabama Academic Libraries, which has recently been established, will facilitate a computerized search among many college and university libraries for needed materials pertaining to state government. The universities with graduate programs are the sites of the most research pertaining to Alabama, and it is there that the researcher will find graduate dissertations and theses that, aside from the substance of their painstaking research, contain excellent bibliographies that give clues to the directions a research effort ought to take. The dissertations, which are frequently on specialized topics unlikely to be treated in the commercial press, are available for purchase in photocopy or machine-readable formats from University Microfilms in Ann Arbor, Michigan.

The University of Alabama is also the site of the major academic law library in the state. There are others in particular communities, but access may be restricted to attorneys. Good law libraries will have complete sets of the *Code,* copies of the present and possibly past Alabama constitutions, case reports, and treatises on legal subjects.

If state government documents are available at all, they may be located in the Archives and History Library. The university libraries also have many state documents. In addition, Alabama and Auburn universities are both federal document depositories. State and local archives are also found in the DOAH library as well as in the larger university libraries.

The researcher using these and other library resources is not left totally to his or her own devices. Libraries are organized to assist the investigator interested in pursuing research concerns. At the DOAH, materials are generally available for use only in the library. However, photocopies of needed materials often can be made. The library has fairly extended hours, including weekends, when it may be more convenient to travel for research purposes. The library has a staff of trained archivists to assist the serious researcher, and there are numerous volumes of indices and book publishers' catalogs to expedite the research process. There is no charge for the use of library materials, although nominal fees are, of course, charged for photocopying. Users of library materials are generally free to make handwritten notes from the sources they are using. The researcher will generally find libraries to be quiet and comfortable places to work where scholarly interests may be pursued without too many unwanted distractions.

If the inquiry concerns the life of some past Alabama political figure, it is first necessary to locate the individual's papers, which may have been deposited in a library. An inquiry to the DOAH or the Alabama or Auburn libraries might be a useful place to start.

Despite the generally helpful attitude of librarians and the presence of abundant materials related to Alabama government and politics, the researcher should nonetheless be prepared for frustration at some point in the investigative process. Almost inevitably, collections of materials will be found to be incomplete, even in major libraries. Some volumes of sets may be absent from the library shelves, and when volumes are located, pages may be missing. Frequently, huge volumes may not have been indexed, thus requiring a tedious page-by-page search for the information the reader is looking for. This is almost inevitable in newspaper research. Sometimes one volume of a newspaper run may be in one location while others are located miles away in another location. Also, issues may be complete but so disarranged as to be extremely difficult to use in any sequential process. In our experience, these problems are rarely the fault of the library staff. Rather, they are frequently attributable to such factors as records and other materials having been lost or destroyed or to budgets that do not permit the acquisition of complete collections and the hiring of the necessary staff to better superintend the use of library holdings.

Despite the inevitable problems, we find that research on topics of interest to us is both challenging and usually absorbing, and we think that other researchers will, too. Here we offer some of the sources of information that serious researchers will probably find most helpful.

Sources

We have referred several times to general histories of Alabama—most notably A. B. Moore's *History of Alabama* (University, Ala.: University Supply Store, 1934) and Charles G. Summersell's *Alabama History for Schools*, 5th ed. (Montgomery: Viewpoint Publications, 1975).

Recent general books on Alabama history, government, and life-styles include three with the basic title *Alabama*. These are Kathryn T. Windom (Huntsville, Ala.: Strode Publishers, 1975), Daniel S. Gray (Dubuque, Ia.: Kendall/Hunt Publishing Co., 1975), and Virginia V. Hamilton (New York: Norton, 1977 and 1984). The Hamilton book was originally published as part of a national bicentennial series. More strictly oriented toward government and politics is David L. Martin's *Alabama State and Local Governments* (Dubuque, Ia.: Kendall/Hunt, 1975, with a revised edition published by the University of Alabama Press in 1985).

If one is interested in particular historical periods, one should consider such volumes as *Politics and Power in a Slave Society: Alabama, 1800–1860*, by J. Mills Thornton (Baton Rouge: Louisiana State University Press, 1978); *Labor Revolt in Alabama: The Great Strike of 1894*, by Robert D. Ward and William W. Rogers (University: University of Alabama Press, 1965); *Populism to Progressivism in Alabama*, by Sheldon Hackney (Princeton, N.J.: Princeton University Press, 1969); *Bourbon Democracy in Alabama, 1874–1890*, by Allen J. Going (Westport, Conn.:

Greenwood Press, 1972); *August Reckoning: Jack Turner and Racism in Post–Civil War Alabama,* by William Rogers (Baton Rouge: Louisiana State University Press, 1973); *The Secessionist Impulse: Alabama and Mississippi in 1860,* by William L. Barney (Princeton, N.J.: Princeton University Press, 1974); *Dixiecrats and Democrats: Alabama Politics, 1942–1950,* by William D. Barnard (University: University of Alabama Press, 1974); and *Selma, Lord, Selma,* by Sheyann Webb and Rachel West Nelson, as told to Frank Sikora (Tuscaloosa: University of Alabama Press, 1980).

One will also find chapters dealing with Alabama in books examining the southern states in general. The most famous of these is the chapter on Alabama in V. O. Key's *Southern Politics in State and Nation.* Key's classic work was re-published in both hard- and softcover editions by the University of Tennessee Press in 1984. A newer general analysis of Alabama political life is Donald S. Strong's chapter in *The Changing Politics of the South,* edited by William C. Havard (Baton Rouge: Louisiana State University Press, 1972). Two other books of this type, and ones that we have found useful in the preparation of this study, are Neal R. Peirce, *The Deep South States of America: People, Politics, and Power in the Seven Deep South States* (New York: Norton, 1974), and Jack Bass and Walter De Vries, *The Transformation of Southern Politics* (New York: New American Library, 1977; reprint of a 1976 Basic Books edition). The latest comprehensive study of southern party politics is that by Alexander P. Lamis, *The Two-Party South* (New York: Oxford University Press, 1984).

A valuable doctoral dissertation dealing with interest groups in the Alabama context is Donna R. Gaston, "An Assessment of the Influence by Lobbyists on Appropriations by the Alabama Legislature to Public Four-Year Universities in Alabama" (University of Alabama, 1982). Carl J. Harris has written an informative historical study of group activity in local politics entitled *Political Power in Birmingham, 1871–1921* (Knoxville: University of Tennessee Press, 1977).

The notes for chapter 2 mention several important sources for research in intergovernmental relations from an Alabama perspective. The student will also find informative such works as Bernard Taper's study *Gomillion* versus *Lightfoot* (New York: McGraw-Hill, 1963) and David J. Garrow's *Protest at Selma* (New Haven: Yale University Press, 1978). A more regional treatment of race-related intergovernmental conflict is Earl Black's study *Southern Governors and Civil Rights: Racial Segregation as a Campaign Issue in the Second Reconstruction* (Cambridge, Mass.: Harvard University Press, 1976). There is a large body of literature on this general subject—the Second Reconstruction, the southern policy of massive resistance, the role of the Citizens Councils, and so forth—so the researcher should have little difficulty in pursuing the subject. An unpublished study focusing specifically on Alabama is James T. Harris's "Alabama Reaction to the Brown Decision: A Case Study in Early Massive Resistance" (Ph.D. dissertation, Middle Tennessee State University, 1978).

For a scholarly periodical that focuses on Alabama, we cite the *Alabama Review* (published quarterly by the Alabama Historical Association). National and regional journals in the fields of history and political science contain occasional articles on Alabama government and politics. One example of an excellent article pertaining to Alabama is Walter Dean Burnham's "The Alabama Senatorial Election of 1962: Return of Inter-Party Competition," *Journal of Politics* 26 (October 1964): 798–829. Other serials likely to be of use to those interested in Alabama government and politics include the *Alabama Municipal Journal* (published by the Alabama League of Municipalities), *The County Commissioner* (published by the Association of County Commissions of Alabama), and the *Alabama Law Review* (edited at the University of Alabama School of Law).

Readers interested in learning about particular Alabama personalities will find extensive biographical and autobiographical materials in university libraries and in the DOAH library. Several books have been published on the life and works of Hugo Black, for example. Virginia Hamilton has written two books about Justice Black that have been published by the University of Alabama Press (1978; softcover edition, 1982). Numerous scholarly and popular books about Governor George Wallace have been published. Wallace's own ideas are best seen in *"Hear Me Out"* (Anderson, S.C.: Droke House, 1968) and *Stand Up for America* (Garden City, N.Y.: Doubleday, 1976). Prominent interpretations of the Wallace phenomenon include Marshall Frady, *Wallace* (New York: World Publishing Co., 1968); Michael Dorman, *The George Wallace Myth* (New York: Bantam Books, 1976); and Wayne Greenhaw, *Watch Out for George Wallace* (Englewood Cliffs, N.J.: Prentice-Hall, 1976). A useful unpublished study is Forrest H. Armstrong, "George C. Wallace: Insurgent on the Right" (Ph.D. dissertation, University of Michigan, 1970). Tinsley Yarbrough's book *Judge Frank Johnson and Human Rights in Alabama* (University: University of Alabama Press, 1981) is an excellent source of information about one of the chief participants in Wallace's running battle with the federal judiciary.

To become more familiar with the civil rights movement, the reader should examine both primary and secondary sources pertaining to the late Dr. Martin Luther King, Jr. Most notable among Dr. King's own works are *I Have a Dream* (Agincourt, Ont.: Book Society of Canada, 1968), *Stride toward Freedom: The Montgomery Story* (New York: Harper & Row, 1958), and *Why We Can't Wait* (New York: Harper & Row, 1964). The latter includes the famous "Letter from the Birmingham

Jail." A well-received biography of Dr. King is David L. Lewis's *King: A Biography*, 2d ed. (Urbana: University of Illinois Press, 1978).

Shorter sketches of notable contemporary Alabamians will be found in such volumes as *Who's Who in the United States, Who's Who in the South and Southwest*, and, on an irregular basis, *Who's Who in Alabama*. From an historical perspective, the researcher will find particularly useful William Garrett's volume *Reminiscences of Public Men in Alabama for Thirty Years* (Spartanburg, S.C.: Reprint Co., 1975) and Willis Brewer's *Alabama: Her History, Resources, War Record and Public Men, from 1540 to 1872* (Spartanburg, S.C.: Reprint Co., 1975). Thomas M. Owen's four-volume *History of Alabama and Dictionary of Alabama Biography* (1921) is another source.

An especially fascinating way to study Alabama is to read novels set in the state. Probably the best known of these is *To Kill a Mockingbird* (Philadelphia: Lippincott, 1960), for which the writer, Harper Lee, won a Pulitzer Prize. Another important book, though less widely known, is *Mud on the Stars* (New York: New American Library, 1955; original copyright, 1942) by William Bradford Huie, one of Alabama's most prolific twentieth-century writers. A third work, set in the same general period as Huie's book (the Great Depression), is Carl Carmer's *Stars Fell on Alabama* (New York: Literary Guild, 1934). We should hasten to add that Carmer's book is not a novel; it contains impressions of life in different parts of Alabama a half century ago. The University of Alabama Press reissued the book in 1985 and plans to reprint works of similar stature in its Alabama Classics Series. One of the most recent novels set in Alabama but dealing with an even more distant period is Mark Childress's *A World Made of Fire: A Story of Alabama at the Turn of the Century* (New York: Knopf, 1984). A nonfiction book of sketches on more recent times in Alabama has been written by Scottie Fitzgerald Smith, the daughter of F. Scott Fitzgerald. Her book is entitled *An Alabama Journal* (Huntsville: Strode, 1976).

Readers interested in bibliographies devoted to Alabama government and politics now have several sources available. The most extensive general bibliography of sources is probably Robert B. Harmon's *Government and Politics in Alabama* (Monticello, Ill.: Council of Planning Librarians, 1978). A good example of available specialized bibliographies is Don Dodd's *The History of Black Politics in Alabama* (Monticello, Ill.: Vance Bibliographies, 1979). Two others, of unpublished materials, are Allen W. Jones's *Theses and Dissertations in Alabama History, 1900–1968* (Tuscaloosa: University of Alabama, 1969) and Exir Brannan's *A Dissertation Bibliography: Alabama* (Ann Arbor, Mich.: University Microfilms, n.d.). A very selective critique of volumes relating to Alabama is Rucker Agee's *Twenty Alabama Books* (Miami, Fla.: E. A. Seeman Publishing Co., 1975).

ALABAMA GOVERNMENT

The Constitution

Professor Malcolm C. McMillan's book *Constitutional Development in Alabama, 1798–1901: A Study in Politics, the Negro, and Sectionalism* (Chapel Hill: University of North Carolina Press, 1955) is an excellent history of the subject. More difficult to comprehend will be the constitution of 1901 itself, with its more than four hundred amendments. Because of its extreme length, the constitution is generally unavailable in any single volume, not excepting the state *Code,* which employs supplements and pocket parts to furnish its users with an updated version of Alabama's much-amended constitution. The minutes (journal) of the 1901 convention that drafted the constitution are generally available in volumes of manageable proportions. Constitutional referenda were discussed at some length earlier in the text. Votes on referenda held in years past are found in the *Official and Statistical Register* (last published in 1975) and, more recently, in the files of the secretary of state and issues of leading daily newspapers.

The Legislative Branch

It is not hard to find data on the processes and products of the state legislature. The most comprehensive source dealing with the legislative product is the *Code,* annotated copies of which are available in law libraries and probably most of the larger college and university libraries. Noncodified session laws are published in *Acts of Alabama,* issued following one or more regular or special legislative sessions. These volumes present acts in the chronological order in which they became laws. In some functional areas—education, for example—separate volumes deal solely with laws pertaining to a particular subject. In recent years the Alabama Women's Commission has made a compilation of laws pertaining especially to women. Pamphlet copies of the acts are distributed before publication and may be found in probate judges' offices relatively soon after their enactment.

Records of legislative proceedings in regular and special sessions (the session journals) are published by the House and Senate. One notable difference between these volumes and the *Congressional Record* is that the Alabama records (as is the case with most states) do not contain legislative debates. One can use these volumes to trace the course of a bill from introduction to its ultimate enactment into law. However, as for who said what (if legislators' comments are available at all), one must look in the daily newspapers that provide the most extensive coverage of legislative developments. Legislative records are routinely filed in the DOAH and university libraries. Legislative daily journals can be located in the secretary of state's office and the DOAH.

Legislative committee reports are not published on a systematic basis. We have referred to important reports of special legislative study committees. Most work, however, is done by the House and Senate standing committees, and their work is not recorded in any complete fashion. Again, to find out what committee members' individual and collective views were on bills referred to the committees it is necessary to consult newspaper records. Official reports, stating the committee's recommendation that a bill "do pass," will be only of marginal benefit. Newspaper research on current topics can be supplemented, of course, by interviews with participants in political events. Harold Stanley's book on the 1971 Senate session, is a fine illustration of how this technique can be used as a research tool. Occasionally, reports of regular and special committees will be drafted in an unusually comprehensive form. These reports are generally filed with the clerk of the House of Representatives and/or the secretary of the Senate.

The House and Senate publish handbooks primarily for the benefit of members. It may be possible, however, to obtain access to these volumes in libraries, and they furnish useful information on legislative procedures and personalities. A book recounting the history of the Senate, whose coauthors include the longtime secretary of the Senate, is *The Role of the Senate in Alabama History,* by McDowell Lee, H. E. Sterkx, and Benjamin B. Williams (Troy, Ala.: Troy State University Press, 1978). In addition, the Alabama Law Institute publishes materials for and about the legislature, as does Auburn University's Office of Public Service and Research. The place for any student of the Alabama legislature to begin, however, is with the late Hallie Farmer's pioneering work *The Legislative Process in Alabama,* published by the University of Alabama Bureau of Public Administration in 1949.

The Executive Branch

The most important primary materials relating to the governor are the gubernatorial messages. Messages delivered to the legislature are published in the volumes of the legislative sessions to which the messages were addressed. There is no systematic arrangement for publication of other executive statements, so there is no state serial comparable to the *Messages and Papers of the Presidents.* However, the researcher may be able to locate the published messages and papers of some governors.

The proclamations and executive orders of the governors are filed in the DOAH, as are recent executive budget documents. A major study of budgeting in Alabama is Joseph C. Pilegge's *Taxing and Spending: Alabama's Budget in Transition* (University: University of Alabama Press, 1978). Two other scholars long associated with the University of Alabama have written discerningly of Alabama's and other states' governors. Coleman B. Ransone, Jr., was the author of *The Office of Governor in the South* (University: Bureau of Public Administration, University of Alabama, 1951), *The Office of Governor in the United States* (University: University of Alabama Press, 1956), and *The American Governorship* (Westport, Conn.: Greenwood Press, 1982). An article pertaining to Alabama and other southern chief executives that urges caution with respect to moves to strengthen gubernatorial power is Robert B. Highsaw's "The Southern Governor—Challenge to the Strong Executive Theme," *Public Administration Review* 19 (Winter 1959): 7–11. An informative book dealing with the governorship is John C. Stewart's *The Governors of Alabama* (Gretna, La.: Pelican Publishing Co., 1975). As to particular governors, a dissertation pertaining to Governor James E. Folsom is Thomas J. Gilliam's "The Second Folsom Administration: The Destruction of Alabama Liberalism" (Ph.D. dissertation, Auburn University, 1975). One should also be aware of George E. Sims's *The Little Man's Big Friend: James E. Folsom in Alabama Politics, 1946–1958* (University: University of Alabama Press, 1985). At the time of writing, another book about Folsom was forthcoming from the University of Georgia Press: *Big Mules and Branchheads: James E. Folsom and Political Power in Alabama,* by Carl Grafton and Anne Permaloff. Earlier we listed a sampling of publications relating to Governor Wallace.

The most useful general reference work on administrative agencies is the *Alabama Government Manual,* now published on an intermittent basis by the Alabama Law Institute at the University of Alabama Law Center. The State of Alabama's annual report, copublished by the state comptroller and the Department of Finance, contains extremely useful financial data. We have made extensive use of it. Works dealing with administrative organization and reorganization are cited in our chapter notes. For more specialized studies, one should consult the individual annual reports published by particular agencies—for example, the Highway Department or the Department of Human Resources. More often than not, though, these reports appear some time after the end of the fiscal year whose activities they describe. Departments and other bureaucratic units also publish brochures that serve as guides to the services offered by the agencies.

The Judicial Branch

Comprehensive collections of the opinions of the Supreme Court of Alabama will be found in almost any law library as well as in the DOAH Library. The same will generally be found true for the decisions of the Courts of Appeals, both before and after this tribunal was split into separate criminal and civil courts. A noteworthy addition to materials on the state judiciary is the annual report now issued by the

Administrative Office of the Courts. The opinions of federal judges in Alabama are, of course, also published, and most are easily accessible in law libraries. The opinions of the attorney general are collected and published quarterly and, like strictly judicial opinions, can be found in most law libraries.

The most prominent legal periodical in Alabama is the *Alabama Law Review.* Practically every issue contains important articles pertaining to matters related to Alabama judicial policy and institutions. Another legal periodical is the *Alabama Lawyer,* the official publication of the Alabama Bar Association. Due to the national importance of legal developments in Alabama, numerous articles pertaining to Alabama may also be assembled from law journals published throughout the United States.

RESEARCH CENTERS AND DATA SOURCES

Research Centers

Illustrating the governmental research centers in the state are those located at the University of Alabama and Auburn University. The Alabama unit is the Center for Social and Policy Studies, formerly the Center for Administrative and Policy Studies, which was the successor to the University's old Bureau of Public Administration. The new center is now part of a larger research organization, the Institute for Social Science Research. The bureau's publication program has been discontinued, so many of its publications are becoming increasingly more difficult to obtain. Auburn's governmental research unit is called the Office of Public Service and Research. An example of the publications it has issued is *Home Rule for Local Governments,* by David L. Martin and Keith J. Ward (rev. ed., 1978). In addition to the Office of Public Service and Research, much material pertaining to Alabama is distributed by the Cooperative Extension Service, which is also located on the Auburn campus.

Fiscal and Economic Data

Fiscal and economic data pertaining to Alabama may be found at the University of Alabama's Center for Business and Economic Research, located within the College of Commerce and Business Administration, and at similar research centers at other institutions. In addition, much information of this type is contained in federal publications, particularly those issued by the Bureau of the Census and the divisions of the Treasury Department. We have made extensive use of the State of Alabama's *Annual Report,* published by the Department of Finance. The *Alabama County Data*

Book, published by the Department of Economic and Community Affairs, is another useful source of statistical data.

Important statistical data will also be found frequently in publications of organizations of city and county officials, most notably the League of Municipalities and the Association of County Commissions. For historically important data, the researcher should consult the *Atlas of Alabama* (University: University of Alabama Press, 1973) which we used extensively in the preparation of chapter 1. Other sources of statistical data may be located by consulting the bibliographies of publications that we have mentioned.

Public Opinion Surveys

There are a number of public opinion polls active in Alabama, one of which is the Capstone Poll, headquartered at the University of Alabama. The Capstone Poll regularly surveys opinions on a wide variety of subjects, not simply at election times. The poll makes its services available to legitimately interested organizations but does not work for particular candidates. In 1984 the university became the headquarters for the Network of State Polls. Thus a substantial amount of survey data pertaining not merely to Alabama but also to many other states is expected to become increasingly accessible to students of state government and politics. Polling is an important new development in Alabama political science, especially to students of voting behavior. Survey data of this sort were hard to come by until recently.

We should note that surveys are also conducted independently by major state newspapers, most significantly by the *Birmingham Post-Herald,* the *Montgomery Advertiser–Alabama Journal,* and the *Birmingham News.*

Campaigns and Election Sources

The student of elections in Alabama will find most useful the study of historically significant elections in the state-published volumes of election data entitled *Alabama Official and Statistical Register.* However, since this volume has not been issued for over a decade, to analyze recent elections it will be necessary to acquire photocopies of needed returns from the office of the secretary of state. Official returns are also usually published in the more comprehensive daily newspapers a few weeks following election day.

As noted in the text, Alabama has some laws on campaign finance. Data that are required to be filed are normally located in the offices of the secretary of state, the secretary of the Senate, the clerk of the House, the State Ethics Commission, or the Federal Election Commission in Washington. The last named is the best source insofar as financial data pertaining to U.S. House, Senate, and presidential primary and general elections are concerned.

News Media

For primary newspaper research into bygone political eras, it is most profitable to consult back issues of such newspapers as the *Montgomery Advertiser,* the *Alabama Journal* (also in Montgomery), the *Selma Times* and the *Selma Journal,* and the *Mobile Register.* The *Montgomery Daily Mail* and the *Selma Daily Messenger* are also helpful for historical data. Since Birmingham is a relatively young city, its newspapers, such as the *Birmingham News* and the *Post-Herald,* become of major importance only around the turn of the century. Many of the historically significant newspapers are available on microfilm. However, it is quite possible that in some instances the reader will have to leaf carefully through very old newspapers in the original form.

We emphasize the importance of the daily press to the serious study of Alabama government and politics, given the incompleteness of official records. It is our view that the best guides to ongoing developments in Alabama are the large-city dailies, such as the *Birmingham News* and the *Post-Herald,* the *Montgomery Advertiser* and the *Alabama Journal,* the *Mobile Press,* and the *Mobile Register.* Several smaller cities also have newspapers that provide extensive coverage of state politics, however. For example, we were able to rely heavily on our local daily, the *Tuscaloosa News,* in the preparation of this study. The broadcast media, of course, can be used to keep tabs on current happenings in the state government. A news program on public television, "For the Record," is directed particularly toward Alabama government and politics.

Newspapers generally are not indexed. However, if the researcher has a fairly accurate notion of when a particular development occurred, it should not be too difficult to find it by scanning the newspapers mentioned above or others during the relevant periods. Some national papers (the *New York Times,* for example) are indexed, and the publication date may be available in these indexes. Through such techniques as these, the researcher can usually find in a fairly short period of time a plentiful amount of information on practically any newsworthy subject.

Notes

CHAPTER ONE

1 This account is partially based on the account of Wallace's life appearing in Jack Bass and Walter DeVries, *The Transformation of Southern Politics: Social Change and Political Consequence since 1945* (New York: New American Library, 1977), pp. 59–71.

2 Charles G. Summersell, *Alabama History for Schools,* 5th ed. (Montgomery: Viewpoint Publications, 1975), p. 486.

3 The best treatment of American state and regional cultures is Daniel J. Elazar, *American Federalism: A View from the States* (New York: Thomas Y. Crowell Co., 1966).

4 The main source of the geographical and historical data presented in this chapter is Neal G. Lineback, ed., *Atlas of Alabama* (University: University of Alabama Press, 1973); here the reference is to p. 10. The atlas was supplemented by Summersell, *Alabama History for Schools;* A. B. Moore, *History of Alabama* (University, Ala.: University Supply Store, 1934); and V. O. Key, Jr., *Southern Politics in State and Nation* (New York: Alfred A. Knopf, 1949), esp. pp. 41–46, 282–83. U.S. Bureau of the Census data were also utilized. We also referred to the interesting commentary appearing in *Hunter* v. *Underwood,* 105 S. Ct. 1916 (1985), on the adoption of the constitutional article on the suffrage that we mention toward the end of this chapter. In this case, the U.S. Supreme Court invalidated Alabama's practice of disfranchising people convicted of a variety of minor crimes involving "moral turpitude."

5 See William H. Stewart, Jr., *The Tennessee-Tombigbee Waterway: A Case Study in the Politics of Water Transportation* (University: Bureau of Public Administration, University of Alabama, 1971).

6 Summersell, *Alabama History for Schools*, pp. 162, 201.

7 A number of documents important in Alabama history are contained in the *Code of Alabama, 1923,* vol. 1, the source of the boundary description of Mississippi Territory, for example.

8 Moore, *History of Alabama*, p. 650.

9 The most significant modern source here is David B. Truman, *The Governmental Process* (New York: Alfred A. Knopf, 1951). The classic source is Federalist Number 10, by James Madison. See any edition of the papers—for example, the 1961 New American Library edition, with an introduction by Clinton Rossiter.

10 Moore, *History of Alabama*, pp. 160–61.

11 Ibid., p. 426.

12 Ibid., pp. 438–39.

13 Key, *Southern Politics*, pp. 42–43.

14 Alexander P. Lamis, *The Two-Party South* (New York: Oxford University Press, 1984), pp. 82–83; and Donald S. Strong, "Alabama: Transition and Alienation," in *The Changing Politics of the South,* ed. William C. Havard (Baton Rouge: Louisiana State University Press, 1972), pp. 451–52; Patrick R. Cotter, "George Wallace and the Changing Party Politics of Alabama," (Paper presented at the 1983 annual meeting of the Southern Political Science Association, Birmingham, November 3–5, 1983), p. 2.

15 Lamis, *Two-Party South*, p. 82.

16 Strong, "Alabama," pp. 433, 440–41.

17 Cotter, "George Wallace," p. 9.

18 See, e.g., Cotter, "George Wallace." The immediately preceding quotation is from Moore, *History of Alabama*, p. 650.

19 For the details of the contest, see the daily press for the period June 27–October 15, 1986. On October 14 the U.S. Supreme Court denied Graddick an expedited review of unfavorable lower-court decisions. Our account of the contest and the subsequent general election relies heavily on the *Tuscaloosa News*. On national coverage see, for example, *New York Times,* June 26, 1986, p. 8 (national edition), and July 10, 1986, p. A21; also *Time,* October 20, 1986, p. 40.

CHAPTER TWO

1 See William H. Stewart, Jr., *Concepts of Federalism* (Lanham, Md.: Center for the Study of Federalism, and the University Press of America, 1984).

2 Edward S. Corwin, *Constitutional Revolution Ltd.* (Claremont, Calif.: Claremont Colleges, 1941), p. 99.

3 21 Howard 509, quoted in U.S. Advisory Commission on Intergovernmental

Relations, *The Federal Role in the Federal System: The Dynamics of Growth* (Washington, D.C.: The Commission, 1981), p. 3.

4 92 U.S. 542 (1876), quoted in ibid.

5 The view that is accepted here is that cooperative federalism, even though it long went unlabeled, is as old as the republic. This position has been most effectively articulated by Morton Grodzins and Daniel J. Elazar. Elazar, in *The American Partnership,* (Chicago: University of Chicago Press, 1963), p. 24, asserted that "federalism in the United States . . . has traditionally been cooperative. . . . [D]ual federalism as demarcation of responsibilities has never worked in practice."

6 David B. Walker, *Toward a Functioning Federalism* (Cambridge, Mass.: Winthrop Publishers, 1981), p. 47.

7 A. B. Moore, *History of Alabama* (University: University Supply Store, 1934), pp. 162–69.

8 Ibid., p. 656.

9 Reo M. Christenson, *Heresies Right and Left: Some Political Assumptions Reexamined* (New York: Harper & Row, 1973), p. 118.

10 This interpretation is found in Eugene P. Dvorin and Arthur J. Misner, *Government in American Society* (Reading, Mass.: Addison-Wesley Publishing Co., 1968), p. 67.

11 See, for example, James T. Harris, "Alabama Reaction to the Brown Decision: A Case Study in Massive Resistance" (Ph.D. dissertation, Middle Tennessee State University, 1978). The Wallace quote appears in the *Birmingham Post-Herald,* January 15, 1963, p. 1.

12 *Gayle* v. *Browder,* 352 U.S. 903 (1956).

13 On the use of this expression, see, for example, Earl Black, *Southern Governors and Civil Rights: Racial Segregation as a Campaign Issue in the Second Reconstruction* (Cambridge, Mass.: Harvard University Press, 1976).

14 Neal Peirce, *The Deep South States of America: People, Politics, and Power in the Seven Deep South States* (New York: W. W. Norton & Co., 1974), p. 239.

15 Ira Sharkansky, *The Maligned States* (New York: McGraw-Hill Book Co., 1972), pp. 6–7, reporting from James L. Sundquist, *Making Federalism Work* (Washington, D.C.: Brookings Institution, 1969), pp. 265–66.

16 Lecture delivered by Frank M. Johnson, Jr., at the University of Alabama, November 4, 1975. Judge Johnson attributes the use of the expression "Alabama Federal Intervention Syndrome" to Wayne McCormack, "The Expansion of Federal Question Jurisdiction and the Prisoner Complaint Caseload," *Wisconsin Law Review* 76, no. 2 (1975): 523–51; syndrome reference is on p. 536.

17 Johnson lecture.

18 See Tinsley E. Yarbrough, *Judge Frank Johnson and Human Rights in Alabama* (University: University of Alabama Press, 1981).

19 The concepts of symmetrical and asymmetrical federalism are most clearly developed in Charles D. Tarlton, "Symmetry and Asymmetry as Elements of Federalism: A Theoretical Speculation," *Journal of Politics* 27 (November 1965): 861–74. The information about religious groups in Alabama that appears later in this paragraph is based on Neal G. Lineback, ed., *Atlas of Alabama* (University: University of Alabama Press, 1973), pp. 50–51.

20 Marshall E. Dimock, *Modern Politics and Administration* (New York: American Book Co., 1937), pp. 54–55.

21 Corwin, *Constitutional Revolution Ltd.*, p. 98.

22 Dvorin and Misner, *Government in American Society,* p. 68.

23 See Max Ways, " 'Creative Federalism' and the Great Society," *Fortune,* January 1966, pp. 120–23ff.

24 A discussion of the impact of federal retrenchment efforts appears in Susannah Calkins and John Shannon, "The New Formula for Fiscal Federalism: Austerity Equals Decentralization," *Intergovernmental Perspective* 8 (Winter 1982): 23–29.

25 Jack C. Plano and Milton Greenberg, comps. *The American Political Dictionary,* 3d ed. (Hinsdale, Ill.: Dryden Press, 1972), p. 38.

26 Constitution of the United States, Article 4, Sections 1, 2.

27 See "Southern Congressmen Present Segregation Manifesto," *Congressional Quarterly Almanac,* vol. 12 (Washington, D.C.: Congressional Quarterly News Features, 1956), pp. 416–17.

28 Donald S. Strong, "Alabama: Transition and Alienation," in *The Changing Politics of the South,* ed. William C. Havard (Baton Rouge: Louisiana State University Press, 1972), pp. 449–50.

29 *Tuscaloosa News,* April 14, 1978, p. 18. For another refusal of extradition, this one by California governor Jerry Brown, see *Birmingham News,* June 13, 1977, pp. 1, 6.

30 D. L. Rosenau, "Those 'Quickie' Alabama Divorces," *Alabama Lawyer* 18 (January 1957): 37–40.

CHAPTER THREE

1 For more on constitutions, see, for example, Carl B. Swisher, *American Constitutional Development* (Cambridge, Mass.: Houghton Mifflin Co., 1943), p. 10; Gabriel A. Almond and G. Bingham Powell, Jr., *Comparative Politics* (Boston: Little, Brown and Co., 1978), pp. 15, 242; Charles R. Adrian, *State and Local*

Governments, 4th ed. (New York: McGraw-Hill Book Co., 1976), p. 80; Russell W. Maddox and Robert F. Fuquay, *State and Local Government* (New York: D. Van Nostrand, 1975), p. 35; and Thomas R. Dye, *Politics in States and Communities,* 3d ed. (Englewood Cliffs, N.J.: Prentice-Hall, 1977), p. 18.

2 Malcolm C. McMillan, *Constitutional Development in Alabama, 1798–1901: A Study in Politics, the Negro, and Sectionalism* (Chapel Hill: University of North Carolina Press, 1955; reprinted by the Reprint Company, Publishers, Spartanburg, S.C., 1978), pp. 358–62; Alabama Constitutional Commission, *Proposed Constitution of Alabama: Report of the Constitutional Commission* (Montgomery: The Commission, 1973), p. vii, the source of the quotation.

3 In Alabama, litigation in federal courts has been a significant source of public policy, especially in such areas as race relations, reapportionment, property tax administration, prisons, and mental health. For an interesting account of recent civil rights litigation in Alabama, see Tinsley E. Yarbrough, *Judge Frank Johnson and Human Rights in Alabama* (University: University of Alabama Press, 1981).

4 McMillan, *Constitutional Development in Alabama,* pp. 365–66.

5 Ibid., pp. viii–ix, 327, 328; Amendment 1, adopted November 3, 1908.

6 Constitution of Alabama, 1901, Sections 50, 197–203; Hallie Farmer, *The Legislative Process in Alabama* (University: Bureau of Public Administration, University of Alabama, 1949), pp. 28–30.

7 A. B. Moore, *History of Alabama* (University: University Supply Store, 1934), p. 650.

8 369 U.S. 186 (1962).

9 377 U.S. 533 (1964).

10 Constitution of Alabama, 1901, Sections 112, 114, 116.

11 Amendment 282. See Donald S. Strong, "Alabama: Transition and Alienation," in *The Changing Politics of the South,* ed. William C. Havard (Baton Rouge: Louisiana State University Press, 1972), pp. 452–53. Sheriffs were permitted to succeed themselves in office by Amendment 35, adopted in 1938. Amendment 284, adopted in 1969, altered the procedure for selecting the state superintendent of education by requiring the appointment of the superintendent by an elective state board of education.

12 Constitution of Alabama, 1901, Sections 117, 132, 173.

13 Ibid., Sections 127, 128.

14 Amendment 323, adopted in 1972, and Amendment 328, adopted in 1973.

15 McMillan, *Constitutional Development in Alabama,* p. vi; Constitution of Alabama, 1901, Article 8.

16 For example, Constitution of Alabama, 1901, Amendment 96, which reduced

the poll tax requirement to two years, and Amendment 207, which reduced the residence requirement from two years to one. See also Constitution of the United States, Amendments 15, prohibiting racial discrimination in voting; 19, providing for women's suffrage; 24, prohibiting the requirement of a poll tax in elections for federal officers; and 26, reducing the voting age to eighteen. Also, see the Voting Rights Act of 1965 and its amendments, and *Harper* v. *Virginia Board of Elections,* 383 U.S. 663 (1966), and *U.S.* v. *Alabama,* 252 F. Supp. 95 (M.D. Ala. 1966), relative to the poll tax; *Hadnott* v. *Amos,* 320 F. Supp. 107 (M.D. Ala. 1970), and *Dunn* v. *Blumstein,* 405 U.S. 330 (1972), invalidating durational residence requirements.

17 Constitution of Alabama, 1901, Article 18 (Sections 284–87), as amended by Amendment 24. See also Amendment 425, which relates to local amendments. Those interested in the process should consult Amendment 425, because it is more complicated than is indicated in the text.

18 See *Harris* v. *Walker,* 199 Ala. 51, 74 So. 40 (1917).

19 Dye, *Politics in States and Communities,* p. 24.

20 Lawrence M. Friedman, *A History of American Law* (New York: Simon and Schuster, 1973), pp. 103–4.

21 McMillan, *Constitutional Development in Alabama,* p. vi.

22 Brookings Institution, Institute for Government Research, *Organization and Administration of the State Government of Alabama,* 5 vols. (Montgomery, 1932), vol. 1, pp. 52–53.

23 Ibid., p. 51. See also A. B. Moore, *History of Alabama,* p. 790; Charles G. Summersell, *Alabama History for Schools,* 5th ed. (Montgomery: Viewpoint Publications, 1975), p. 495.

24 Quoted in William H. Stewart, Jr., *The Alabama Constitutional Commission: A Pragmatic Approach to Constitutional Revision* (University: University of Alabama Press, 1975), p. 6.

25 This and the preceding paragraph draw on ibid., pp. 3–4; McMillan, *Constitutional Development in Alabama,* p. viii; and Alabama Constitutional Commission, *Proposed Constitution of Alabama, Report of the Constitutional Commission* (Montgomery, 1973), pp. vii–viii.

26 Albert L. Sturm, "State Constitutions and Constitutional Revision, 1976–1977," *Book of the States, 1978–79* (Lexington, Ky.: Council of State Governments, 1978), pp. 194, 201.

27 Ibid., p. 198.

28 Stewart, *Alabama Constitutional Commission,* p. 7.

29 Ibid., pp. 8–10; Act 753, *Acts of Alabama,* Regular Session, 1969, p. 1330.

30 Stewart, *Alabama Constitutional Commission,* pp. 9–12; Act 95, *Acts of Alabama,* Organizational, Special, and Regular Sessions, 1971, vol. 1, p. 165.

31 Alabama Constitutional Commission, *Proposed Constitution of Alabama*. The comments that follow in the text are drawn from this document.

32 Ibid., p. v.

33 Sturm, "State Constitutions and Constitutional Revision, 1972–1973," Council of State Governments, *Book of the States, 1974–1975*, p. 9; Charles Press and Kenneth VerBurg, *State and Community Governments in the Federal System* (New York: John Wiley and Sons, 1979), p. 176.

34 The concept is well known, but this terminology is drawn from Press and VerBurg, *State and Community Governments*, p. 180.

35 James D. Thomas, *Adoption of Annual Legislative Sessions: The Case of Alabama* (University: Bureau of Public Administration, University of Alabama, 1976), pp. 6, 8. The amendment was proposed by Act 1264 of the 1971 regular session. For a discussion of the proposal's legislative history, see Stewart, *Alabama Constitutional Commission*, pp. 36–38. The measure proposed was not the one sponsored by the commission but one derived from another source—the chairman of the legislative committee mentioned in the text.

36 Alabama Constitutional Commission, *A New Constitution for the Alabama Court System: The Judicial Article—Proposed Amendment Number 2* (Columbiana, Ala.: The Commission, 1973).

37 Thomas, *Annual Legislative Sessions*, p. 11. The judicial article became Amendment 328, mentioned earlier in the chapter.

38 The amendment was proposed by Act 2, Second Special Session, 1975. Thomas, *Annual Legislative Sessions*, pp. 11–12, 20. The proposal became Amendment 339.

39 McMillan, *Constitutional Development in Alabama*, pp. vii, 329, 358.

40 See V. O. Key, Jr., *Southern Politics in State and Nation* (New York: Alfred A. Knopf, 1949). Key entitled his chapter on Alabama, "Alabama: Planters, Populists, 'Big Mules.' " The term was commonly used in the state and was especially associated with Governor Folsom.

41 L. Harmon Zeigler and Hendrik van Dalen, "Interest Groups in State Politics," in *Politics in the American States*, ed. Herbert Jacob and Kenneth N. Vines, 3d ed. (Boston: Little, Brown and Co., 1976), p. 98.

42 See, for example, *Montgomery Advertiser*, January 1, 1978, p. 14B; November 5, 1978, pp. 9–10. Also, see Jack Bass and Walter DeVries, *The Transformation of Southern Politics: Social Change and Political Consequence since 1945* (New York: New American Library, 1977), p. 73. Bass and DeVries note the continuing influence of land interests.

43 See Stewart, *Alabama Constitutional Commission*, p. 117.

44 The news media, of course, maintained a continuing record of this activity. For the examples cited here, see *Montgomery Advertiser*, January 18, 1979, p. 3;

January 30, 1979, pp. 1, 2; March 1, 1979, p. 17; and March 2, 1979, p. 9. This document, as introduced, was Senate Bill 40. The Alabama Law Institute published a version of it.

45 *Tuscaloosa News,* April 14, 1983, pp. 1, 3; April 18, 1983, p. 4.

46 The constitution was proposed by Act 83–683. Secretary of State Don Siegelman made printed copies available.

47 *Tuscaloosa News,* September 18, 1983, p. 22A; September 26, 1983, p. 1; September 27, 1983, p. 9; October 1, 1983, p. 4; October 12, 1983, p. 11; October 13, 1983, p. 11; October 17, 1983, p. 20; October 22, 1983, p. 3; November 2, 1983, p. 1. The Constitutional Commission had expressed some doubt as to whether the legislature could submit a whole constitution to the voters as a single constitutional amendment. It suggested that its proposed amendment article, which did permit wholesale revision by constitutional amendment, could first be adopted as one way of removing these doubts. See Alabama Constitutional Commission, *Proposed Constitution of Alabama,* pp. vi–vii, 141–43. Some state courts have held that a completely revised, or new, constitution can be proposed by the legislature. See Daniel R. Grant and H. C. Nixon, *State and Local Government in America* (Boston: Allyn and Bacon, 1982), pp. 113, 116–17. For the Georgia experience, see Tip H. Allen, Jr., and Coleman B. Ransone, Jr., *Constitutional Revision in Theory and Practice* (University: Bureau of Public Administration, University of Alabama, 1962), pp. 134–36.

CHAPTER FOUR

1 Clyde F. Snider, *American State and Local Government,* 2d ed. (New York: Appleton-Century-Crofts, 1965), pp. 213–14; Richard A. Thigpen and Coleman B. Ransone, Jr., eds., *Alabama Government Manual* (University: Alabama Law Institute, 1982), p. 441.

2 Hallie Farmer, *The Legislative Process in Alabama* (University: Bureau of Public Administration, University of Alabama, 1949), p. 21.

3 The following paragraphs draw on James D. Thomas and L. Franklin Blitz, *The Alabama Legislature* (University: Bureau of Public Administration, University of Alabama, 1974), pp. 6–7. The court case mentioned is *Sims* v. *Amos,* 336 F. Supp. 924 (M.D. Ala. 1972).

4 See William H. Stewart, Jr., "Reapportionment with Census Districts: The Alabama Case," *Alabama Law Review* 24 (Summer 1972): 698–99.

5 Ibid., p. 706.

6 See, e.g., Office of Secretary of State, Elections Division, "Alabama Elections Update," vol. 2, no. 2 (August 20, 1982), p. 1. See also *Tuscaloosa News,* April

12, 1983, p. 1. Actually, the legislature drafted several reapportionment plans. It worked from 1981 until 1983 to produce the approved plan.

7 Constitution of Alabama, 1901, Section 47 and *Code of Alabama, 1975,* Section 36–2–1; Farmer, *Legislative Process in Alabama,* p. 4; Robert L. McCurley, Jr., and James D. Thomas, eds., *The Legislative Process: A Handbook for Alabama Legislators* (University: Alabama Law Institute, 1980), p. 5.

8 McCurley and Thomas, *Legislative Process,* p. 5. Farmer, *Legislative Process in Alabama,* p. 9; McDowell Lee, H. E. Sterkx, and Benjamin B. Williams, *The Role of the Senate in Alabama History* (Troy, Ala.: Troy State University Press, 1978), pp. 101–2; Constitution of Alabama, 1901, Sections 46 and 53.

9 Constitution of Alabama, 1901, Amendment 57. This discussion is partially based on Thomas and Blitz, *Alabama Legislature,* p. 8.

10 See Act 79–7, Senate Joint Resolution 13, *Acts of Alabama,* Organizational Session, 1979. Also, see *Tuscaloosa News,* January 14, 1980, p. 3; January 22, 1981, p. 35; November 16, 1983, p. 1; November 22, 1983, p. 1; November 23, 1983, p. 1. Interestingly, the monthly expense allowance was reduced in 1983 from a proposed $700 to $600 through the process of executive amendment. In the summer of 1987, after this manuscript was sent to the press, the legislators changed their per diem from $85 to $40 and their monthly expense allowance to $1,900. The change increased their "base pay" considerably. See *Tuscaloosa News,* June 14, 1987, pp. 1A and 15A.

11 The following material has been adapted from Thomas and Blitz, *Alabama Legislature,* pp. 13–15. Also consulted were Alabama Legislative Reference Service, *A Manual for Alabama Legislators* (1959) and McCurley and Thomas, *Legislative Process,* pp. 11–12.

12 This discussion of legislative sessions is largely taken from James D. Thomas, *Adoption of Annual Legislative Sessions: The Case of Alabama* (University: Bureau of Public Administration, University of Alabama, 1976), pp. 2–6, 11–12, 23–24; also Thomas and Blitz, *Alabama Legislature,* pp. 8–11; Farmer, *Legislative Process in Alabama,* pp. 5–9, 202–3, 259–60; Malcolm C. McMillan, "The Making of Alabama's Six Constitutions, 1819–1901," in Alabama Constitutional Commission, *Proposed Constitution of Alabama: Report of the Constitutional Commission* (Montgomery, 1973), p. 162; and McMillan, *Constitutional Development in Alabama,* pp. vii, 333–36.

13 Amendment 39.

14 Amendment 57.

15 Two state study groups recommended the adoption of annual sessions. Also, the Citizens Conference on State Legislatures (a national organization interested in the improvement of American legislatures, later known as Legis 50) made a

similar recommendation. The reports are Legislature of Alabama, Legislative Reform Study Committee, *Improving the Alabama Legislature* (Montgomery, 1970), Alabama Constitutional Commission, *Proposed Constitution of Alabama,* and Citizens Conference on State Legislatures, *The Sometime Governments: A Critical Study of the 50 American Legislatures* (New York: Bantam Books, 1971; reprinted by the Citizens Conference, Kansas City, Mo., 1973), with support for annual legislative sessions expressed on p. 169.

16 Alabama Constitutional Commission, *Proposed Constitution of Alabama,* p. 67.

17 The amendment was proposed by Act 2, Legislature of Alabama, Second Special Session, 1975. Upon its ratification it became Amendment 339.

18 In this chapter we have drawn our information on the legislative process in Alabama largely from Alabama Legislative Reference Service, *Manual for Alabama Legislators* (1959); McDowell Lee, *Alabama's Legislative Process and Legislative Glossary* (Montgomery, n.d.); Thomas and Blitz, *Alabama Legislature;* Farmer, *Legislative Process in Alabama;* Lee, Sterkx, and Williams, *Role of the Senate,* pp. 101–9; Robert L. McCurley, Jr., and James D. Thomas, eds., *The Legislative Process: A Handbook for Alabama Legislators* (University: Alabama Law Institute, 1980); Legislative Reference Service, "Legislative Processes and Procedures," *Senate Manual, State of Alabama, 1975–1979* (Revised March 1977), pp. 60–84; and the 1979 printed rules of the two houses of the legislature.

19 See *Code of Alabama, 1975,* Sections 29–7–1 through 29–7–7. Descriptions of the agencies that constitute the legislative branch may be found in Thigpen and Ransone, *Alabama Government Manual.*

20 McCurley and Thomas, *Legislative Process,* p. 43.

21 Council of State Governments, *The Book of the States, 1980–81* (Lexington, Ky.: The Council, 1980), pp. 104–5.

22 Robert L. McCurley, Jr., ed., *The Legislative Process* (University: Alabama Law Institute, 1984), p. 76.

23 This is a point usually made by students of the legislative process. The quotation here is from Harold W. Stanley, *Senate vs. Governor, Alabama, 1971: Referents for Opposition in a One-Party Legislature* (University: University of Alabama Press, 1975), p. 52.

24 Ibid., p. 56; McCurley and Thomas, *Legislative Process,* p. 47. In both houses, committee meetings may be called by a majority of the committee members.

25 Farmer, *Legislative Process in Alabama,* p. 157.

26 Alan Rosenthal, *Legislative Performance in the States: Explorations of Committee Behavior* (New York: Free Press, 1974), pp. 35, 42.

27 Farmer, *Legislative Process in Alabama,* pp. 156–57, 159.

28 *Improving the Alabama Legislature*, p. 14.

29 Stanley, *Senate vs. Governor*, p. 53.

30 Ibid., pp. 54, 61.

31 Farmer, *Legislative Process in Alabama*, pp. 64, 161; Malcolm E. Jewell, *The State Legislature: Politics and Practice* (New York: Random House, 1969), pp. 46–47; McCurley and Thomas, *Legislative Process*, p. 50; and Lee, Sterkx, and Williams, *Role of the Senate*, p. 105.

32 Farmer, *Legislative Process in Alabama*, pp. 276–309; Thomas and Blitz, *Alabama Legislature*, pp. 38–46. For national and regional data on legislative composition, see *U.S. News & World Report*, December 17, 1979, p. 74.

33 Thomas and Blitz, *Alabama Legislature*, pp. 38–46.

34 Charles Press and Kenneth VerBurg, *State and Community Governments in the Federal System*, 2d ed. (New York: John Wiley and Sons, 1983), p. 247.

35 See *Improving the Alabama Legislature* and *The Sometime Governments*, cited in note 15. This account is partially based on Thomas and Blitz, *Alabama Legislature*, pp. 48–52; and James D. Thomas, "Legislature Given Plan for Modernization," *Tuscaloosa News*, December 6, 1970, p. E2; *Senate Manual;* and the 1979 legislative rules.

36 Amendment 339.

37 Lee, Sterkx, and Williams, *Role of the Senate*, p. 109.

38 *Improving the Alabama Legislature*, p. i.

39 Betty B. Hardee, *Legislative and Citizen Attitudes about Public Issues in Alabama, 1983* (Tuscaloosa [University]: Center for Administrative and Policy Studies, University of Alabama, 1983), p. 17.

40 Capstone Poll, University of Alabama, Spring 1983. The alternative choices were "fair" and "poor". The ratings in Alabama during the period 1980–1983 were roughly similar to a national survey of citizens' perceptions of their state legislatures conducted in the summer of 1979 (31 percent). See Malcolm E. Jewell, ed., *Comparative State Politics Newsletter* (Lexington: Department of Political Science, University of Kentucky, October 1980), pp. 17–18.

CHAPTER FIVE

1 Constitution of Alabama, 1901, Sections 113ff.

2 See, for example, Coleman B. Ransone, Jr., *The American Governorship* (Westport, Conn.: Greenwood Press, 1982), pp. 97, 162, 177.

3 Ibid., p. 84.

4 See *Montgomery Advertiser*, September 27, 1985, p. 1C.

5 Hallie Farmer, *The Legislative Process in Alabama* (University: Bureau of Public

Administration, University of Alabama, 1949), pp. 167–93. The following discussion is based largely on this study.

6 Ibid., p. 187.

7 William D. Barnard, *Dixiecrats and Democrats: Alabama Politics, 1942–1950* (University: University of Alabama Press, 1974), pp. 77–80, 144–46.

8 Farmer, *Legislative Process in Alabama*, p. 303. Our interpretation here follows Farmer, p. 189.

9 Council of State Governments, *The Book of the States, 1980–81* (Lexington, Ky.: The Council, 1980), p. 103.

10 On the individual nature of Alabama politics, see, e.g., V. O. Key, Jr., *Southern Politics in State and Nation* (New York: Random House, 1949), pp. 39, 46–52.

11 Farmer, *Legislative Process in Alabama*, p. 167.

12 Harold W. Stanley, *Senate vs. Governor, Alabama, 1971: Referents for Opposition in a One-Party Legislature* (University: University of Alabama Press, 1975), p. 20. *Montgomery Advertiser,* November 19, 1978, p. 20A; January 4, 1979, p. 13; January 15, 1979, p. 14; and Jack Bass and Walter DeVries, *The Transformation of Southern Politics: Social Change and Political Consequence since 1945* (New York: New American Library, 1977), p. 75.

13 Stanley, *Senate vs. Governor,* pp. 13–30, 95. The quotations are from pp. 13 and 17.

14 *Tuscaloosa News,* October 10, 1982, p. 1.

15 See, e.g., Stanley, *Senate vs. Governor,* pp. 18–19, 95.

16 Ibid., p. 15.

17 Legislature of Alabama, Legislative Reform Study Committee, *Improving the Alabama Legislature* (Montgomery, 1970), p. 1. See Daniel R. Grant and H. C. Nixon, *State and Local Government in America* (Boston: Allyn and Bacon, 1982), pp. 252–54, for a general discussion, and the *Tuscaloosa News,* December 18, 1983, pp. 1A, 3A, for a commentary on the Alabama experience.

18 Again, in treating the lawmaking process, we have based our account on Robert L. McCurley, Jr., and James D. Thomas, eds., *The Legislative Process: A Handbook for Alabama Legislators* (University: Alabama Law Institute, 1980); James D. Thomas and L. Franklin Blitz, *The Alabama Legislature* (University: Bureau of Public Administration, University of Alabama, 1974); McDowell Lee, *Alabama's Legislative Process and Legislative Glossary* (Montgomery, n.d.); Farmer, *Legislative Process in Alabama;* and Legislative Reference Service, *A Manual for Alabama Legislators* (Montgomery, 1959). As to the amendatory veto, see Larry Sabato, *Goodbye to Good-Time Charlie* (Washington, D.C.: CQ Press, 1983), p. 77.

19 Farmer, *Legislative Process in Alabama,* pp. 179, 183. The governor's veto power is described in the Constitution of Alabama, 1901, Sections 125, 126.

20 Ransone, *American Governorship,* p. 72.

21 Ibid., pp. 48–83; Sabato, *Goodbye to Good-Time Charlie,* pp. 147–48.

22 Ransone, *American Governorship,* p. 55.

23 Stanley, *Senate vs. Governor,* pp. 15–16.

24 Here we are following Robert L. Lineberry's treatment of the presidency in his *Government in America: People, Politics, and Policy* (Boston: Little, Brown and Co., 1983), p. 400.

25 The source for much of the data presented in this section is John C. Stewart, *The Governors of Alabama* (Gretna, La.: Pelican Publishing Co., 1975).

26 Ibid., *passim.*

27 Ibid.

28 Other writers make a similar point. See, e.g., Grant and Nixon, *State and Local Government,* p. 259. Also, U.S. Advisory Commission on Intergovernmental Relations, *The Question of State Government Capability* (Washington, D.C.: The Commission, 1985), p. 127.

29 Again, we are influenced by Lineberry's treatment of the presidency in *Government in America.*

30 Charles Press and Kenneth VerBurg, *State and Community Governments in the Federal System,* 2d ed. (New York: John Wiley and Sons, 1983), p. 301.

31 Ibid., pp. 301–19; Ransone, *American Governorship,* p. 120.

32 Charles G. Summersell, *Alabama History for Schools,* 5th ed. (Montgomery: Viewpoint Publications, 1975), pp. 494–505; A. B. Moore, *History of Alabama* (University: University Supply Store, 1934), pp. 666–72, 765–66; Press and VerBurg, *State and Community Governments,* pp. 321–22.

33 Bass and DeVries, *Transformation of Southern Politics,* p. 57.

CHAPTER SIX

1 See, for example, the essays presented in Francis E. Rourke, ed., *Bureaucratic Power and National Politics,* 2d ed. (Boston: Little, Brown and Co., 1972).

2 The methods of selecting administrative officers in Alabama state government are presented in Richard A. Thigpen and Coleman B. Ransone, Jr., eds., *Alabama Government Manual* (University: Alabama Law Institute, 1982). The 1982 edition, along with earlier editions of this publication, edited by Ransone and issued by the University of Alabama's Bureau of Public Administration, are

the source of much of the information on agency organization and functions presented in this chapter.

3 The source of most of the administrative statistics presented in this section is William H. Stewart, Jr., *The Growth of State Administration in Alabama: A Contemporary Reassessment* (University: Bureau of Public Administration, University of Alabama, 1978). The number of governing authorities is smaller than the number of administrative agencies presented earlier in the chapter because in thirty-nine instances more than one agency was directed by the same head or heads.

4 Recently the name of the Department of Pensions and Security was changed to the Department of Human Resources. With respect to the Alcoholic Beverage Control Board, see William H. Stewart, Jr., *Government and Alcohol* (University: Bureau of Public Administration, University of Alabama, 1973), p. 12.

5 The principal source for the financial data presented in this chapter is State of Alabama, *Annual Report: Fiscal Year Ending September 30, 1985* (Montgomery: Office of the State Comptroller, 1985).

6 Thigpen and Ransone, *Alabama Government Manual*, p. 18.

7 This discussion of the policy-making process is based to a great extent on Larry N. Gerston, *Making Public Policy* (Glenview, Ill.: Scott, Foresman and Co., 1983), pp. 5ff.

8 Education is the only service function mentioned in the original articles of the constitution of 1901. See Article 12, sections 256–70.

9 This discussion on local educational organization draws on James D. Thomas, *A Manual for Alabama County Commissioners*, rev. ed. (University: Bureau of Public Administration, University of Alabama, 1979), pp. 54–56.

10 The principal sources for these statistics are: National Education Association, *Rankings of the States, 1985* (Westhaven, Conn.: NEA Publications, 1986), pp. 41–42; and the *Digest of Educational Statistics, 1985–86* (Washington, D.C.: Center for Statistics, Office of Educational Research and Improvement, U.S. Department of Education, 1986), p. 81.

11 Stephen D. Gold, *State and Local Fiscal Relations in the Early 1980s* (Washington, D.C.: Urban Institute Press, 1983), p. 20.

12 411 U.S. 59 (1973).

13 The statistics presented in this section have been derived from various annual editions of the *Statistical Abstract of the United States* (Washington, D.C.: U.S. Government Printing Office) and of the annual report of the Alabama Department of Education.

14 Much of the material in the following paragraphs is from recent annual reports of the State Highway Department. Jack Bass and Walter De Vries, in *The Transfor-*

mation of Southern Politics: Social Change and Political Consequence since 1945 (New York: New American Library, 1977), p. 73, mention the political character of highway spending decisions.

15 Gold, *State and Local Fiscal Relations,* p. 14.

16 Ibid., p. 20.

17 This discussion is partially based on Thomas, *Manual for County Commissioners,* pp. 51–53, 56–57.

18 Jeffrey D. Straussman, *Public Administration* (New York: Holt, Rinehart and Winston, 1985), p. 304.

19 Ibid.

20 Ibid.

21 *Tuscaloosa News,* March 13, 1985, p. 11; *Montgomery Advertiser,* October 2, 1984, pp. 1A, 2A.

22 Gold, *State and Local Fiscal Relations,* p. 20.

23 State of Alabama, *Annual Report, 1985,* pp. 7–8.

24 This account of property tax administration in Alabama draws on Thomas, *Manual for County Commissioners,* pp. 45, 72–78, 102–4.

25 The case was originally filed as *Hornbeak et al.* v. *Rabren.* The federal court's decision ordering a reappraisal program was issued as *Weissinger* v. *Boswell* on July 29, 1971. See 330 F. Supp. 615 (M.D. Ala. 1971). Previous conditions are described in a classic study, *The Alabama Revenue System, Report of the Revenue Survey Committee, An Interim Committee of the 1947 Legislature* (Montgomery, 1947).

26 See *McCarthy* v. *Jones,* 449 F. Supp. 480 (S.D. Ala. 1978). The Lid Bill became Amendment 373. See Bass and De Vries, *Transformation of Southern Politics,* p. 73, on landowner involvement in the politics of property tax assessments.

27 U.S. Department of Commerce, Bureau of the Census, *Statistical Abstract of the United States: 1986* (Washington, D.C.: U.S. Government Printing Office, 1985), p. 272.

28 Gold, *State and Local Fiscal Relations,* pp. 62–63.

29 For an analysis of recent trends in Alabama budgeting, see Joseph C. Pilegge, *Taxing and Spending: Alabama's Budget in Transition* (University: University of Alabama Press, 1978). Act 83–438 provides that the budget officer need no longer be appointed under the merit system.

30 Still valuable as a source of budgetary information is Paul E. Alyea, *Alabama's Balancing Budget* (University: Bureau of Public Administration, University of Alabama, 1942).

31 *Tuscaloosa News,* September 30, 1985, p. 9.

32 For a recent analysis of this agency, see Robert J. Freeman and John R. Cooper,

Governmental Auditing in Alabama: A Preliminary Study (Montgomery: Joint Legislative Committee on State Auditing, Alabama Legislature, 1975), pp. 29–45. The Auditor's Office, discussed earlier in this chapter, is treated on pp. 20–28 of this study.

33 Charles Press and Kenneth VerBurg, *State and Community Governments in the Federal System,* 2d ed. (New York: John Wiley and Sons, 1983), pp. 367–69.

34 The source for the information presented here is *The Alabama Merit System—1985: Annual Report of the State Personnel Department* (Montgomery: The Department, n.d.).

35 See the general discussion in Charles Warren, "State Governments' Capacity: Continuing to Improve," *National Civic Review,* May 1982, pp. 234ff.

36 Arthur E. Buck, *The Reorganization of State Governments in the United States* (New York: Columbia University Press, 1938). The list here is quoted, slightly expanded, and paraphrased from Buck, pp. 14–28.

37 See William H. Stewart, Jr., "Governor Frank Murray Dixon and Reform of State Administration in Alabama," in *The Public Life of Frank M. Dixon: Sketches and Speeches* (Montgomery: Alabama State Department of Archives and History, 1979), pp. 15–30.

38 This assertion is supported mostly by a table based on the *Code* issue years for the period 1823–1938 and the Bureau of Public Administration government manual publication years for 1942–1976. The table appears in Stewart, *State Administration in Alabama,* p. 34. Our discussion of the reorganization movement is partially based on this source.

39 For a discussion of Alabama's sunset law, see Pilegge, *Taxing and Spending,* pp. 75–77.

40 *Tuscaloosa News,* November 15, 1984, p. 1.

41 See, e.g., Robert B. Highsaw, "The Southern Governor—Challenge to the Strong Executive Theme," *Public Administration Review* 19 (Winter 1959): 7–11.

CHAPTER SEVEN

1 Constitution of Alabama, 1901, Amendment 323.

2 *Ward* v. *Village of Monroeville,* 409 U.S. 57 (1972).

3 See *Proposed Constitution of Alabama: Report of the Constitutional Commission* (Montgomery, 1973), p. 98.

4 The proposed judicial article, upon its adoption, became Amendment 328. It was implemented by Act 1205, Legislature of Alabama, Regular Session, 1975.

5 Henry R. Glick, *Courts, Politics, and Justice* (New York: McGraw-Hill, 1983), pp. 125–27, 164–84.

6 The basic sources of the information about the Alabama judiciary in this chapter are Alabama Legislative Reference Service, *Alabama Courts* (Montgomery, 1954); the *Code of Alabama, 1975;* Act 1205; an analysis of Act 1205 prepared by the then State Department of Court Management; Alabama Constitutional Commission, *A New Constitution for the Alabama Court System: The Judicial Article, Proposed Amendment Number 2* (Columbiana, Ala.: The Commission, 1973); and James D. Thomas, *A Manual for Alabama County Commissioners,* rev. ed. (University: Bureau of Public Administration, University of Alabama, 1979). All 1983 statistics are from Alabama Administrative Office of Courts, *Alabama Judicial System Annual Report: Fiscal Year 1983; October 1, 1982, to September 30, 1983* (Montgomery: The Office, n.d.), pp. 2–24. For the political significance of probate judges, see V. O. Key, Jr., *Southern Politics in State and Nation* (New York: Alfred A. Knopf, 1949), p. 53.

7 *Code of Alabama, 1975,* Sections 12–11–2 and 12–17–20, as amended; Alabama Judicial System, *Annual Report, 1983,* p. 9.

8 The change in designation from circuit solicitor to district attorney was accomplished by Amendment 226, adopted in 1965. This section is based largely on Thomas, *Manual for County Commissioners,* pp. 38–39.

9 Ibid., p. 44.

10 *Code of Alabama, 1975,* Sections 12–16–55 through 12–16–63.

11 *Tuscaloosa News,* November 15, 1983, pp. 1, 3.

12 The legislative vehicle for the creation of the courts of appeals was S. 237, Legislature of Alabama, Regular Session, 1969, effective October 1, 1969.

13 *Code of Alabama, 1975,* Sections 12–3–9 and 12–3–10. See also Hugh Maddox, James H. Faulkner, and William C. Younger, eds., *Alabama Appellate Courts, 1981: Supreme Court, Court of Criminal Appeals, Court of Civil Appeals* (Montgomery: Alabama Supreme Court, and the State Law Library, 1981), pp. 17, 24.

14 S. 59, Legislature of Alabama, Regular Session, 1969, approved August 29, 1969. The size of the Supreme Court was increased from seven to nine members.

15 Maddox, Faulkner, and Younger, *Alabama Appellate Courts,* pp. 16, 11, 14. See Robert J. Frye, *The Alabama Supreme Court: An Institutional View* (University: Bureau of Public Administration, University of Alabama, 1969), pp. 29–34, for a discussion of the social characteristics of Alabama Supreme Court justices.

16 See Maddox, Faulkner, and Younger, *Alabama Appellate Courts,* p. 5.

17 Frye, *Alabama Supreme Court,* pp. 41, 44, 46–47; James N. Bloodworth,

"Remodeling the Alabama Appellate Courts," *Alabama Law Review* 23 (Spring 1971): 355–56; Herbert Jacob, *Justice in America: Courts, Lawyers, and the Judicial Process* (Boston: Little, Brown and Co., 1978), pp. 217–18.

18 Frye, *Alabama Supreme Court,* pp. 41, 55.

19 Ibid., p. 55.

20 Jacob, *Justice in America,* p. 219.

21 Frye, *Alabama Supreme Court,* pp. 83–84.

22 Ibid., pp. 58–59.

23 Ibid., pp. 55, 59, 60, 85–86.

24 See, e.g., *Jackson* v. *City of Florence,* 294 Ala. 592, 320 So. 2d 68 (1975); *Lorence* v. *Hospital Board of Morgan County,* 294 Ala. 614, 320 So. 2d 631 (1975); and related cases. Also, *Peddycoart, et al.* v. *City of Birmingham,* 354 So. 2d 808 (Ala., 1978); and *Tuscaloosa News,* December 1, 1983, p. 14. Samuel H. Fisher III, a graduate student in the Department of Political Science, University of Alabama, found in a 1982 study of dissent in the Alabama Supreme Court that after the 1969 reorganization the dissent rate increased significantly. Fisher also brought to our attention the article by former justice Bloodworth cited in note 17. See also *Montgomery Advertiser–Alabama Journal,* January 19, 1975, p. 5A.

25 See, e.g., *Tuscaloosa News,* July 15, 1979, p. 3A.

26 For variations, see, e.g., Amendments 83 and 110, applicable to Jefferson County, and 334, applicable to Madison County. Also, see the new judicial article, Section 6.14.

27 Henry R. Glick and Kenneth N. Vines, *State Court Systems* (Englewood Cliffs, N.J.: Prentice-Hall, 1973), p. 12.

28 *Alabama Lawyer* 28 (April 1967): 190–92.

29 Ibid., pp. 191–92.

30 The agencies that constitute the judicial branch are described in Richard A. Thigpen and Coleman B. Ransone, Jr., eds., *Alabama Government Manual* (University: Alabama Law Institute, 1982), pp. 461–89. On the Administrative Office of Courts, see also Maddox, Faulkner, and Younger, *Alabama Appellate Courts,* p. 33, and the FY 1983 annual report, pp. 2–6.

31 See Council of State Governments, *The Book of the States, 1978–1979* (Lexington, Ky.: The Council, 1978), p. 80.

32 Herbert Jacob, *Justice in America: Courts, Lawyers, and the Judicial Process,* 4th ed. (Boston: Little, Brown and Co., 1984), pp. 128–29.

33 *Tuscaloosa News,* September 17, 1983, p. 3.

34 C. C. Torbert, Jr., chief justice of the Alabama Supreme Court, (Speech deliv-

ered at the 1984 annual conference, Alabama Political Science Association, Auburn, Ala., April 7, 1984), p. 4.

CHAPTER EIGHT

1 V. O. Key, Jr., *Southern Politics in State and Nation* (New York: Alfred A. Knopf, 1949), pp. 395–99. For an extensive account of Alabama politics during the period under consideration, see William D. Barnard, *Dixiecrats and Democrats: Alabama Politics, 1942–1950* (University: University of Alabama Press, 1974), pp. 59–71.
2 John F. Bibby et al., "Parties in State Politics," in *Politics in the American States,* ed. Virginia Gray, Herbert Jacob, and Kenneth N. Vines, 4th ed. (Boston: Little, Brown and Co., 1983), p. 76.
3 In 1956 one elector defected from his announced intention of supporting the Democratic national ticket. In other instances, voters were aware when they cast their ballot that some other individuals besides the nominees of the Democratic National Convention would get all or part of Alabama's electoral votes should the Democratic slate of electors triumph over other slates.
4 This section is based on Austin Ranney, "Parties in State Politics," in *Politics in the American States: A Comparative Analysis,* ed. Herbert Jacob and Kenneth N. Vines, 3d ed. (Boston: Little, Brown and Co., 1976), pp. 58–65. The seven one-party Democratic states are, in descending order of Democratic dominance, Louisiana, Alabama, Mississippi, South Carolina, Texas, Georgia, and Arkansas. The four southern modified one-party states are North Carolina, Virginia, Tennessee, and Florida. Discussions of Alabama one-party politics may be found, for example, in Key, *Southern Politics,* and in Donald S. Strong, "Alabama: Transition and Alienation," in *The Changing Politics of the South,* ed. William C. Havard (Baton Rouge: Louisiana State University Press, 1972), pp. 427–71.
5 Malcolm Jewell and David M. Olson, *American State Political Parties and Elections* (Homewood, Ill.: Dorsey Press, 1982), pp. 213–14.
6 Bibby et al., "Parties in State Politics," p. 66.
7 Ibid., p. 68.
8 Cited in Alexander P. Lamis, *The Two-Party South* (New York: Oxford University Press, 1984), p. 85.
9 Bibby et al., "Parties in State Politics," p. 91.
10 Ranney, "Parties in State Politics," p. 64; Key, *Southern Politics,* pp. 280–83.
11 The erosion of solid regional loyalty to the Democratic party and the growth of

Republican support is best examined in Donald S. Strong, *Urban Republicanism in the South* (University: Bureau of Public Administration, University of Alabama, 1960), which was used as a source of information in this paragraph. Also, see Strong, "Alabama," pp. 441–42, and Jack Bass and Walter DeVries, *The Transformation of Southern Politics: Social Change and Political Consequence since 1945* (New York: New American Library, 1977), pp. 27–29, 78–81, which also has a chapter directed particularly to Alabama politics.

12 *Birmingham Post-Herald*, November 13, 1984, p. 1C.

13 Thomas R. Dye, *Politics in States and Communities*, 3d ed. (Englewood Cliffs, N.J.: Prentice-Hall, 1977), pp. 97–98.

14 Ibid., p. 99.

15 These examples were taken from Charles R. Adrian, *State and Local Governments*, 4th ed. (New York: McGraw-Hill Book Co., 1976), p. 125. Adrian says that, in addition to partisanship, "It seems likely that local political styles and probably other factors are also significant" (p. 125).

16 Dye, *Politics in States and Communities*, p. 100. Key's chapter 14 in *Southern Politics* is a classic discussion of the "Nature and Consequences of One-Party Factionalism."

17 Charles Press and Kenneth VerBurg, *State and Community Governments in the Federal System* (New York: John Wiley and Sons, 1979), pp. 528–29.

18 Dye, *Politics in States and Communities*, p. 100.

19 Press and VerBurg, *State and Community Governments*, p. 532.

20 In addition to the University of Alabama's Capstone Poll, this paragraph draws on Patrick Cotter, "Partisanship and the Chance for a Political Realignment in Alabama," *Birmingham News*, July 21, 1985, p. 2D.

21 Strong, "Alabama," p. 463.

22 *Birmingham News*, December 30, 1984, p. 2A.

23 The 1980 statistics were reported in Lamis, *Two-Party South*, pp. 214–17. Here we used the table on p. 214.

24 *Birmingham Post-Herald*, April 1, 1984, p. 20A.

25 Cotter, "Partisanship," p. 2D; Lamis, *Two-Party South*, p. 216.

26 Ibid., p. 217. The story about the Republican candidate is from the *Birmingham News*, February 9, 1986, p. 1C.

27 Partially based on Lamis, *Two-Party South*, pp. 91–92. For a brief discussion of recent developments in the state Republican party, see William H. Stewart, "Alabama," in *The 1984 Presidential Election in the South*, ed. Robert P. Steed (New York: Praeger Publishers, 1986).

28 University of Alabama, Capstone Poll.

29 Michael Engel, *State and Local Politics* (New York: St. Martin's Press, 1985), p. 239.

30 Here we draw on Sarah McCally Morehouse, *State Politics, Parties and Policy* (New York: Holt, Rinehart and Winston, 1981), pp. 106–8, 117; and *Tuscaloosa News*, October 9, 1983, p. 21A, and December 29, 1985, p. 1A.

31 See, for example, L. Harmon Zeigler, "Interest Groups in the States," in *Politics in the American States*, pp. 99ff.

32 Ibid., p. 112, drawing on Morehouse, *State Politics*.

33 Zeigler, "Interest Groups," p. 113.

34 Ibid., pp. 114–15.

35 Tish Pool, "Profile of a Lobbyist," *Alabama Magazine*, 48 (January 1985): 30.

36 Zeigler, "Interest Groups," p. 98.

37 Ibid., p. 99.

38 Pool, "Profile of a Lobbyist," p. 31; also, information supplied by Pool, a former graduate student in the Department of Political Science of the University of Alabama, that does not appear in the printed article. We used the information on several occasions in the preparation of this section.

39 Pool, "Profile of a Lobbyist," p. 30.

40 Zeigler, "Interest Groups," p. 121.

41 Wayne McMahan, "Grassroots Involvement in Legislative and PAC Programs" (Paper delivered at the Regional PAC Legislative Workshop, American Dental Association, Minneapolis, October 29, 1983), p. 57.

42 Ibid., p. 67.

43 Ibid., p. 63.

44 Pool, "Profile of a Lobbyist," p. 30.

45 The following section draws heavily on the *Tuscaloosa News*, December 27, 1982, p. 15.

46 *Birmingham News*, February 26, 1984, p. 2A.

47 Ibid., April 1, 1984, p. 20A.

48 For brief discussions of the activities of the Eagle Forum related to textbooks, see, for example, *Tuscaloosa News*, March 29, 1986, p. 5; and *Birmingham News*, March 27, 1986, p. 4A, and April 6, 1986, p. 6A.

CHAPTER NINE

1 A classic discussion of this subject appears in Donald S. Strong, *Registration of Voters in Alabama* (University: Bureau of Public Administration, University of Alabama, 1956). Our account is partially based on this study. Detailed explana-

tions of election administration may be found in Robert L. McCurley, Jr., and James D. Thomas, eds., *Alabama Election Handbook* (University: Alabama Law Institute, 1980), and Robert S. Montjoy, *State of Alabama Election Officials' Handbook* (Auburn, Ala.: Office of Public Service and Research, Auburn University, n.d.). These publications, the *Code of Alabama,* and James D. Thomas, *A Manual for Alabama County Commissioners* (University: Bureau of Public Administration, University of Alabama, 1963–79), were used in the preparation of the parts of this chapter that concern the conduct of elections.

2 See *Dunn* v. *Blumstein,* 405 U.S. 330 (1972); *Hunter* v. *Underwood,* 105 S. Ct. 1916 (1985).

3 See particularly *Harper* v. *Virginia Board of Elections,* 383 U.S. 663 (1966). Also, Frederic D. Ogden, *The Poll Tax in the South* (University: University of Alabama Press, 1958).

4 See Amendment 91. This amendment was proposed by Acts 1951, p. 760, submitted December 11, 1951, and proclaimed ratified December 19, 1951. See Professor Strong's incisive analysis of this amendment in Strong, *Registration of Voters,* chap. 4. The 1946 amendment was invalidated in *Davis* v. *Schnell,* 81 F. Supp. 872 (S.D. Ala. 1949). Section 181 of the constitution, as amended by Amendment 91, was subsequently repealed by Amendment 223, adopted in 1965. With respect to the 1946 amendment, see V. O. Key, Jr., *Southern Politics in State and Nation* (New York: Alfred A. Knopf, 1949), pp. 632–35; Strong, *Registration of Voters,* pp. 21–25; William D. Barnard, *Dixiecrats and Democrats: Alabama Politics, 1942–1950* (University: University of Alabama Press, 1974), pp. 59–71; and McDowell Lee, H. E. Sterkx, and Benjamin B. Williams, *The Role of the Senate in Alabama History* (Troy, Ala.: Troy State University Press, 1978), pp. 81–82.

5 These statistics were cited in Donald S. Strong, *Negroes, Ballots, and Judges: National Voting Rights Legislation in the Federal Courts* (University: University of Alabama Press, 1970), pp. 90–91. On the application of the Voting Rights Act to Alabama, mentioned in the preceding paragraph, see another work by Strong: "Alabama: Transition and Alienation," in *The Changing Politics of the South,* ed. William C. Havard (Baton Rouge: Louisiana State University Press, 1972), pp. 453–54.

6 Rules of the Democratic Party in Alabama, quoted in William H. Stewart, Jr., *Voter's Guide to the 1976 Elections* (University: Bureau of Public Administration, University of Alabama, 1976), p. 9.

7 *Code of Alabama, 1975,* Section 17–16–18.

8 Alabama Republican Party, *Alabama Republican Platform, 1974.*

9 James E. Folsom, 1962 campaign brochure.

10 *Life,* June 3, 1946, p. 3.

11 *Birmingham Post-Herald,* April 20, 1970, p. 22.

12 *Newsweek,* March 12, 1962, p. 35.

13 *Time,* March 15, 1948, p. 30.

14 *Cavalier,* May 1959, p. 48.

15 See, e.g., *Birmingham News,* April 14, 1962, p. 5.

16 See, e.g., *Birmingham Post-Herald,* May 30, 1962, p. 1.

17 *Nation,* August 31, 1946, p. 241.

18 This section draws on Strong, "Alabama," pp. 456–57.

19 Here we are indebted to Margaret K. Latimer, "A Challenge to Incumbents: The Value of Media Communication in Alabama Senate Races, 1982" (Paper presented to the annual meeting of the Southern Political Science Association, Birmingham, November 3–5, 1983).

20 Ibid., p. 2.

21 Ibid., p. 9.

22 Ibid., p. 10.

23 Ibid., p. 12.

24 Ibid., pp. 13–14, 25.

25 Jeffrey E. Cohen, Patrick R. Cotter, and Philip B. Coulter, "The Changing Structure of Southern Political Participation: Mathews and Prothro 20 Years Later," *Social Science Quarterly* 64 (September 1983): 540. This study builds on Donald Mathews and James Prothro, *Negroes and the New Southern Politics* (New York: Harcourt, Brace, 1966).

26 *Tuscaloosa News,* December 30, 1984, p. 6A.

27 Cohen et al., "Southern Political Participation," p. 540.

28 These statistics were derived from John F. Bibby et al., "Parties in State Politics," in *Politics in the American States,* ed. Virginia Gray, Herbert Jacob, and Kenneth N. Vines, 4th ed. (Boston: Little, Brown and Co., 1983), p. 63.

29 These statistics appeared in Thomas E. Cavanagh, *The Impact of the Black Electorate* (Washington, D.C.: Joint Center for Political Studies, 1984), p. 8.

30 *Tuscaloosa News,* November 4, 1984, p. 24A. It is generally recognized that these figures are inflated, because a number of county voter lists are badly in need of updating.

31 Quoted in *Birmingham News,* February 17, 1985, pp. 1D, 4D, on which this section draws extensively.

32 Latimer, "Challenge to Incumbents," p. 7.

CHAPTER TEN

1 See Brookings Institution, Institute for Government Research, *Report on a Survey of the Organization and Administration of the State and County Governments of Alabama*, 5 vols. (Montgomery, 1932), vol. 5, pt. 4, pp. 16–22, and Hallie Farmer, *The Legislative Process in Alabama* (University: Bureau of Public Administration, University of Alabama, 1949), pp. 217–55. Our discussion here is based mainly on these sources and on James D. Thomas, *A Manual for Alabama County Commissioners*, rev. ed. (University: Bureau of Public Administration, University of Alabama, 1979), pp. 12–15.

2 The rule was formulated by Judge John F. Dillon of Iowa. See his *Commentaries on the Law of Municipal Corporations*, 2d ed. (New York: James Cockcroft & Co., 1873), p. 173. Also, see Duane Lockard, *The Politics of State and Local Government* (New York: Macmillan Co., 1969), pp. 120, 129.

3 Thomas, *Manual for County Commissioners*, pp. 11–12.

4 Farmer, *Legislative Process in Alabama*, p. 240. The decision referred to in the text is *Peddycoart, et al.* v. *Birmingham*, 354 So. 2d 808 (Ala., 1978), which will be discussed in some detail later in this chapter.

5 Committee for Economic Development, *Modernizing Local Government* (New York: The Committee, 1966), p. 48.

6 Ellis C. Rainey, Jr., "County Home Rule," in the *County Year Book 1978* (Washington, D.C.: National Association of Counties, and the International City Management Association, 1978), p. 56.

7 Alabama Constitutional Commission, *Proposed Constitution of Alabama: Report of the Constitutional Commission* (Montgomery, 1973), pp. 126–29.

8 *Proposed 1979 Constitution for the State of Alabama*, printed version prepared by the Alabama Law Institute.

9 S. 40, Legislature of Alabama, Regular Session, 1979, pp. 53–54 (engrossed copy).

10 In this section we follow Thomas, *Manual for County Commissioners*, Brookings Institution, *Report*, vol. V, pt. 4, pp. 16–22; and Farmer, *Legislative Process in Alabama*, pp. 217–55.

11 Farmer, *Legislative Process in Alabama*, p. 219.

12 Ibid.

13 *Peddycoart* v. *City of Birmingham;* Thomas, *Manual for County Commissioners*, pp. 14–16.

14 Farmer, *Legislative Process in Alabama*, pp. 248–51.

15 Ibid., pp. 248–49.

16 Ibid., p. 252.

17 See Brookings Institution, *Report*, vol. V, pt. 4, pp. 22ff.

18 Farmer, *Legislative Process in Alabama*, pp. 252–53.

19 See William H. Stewart, "Local and State Government in the South," in *Encyclopedia of Southern History*, ed. David C. Roller and Robert W. Twyman (Baton Rouge: Louisiana State University Press, 1979).

20 William H. Stewart, Jr., *The Alabama Constitutional Commission* (University: University of Alabama Press, 1975), pp. 86ff.

21 Frederick M. Wirt, "The Dependent City: External Influences on Local Autonomy" (Paper presented at the annual meeting of the American Political Science Association, Chicago, September 1–4, 1983), p. 5.

22 Thomas A. Henderson and F. Glenn Abney, "The State Legislator and Intergovernmental Relations: The Job of Local Governance," p. 12, unpublished paper in possession of William H. Stewart.

23 Charles R. Adrian, *State and Local Governments*, 3d ed. (New York: McGraw-Hill Book Co., 1972), p. 90.

24 This list was largely adapted from Clyde F. Snider, *American State and Local Government*, 2d ed. (New York: Appleton-Century-Crofts, 1965), pp. 65–69.

25 Unless otherwise noted, the illustrations of state-local administrative relations that follow have been taken from Richard A. Thigpen and Coleman B. Ransone, Jr., eds., *Alabama Government Manual* (University: Alabama Law Institute, 1982).

26 Joseph F. Zimmerman, "State-Local Relations: The State Mandate Irritant," *National Civic Review* 65 (December 1976): 548.

27 Ibid.

28 U.S. Advisory Commission on Intergovernmental Relations, *In Brief: State Mandating of Local Expenditures* (Washington, D.C.: U.S. Government Printing Office, 1978), p. 8.

29 Perry C. Rocquemore, Jr., "The Legal Viewpoint: State-Mandated Training for Municipal Personnel," *Alabama Municipal Journal* 41 (February 1984): 16–17ff.

30 Steven D. Gold, *State and Local Fiscal Relations in the Early 1980s* (Washington, D.C.: Urban Institute Press, 1983), p. 13. Forty-nine states participated in the survey Gold reported on.

31 *Tuscaloosa News*, September 19, 1985, pp. 1, 3.

CHAPTER ELEVEN

1 This section relies heavily on the 1963, 1975, and 1979 editions of James D. Thomas, *A Manual for Alabama County Commissioners* (University: Bureau of

Public Administration, University of Alabama) and the works cited therein, especially the Brookings Institution report mentioned in note 4, below. Unless otherwise indicated, the references are to the 1979 edition of this manual. Here, the reference is to p. 4. See also Clyde F. Snider, *American State and Local Government*, 2d ed. (New York: Appleton-Century-Crofts, 1965), pp. 359, 361.

2 *Code of Alabama, 1975*, Section 11–1–5.

3 Thomas, *Manual for County Commissioners*, pp. 20–22.

4 Ibid., pp. 24–31; Snider, *State and Local Government*, pp. 362–63; Brookings Institution, Institute for Government Research, *County Government in Alabama*, vol. 5, pt. 4, of *Report on a Survey of the Organization and Administration of the State and County Governments of Alabama* (Montgomery, 1932), pp. 60–76.

5 Thomas, *Manual for County Commissioners*, pp. 21, 32–34; V. O. Key, Jr., *Southern Politics in State and Nation* (New York: Alfred A. Knopf, 1949), p. 53.

6 Thomas, *Manual for County Commissioners*, pp. 72, 79–89. See also Thomas I. Dickson, Jr., *A Summary of County Finance Trends in Alabama, 1950–1975* (Auburn, Ala.: Office of Public Service and Research, Auburn University, 1977).

7 Thomas, *Manual for County Commissioners*, pp. 4, 31–32; 1963 edition, pp. 20–22.

8 Thomas, *Manual for County Commissioners*, pp. 4–6.

9 Committee for Economic Development, *Modernizing Local Government* (New York: The Committee, 1966), p. 48.

10 Thomas, *Manual for County Commissioners*, pp. 5, 35.

11 See Constitution of Alabama, 1901, Amendment 375.

12 For a more extensive discussion of municipal government than appears here, see Joseph C. Pilegge, Jr., *Alabama Municipalities* (University: Alabama League of Municipalities, and the Bureau of Public Administration, University of Alabama, 1972). This publication, along with the *Code of Alabama* and a 1955 publication of the League of Municipalities, *Some Facts about Municipal Government in Alabama*, were used in the preparation of this part of the chapter.

13 Weldon Cooper, *Municipal Government and Administration in Alabama* (University: Bureau of Public Administration, University of Alabama, 1940), p. 68.

14 Ibid., p. 53.

15 Perry C. Rocquemore, Jr., "The Council-Manager Act of 1982," *Alabama Municipal Journal* 40 (November 1982): 16–18, 24–25. The statute is codified as Sections 11–43A–1 through 11–43A–52 of the *Code of Alabama, 1975*.

16 League of Municipalities, *Municipal Government in Alabama*, pp. 50–55; Pilegge, *Alabama Municipalities*, chap. 6.

17 League of Municipalities, *Municipal Government in Alabama*, p. 47; Pilegge, *Alabama Municipalities*, pp. 68–70. The exercise of extraterritorial power by

Alabama municipalities was upheld by the U.S. Supreme Court in *Holt Civic Club* v. *Tuscaloosa,* 58 L. Ed. 2d 292 (1978).

18 League of Municipalities, *Municipal Government in Alabama,* pp. 47–48.

19 *Roberson* v. *Montgomery,* 285 Ala. 421, 233 So. 2d 69 (1970).

20 Pilegge, *Alabama Municipalities,* p. 70. The city of Montgomery is an exception. Its zoning power was extended by special legislation enacted in 1971; ibid. See also, *Alabama Municipal Journal* 30 (April 1973): 9.

21 League of Municipalities, *Municipal Government in Alabama,* p. 55; U.S. Advisory Commission on Intergovernmental Relations, *Regionalism Revisited: Recent Areawide and Local Responses* (Washington, D.C.: The Commission, 1977), pp. 5, 28; Pilegge, *Alabama Municipalities,* pp. 74–75.

22 Good treatments of the subject include U.S. Advisory Commission on Intergovernmental Relations, *Alternative Approaches to Governmental Reorganization in Metropolitan Areas* (Washington, D.C.: The Commission, 1962), which was the reference used here; and John C. Bollens and Henry J. Schmandt, *The Metropolis: Its People, Politics, and Economic Life* (New York: Harper & Row, 1970), chaps. 11–14.

23 U.S. Advisory Commission on Intergovernmental Relations, *Regionalism Revisited,* p. 28.

24 Bollens and Schmandt, *Metropolis,* chap. 13; on the Lakewood Plan, see pp. 361–64.

25 Donald S. Strong, "Alabama: Transition and Alienation," in *The Changing Politics of the South,* ed. William C. Havard (Baton Rouge: Louisiana State University Press, 1972), p. 445.

26 A. B. Moore, *History of Alabama* (University, Ala.: University Supply Store, 1934), p. 650.

27 See, e.g., Strong, "Alabama," p. 432.

28 Donald S. Strong, *Urban Republicanism in the South* (University: Bureau of Public Administration, University of Alabama, 1960), esp. pp. 1–29; Strong, "Alabama," pp. 427–71.

29 Strong, "Alabama," pp. 465–66.

30 See *Tuscaloosa News,* August 9, 1984, p. 16.

31 Margaret K. Latimer, "A Challenge to Incumbents: The Value of Media Communication in Alabama Senate Races, 1982" (Paper presented at the annual meeting of the Southern Political Science Association, Birmingham, November 3–5, 1983), pp. 11, 12–13.

32 Key, *Southern Politics,* p. 53.

33 See table 10 in chapter 9.

34 *Tuscaloosa News,* September 13, 1984, p. 13.

35 Brookings Institution, *County Government in Alabama*, p. 21.

36 Strong, "Alabama," p. 445.

37 Margaret K. Latimer, "Black Political Representation in Southern Cities: Election Systems and Other Causal Variables," *Urban Affairs Quarterly* 15 (September 1979): 66.

38 Ibid., p. 73. See also U.S. Commission on Civil Rights, *Fifteen Years Ago . . . Rural Alabama Revisited* (Washington, D.C.: U.S. Commission on Civil Rights, 1983), p. 1. The special election of July 29, 1969, in which blacks gained control of the Greene County Commission is described in Milton L. Boykin, "The Emergence of a Black Majority: An Analysis of Political Participation in Greene County, Alabama" (Ph.D. dissertation, Department of Political Science, University of Alabama, 1972). The report by the Alabama Democratic Conference entitled *1984 Population Profile of Selected Municipalities in Alabama* (January 1984) identifies over 180 black elected officials in some 250 of the state's cities and towns.

39 U.S. Commission on Civil Rights, *Fifteen Years Ago*, p. 1.

40 Ibid., p. 2.

41 Latimer, "Black Political Representation in Southern Cities," presents an interesting treatment of this point.

42 *Bolden* v. *Mobile*, 423 F. Supp. 384 (S.D. Ala. 1976). The case is treated at some length in William H. Stewart, "The Voting Rights Act of 1965 and Local Electoral Systems," in *The State of American Federalism: 1981*, ed. Stephen L. Schechter (Washington, D.C.: University Press of America and Publius Books, 1983). *Mobile* v. *Bolden*, 446 U.S. 55 (1980); *Tuscaloosa News*, August 23, 1984, p. 14.

43 Alabama Democratic Conference, *1984 Population Profile*.

44 This section is based on Charles Press and Kenneth VerBurg, *State and Community Governments in the Federal System*, 2d ed. (New York: John Wiley and Sons, 1983), chap. 11.

CHAPTER TWELVE

1 See, for example, the *Yearbook of American and Canadian Churches*, ed. Constant H. Jacquet, Jr., 1983 and 1984 editions (Nashville: Abingdon Press, 1983, 1984), pp. 225, 231, 237, which show increases overall for such conservative groups as the Assemblies of God (from about 1.8 million in 1981 to 1.9 million in 1982) and losses for mainline denominations, including the United Methodist Church (from 9.5 million in 1980 to 9.4 million in 1981).

2 K. Patel and Gary Rose write about conservatism among college students in

"Youth, Political Participation, and Alienation: A Case-Study of College Students in the Bible Belt," *Youth & Society* 13, no. 1 (1981): 57–75.

3 See, for example, Department of Economic and Community Affairs, State Planning Division, *Alabama Regional Economic Outlook, 1983: Twelve Regional Planning and Development Districts* (Montgomery: The Department, 1983), p. 4.

4 *Tuscaloosa News,* September 12, 1984, p. 18; September 13, 1984, p. 3.

5 John S. Reed, *The Enduring South: Subcultural Persistence in Mass Society* (Chapel Hill: University of North Carolina Press, 1976), pp. 1–3, quoted statement is from p. 3. The title of Reed's book indicates his thesis—that regional differences still remain in the South.

6 Ibid., p. 2. For an interesting commentary on Alabama economic development policy, see Dennis J. Gayle and Thomas M. Gunther, *Towards Economic Development for Alabama: New Perspectives* (Tuscaloosa [University]: Center for Administrative and Policy Studies, 1983).

7 Our comments are largely based on census data supplied by the University of Alabama's Center for Business and Economic Research.

SUGGESTIONS FOR FURTHER READING

1 This section has been patterned after Robert Miewald and Robert Sittig, "Nebraska: Documents and Sources," *News for Teachers of Political Science* (Washington, D.C.: American Political Science Association, 1984), pp. 15–18.

Index